Weequahic High School Yearbook Photograph, 1938:
"Good at fight, but better at play.
Godlike in giving, but the devil to pay."

SWEDE

Weequahic's Gentle Giant

Robert G. Masin

iUniverse, Inc.
New York   Bloomington

SWEDE
Weequahic's Gentle Giant

iUniverse books may be ordered through booksellers or by contacting:

iUniverse
1663 Liberty Drive
Bloomington, IN 47403
www.iuniverse.com
1-800-Authors (1-800-288-4677)

Because of the dynamic nature of the Internet, any Web addresses or links contained in this
book may have changed since publication and may no longer be valid.

ISBN: 978-1-4401-4433-2 (sc)
ISBN: 978-1-4401-4435-6 (cloth)
ISBN: 978-1-4401-4434-9 (ebk)

Printed in the United States of America

iUniverse rev. date: 7/8/2009

Contents

INTRODUCTION

Every summer my wife Susie, our children Julie and Max, and I vacation for a week in Sun Valley, Idaho. For many of those years, my father was able to join us.

One day in July 1996 we were at the large community pool near our rented condo. I was standing with my father, chatting as we "lifeguarded," watching the family play in the water. At one point he removed his baseball cap, sneakers, and sunglasses, and strolled to the diving board at the deep end of the pool. Watching him execute a jackknife off the one-meter board, I was so astounded and delighted by his dive that I could only shake my head in wonder. Here was this big, muscular, freakishly fit man, performing a perfect dive: great spring, beautiful form, and barely a ripple as he entered the water. Considering the fact that he was then seventy-six years old and probably had not attempted a dive in decades, he clearly earned a "10." I stood there in awe, wishing others could see what I had just seen. It was another great reminder that athletically and physically, my father, Seymour "Swede" Masin, was different than the rest of us.

Of course, there have forever been great all-around athletes, and there will be forever. But not many had all of the natural physical attributes as Swede: size, speed, quickness, strength, power, uncanny leaping ability, explosiveness, hands like vises, smarts, endurance, and gracefulness.

But the reason for this book goes far beyond my father's athletic ability. Virtually everyone who knew him gushed about him as a person first, and an athletic phenomenon second. Indeed, I have always been surprised that the comments found in his high school and college yearbooks did *not* refer to my father's success in sports. His Weequahic High School (Newark, New Jersey) yearbook caption read, "Godlike in giving, but the devil to pay," referencing his generosity. His Panzer College yearbook caption read "Panzer's loss is the world's gain."

As yearbook captions go, this was pretty serious stuff for someone whose persona to the outside world was that of a big, strong jock. It appeared as though the yearbook staff members wanted to go out of their way to respect him as Swede the Man rather than simply Swede the Athlete.

Initially, I intended this book to be a family history, targeting a very narrow audience. Then, as I started my research, I was astonished by the way my father was described and remembered.

World-class athletes of the past—such as Monte Irvin, Al Attles, and Lonnie Wright—offered glowing comments about my father, both as an athlete and as a man.

The nationally syndicated sportswriter, Jerry Izenberg, who has rubbed elbows with many world-famous athletes, told me matter-of-factly, "Your father was God-like."

Then I called Hal Braff, Weequahic High School Class of 1952, and *the* mover and shaker of the school's remarkable alumni association. I introduced myself, mentioned the book I was working on, and then asked Hal if he knew of my father.

"Did I know of your father?" he asked aloud—as if trying to recall. But then his response revealed something else: "Let's see, there was Superman … and then there was your father. He was huge: a legend."

"God-like?" "Superman?" This was the same unassuming guy I played hide and seek with? Wow.

The first memory I have of my father was in 1951, when I was three. We were living in a small garden apartment in Orange, New Jersey, and my father must have chastised me for something. (I'm sure it was a bum rap). So I ran over to where he was sitting, kicked him in the shin, and then, crying, made a beeline to my mother for protection. I can't imagine I did much damage to my father's leg, but it was the thought that counted. After that incident my behavior got much better. Sure, I was still kicking him in the shins and hiding behind my mother well into my thirties, but I no longer cried as much.

The last memory I have of my father was exactly fifty-four years later, in 2005. It was September 10, and I was sitting next to my father in a nursing home near the Jersey Shore, gently holding his arm, watching him take his final breaths. As I was staring at him, my mind was racing, thinking back to some of the memories, anecdotes, and incidents that we shared together.

The things that initially came to mind were about as random as can be. I remembered his intensity as he worked with me during my lengthy rehabilitation for the serious knee injury I suffered in high school; I remembered my longest day ever—waiting for my father to come home the day I burned the toilet seat with a book of matches (I kid you not); I remembered the absolute security I felt when he arrived at my sporting events, from Little League baseball games through college football games; I remembered, as a young boy, standing next to him in the bathroom most mornings, watching him shave, when he would invariably put a dab of shaving cream on my nose; I remembered asking my father to flex his bicep, only to be informed that he didn't have one; I remembered playing hide and seek with him, and watching as my kids, Julie and Max, played the same game with him decades later; I remembered his wit, his strong singing voice, his playfulness, and his gentleness; I remembered how remarkably friendly he was to *everyone;* I remembered how much I loved being with him, as he was the *greatest* of company; and I remembered how low I felt when I let him down (which was at least every report card day).

Although I am sure he knew it, I don't recall ever—not once in my whole life—telling my father I loved him. It may be a little late, but I'm telling him now. And hopefully this book, which tries to reconstruct his life as best as I can, will get through to my father. Because when this gentle giant passed away in September 2005, the world's loss was heaven's gain. Here's to you, Swede.

CHAPTER ONE:
"YOU'RE SWEDE MASIN'S KID?!"

My siblings—Dale, Patty, and Doug—and I have each heard this question more than a thousand times. Yet, even after hearing the same question over and over again, and hearing all the over-the-top accolades and affection people have felt for my father, I never quite realized how special he was until I started working on this book. Clearly, it is human nature for people, when asked, to say nice things about your family members. But in talking with all sorts of people about my father, their reaction was almost always one of awe and admiration.

Surprisingly, it was not just Swede's contemporaries. Indeed, what blew me away was hearing the way people from generations removed from my father (some who never knew him personally) would describe him and/or his persona.

People I knew of, but had never really known (and in many cases had never met), gushed about my father. One common thread was the way that people would describe Swede. They seemed to be stating facts, not opinions—as if it were obvious to everyone. "Of course, I knew of him. He's a legend." "We all tried to emulate Swede Masin." "He was a giant. A gentle giant." "*Everybody* knew of your father." "We all worshipped your father."

* * * *

Seymour "Swede" Masin was an interesting guy.

He was a physical marvel, as strong as anyone I've ever known; yet he was gentle as a lamb, and his strength and power were rarely exhibited.

He owned a booming, intimidating voice when he was riled; yet he was very soft-spoken.

He could be a very strict parent, with a low tolerance for bad and especially mean behavior; yet he gave his kids plenty of space to mature on their own.

He was not at all comfortable showing affection; yet his kids clearly knew of his uncompromising love for them.

He had an aversion to spending money unless it was based on need; yet he was extremely generous with people who were less fortunate.

He fretted about the fate of the world; yet he was often very carefree with a terrific sense of humor.

He *loved* sports and games his whole life; yet he never took them too seriously and hoped his kids would follow his example.

He was the most wonderful of sons. He never wanted to upset or disappoint his parents; yet he temporarily broke their hearts when he married out of his faith.

He was an *extremely* aggressive competitor who wanted to win very badly; yet when the game was over, it was over.

He was *very* independent of thought, was never a follower, and had his own distinctive view of the world; yet he sometimes seemed to lack confidence in himself.

He grew up competing with and against macho jocks; yet he seemed more comfortable in the presence of women than men.

He was very proud of his Jewish faith; yet he never wore his religion on his sleeve.

He was often referred to as a "legend" by those who knew *of* him; yet that moniker embarrassed and puzzled him.

He was idolized by many; yet he was the most humble, unassuming person I've ever known.

He revered his parents, his brother, other loved ones, his teammates, his coaches, his competitors, his teachers, and surely his friends; yet I don't think he ever realized he was revered back by all of them.

He was a real man, as macho as could be; the word *mensch* was invented for him; yet he never, ever, tried to *act* macho.

He was a little over six feet tall, and 200-plus pounds of muscle. A big, strapping guy for sure; yet in my eyes as a youngster, I knew he was not just a big man. He was the biggest, strongest man in the world. Not a doubt in my mind.

Closer to home, my Aunt Shirley, to whom I've always been close, said it succinctly: "Swede was the greatest son, the greatest brother, and the greatest father. Period." She knew Swede since he was a teenager; few have a better perspective than her on the subject of Swede.

My sister Patty likes to tell the story of when she was a teenager, at a friend's Bar Mitzvah. One of the adult guests found out that her father was Swede. She said he beamed with excitement and proceeded to march Patty around the room. He took her to each guest table: "You know who this is?!

She's Swede Masin's kid!" And the guests would fawn over Patty because of who her father was. I heard it so many times! And each time the person confirming the information would be smiling and thrilled. These incidents were such eye-openers for us!

Like Patty, my sister Dale and my brother Doug still get asked if they are related to Swede. We're amazed at how many people still recall his athletic greatness and notoriety so many decades after he competed.

For instance, while working a tradeshow in Las Vegas for the Columbia Sportswear Company, I was asked to meet with a new customer. While chatting, we discovered we had both grown up in South Orange, New Jersey. So he and I compared notes: people we both knew, teachers, etc. He was about five years older than me, so we had limited mutual acquaintances. But suddenly he said, "Wait, is your father Swede Masin, that great Jewish athlete from Newark?!"

His question caught me off guard, as this was the first time my father's athleticism was limited to his religion, even though there must have been much pride among the local Jewish community for "their" star athlete. Like any other ethnic group, Jews were bound to be proud of "their own." The many people of the Jewish faith in and around Newark in the 1930s and 1940s had in Swede a super star they could claim was one of them.

In any event, the gentleman from South Orange certainly raved about my father's reputation and legendary status, which greatly impressed my Columbia Sportswear colleagues at the tradeshow. And once again it ignited a new round of taunting from my Columbia buddies: "If your father was such a great athlete, what happened to you?" The "what happened to you?" question came up frequently throughout my life—but usually from people who were simply teasing me. At least they were up front about it. I am sure there were plenty of other people who used to *think* that, but were kind enough not to mention it.

In reality, I can't express how invigorated it would make me feel when those frequent episodes occurred. I loved to hear people praise him. The highest praise came from people who knew him personally. Those were the folks who loved him as a man. I would always look forward to telling him about these spontaneous conversations with people: the recognition of the "legendary Swede." And my father always reacted the same way ... humbly. He would always claim there was much exaggerating going on. "Yeah, the older I get, the better I was."

In July 2007, my family and I made a trip to the East Coast, and were having dinner with my Aunt Shirley at the Crestmont Country Club in West Orange, New Jersey. We had just sat down at the table when some of my aunt's friends came over to greet her. First were Julius and Sunya Lehrhoff, and when

Julius heard I was Swede's son he immediately began to glow. Although he had not attended Weequahic—instead he went to rival South Side High—Julius had frequently played paddle ball with my father at the swim club, and could not stop telling me how hard Swede could hit the ball. "Nobody hit the ball like your father!" He added, "One day, I was playing against your father, and I drifted in front of him as he was about to hit. The ball hit me in the back, went through my body, and came out my chest!" Sure, he was exaggerating, but even the passage of many years could not stop him from vividly recalling the impact of one of Swede's shots. More importantly, when Julius became serious, he confided, "You know, your father did not have an enemy in the whole world. He was one of a kind." So there I was, back in New Jersey after a long absence, and already the common exclamations of "you're Swede Masin's kid?!" were back.

Milton Luria is a graduate of Weequahic High School (Class of 1939) who had played football with my father. He heard I was working on this book and wanted to talk to me about Swede. After Milton had described Swede's exceptional athletic ability, he took care to emphasize my father's nature. "Your father was one of the nicest people I have ever known. He was shy and *so* unassuming; he never realized how great he was. On the football field, he was our one star, and other teams were all laying for him. They were looking to clobber him. When they did, he never complained about his linemen. He never said a bad word about anyone. We all worshipped him."

So did I.

The praise keeps coming. Hal "Peanuts" Lefcourt and "Zoom" Fleisher were a few years behind my father at Weequahic. When I introduced myself to Hal by phone, he was *so* excited and animated as he embarked on his praise for Swede. "Your father was the most prolific athlete *ever* to grace the corridors of Weequahic High School and Panzer College … Nobody came *close* to having a body like his! … And he never said a word [about himself]. He just did it! … We all tried to emulate Swede." During our telephone conversation, it sounded to me as if Hal was becoming very emotional. Like most of the Weequahic crowd, he exudes pride in his old neighborhood, teammates, classmates, and friends. Of my mother, Estelle Lepore back in the day, he joked, "We *all* wanted to marry your mother!" Then he said something that grabbed my attention: "You have *no idea* about the blood you have in your body!" He asked if I have kids. After replying yes, I have two, he exclaimed: "Tell them they have *no idea* about the blood in their bodies!" It was a fun, exhilarating conversation for me, one that I quickly shared with my wife and kids. There is nothing better than to hear someone, in this case a man with whom I had never conversed, speak so highly of my parents. And he wanted to make sure that I understood how lucky I was to have such parents. Fortunately, it is something I have *always* understood.

Likewise, "Zoom" Fleisher was a terrific basketball player for Weequahic. In fact, his name was familiar because my father used to talk about him as one of Weequahic's greats. He was in the same class as my mother; she was on the cheerleading squad that rooted for him in football and basketball. Like many others, he remarked about Swede's temperament. "He was not only a super guy, but he was the sweetest of guys … You should be very proud of both of them." This is yet another reminder of the impact both my parents had on friends way back when.

In the very first sentences of Philip Roth's Pulitzer Prize-winning novel, *American Pastoral* (the book in which my father was considered the inspiration for the main character, one Seymour "Swede" Levov), the author describes how the "Swede" was a magical name in Newark during the pre-war years. Well, I occasionally catch myself getting caught up in a fact-or-fiction conversation with myself. Because based on the gracious, indeed, reverent way in which people describe my father, there *did* seem to be some magic associated with the Swede from Weequahic.

One day my cousin Richard (Uncle Leo and Aunt Shirley's son, four years my senior) and I were talking sports, and I joked that my name was never in the paper without it saying "Bob Masin, son of legendary Newark all-everything athlete Swede Masin." Richard replied "Big deal. What are you complaining about? My name was never in the paper without it saying, "Richard Masin, *nephew* of legendary Newark all-everything athlete Seymour 'Swede' Masin." Of course I wasn't complaining. I *loved* being mentioned with my father's name. Thank God it never dawned on me that some people might start comparing me to the big guy.

My college football and baseball teammate, Bruce Fad, and I have remained very close. He and a handful of other buddies frequently communicate via email. His moniker for me is SMK (Swede Masin's Kid).

It's odd, but growing up I don't remember being overly conscious of Swede's stardom as an athlete. In retrospect, he worked hard at downplaying his accomplishments. And he always went overboard in emphasizing schoolwork and de-emphasizing sports.

I recall conversations with Swede my first year in both high school and college when he suggested I quit the football team. He wanted to make sure I would not let sports interfere with my education and was particularly wary of the commitment needed to play college football. He wanted to make sure it was going to be fun for me—and he also didn't want me getting injured.

It was clear my father walked a delicate line with his children. He *loved* sports. He *loved* competing in games. He *never* missed our games. But at the same time he didn't want us to feel the pressure of being compared to him.

If I asked my father to "play catch," whether with a football or baseball, he was always there. As a father myself, I now know that playing catch is also a great opportunity for parents and children to talk with each other. With Swede, the practice of playing catch continued, even when my father was well into his seventies. Whenever I visited him, there was always a ball nearby, ready to be thrown and caught.

When I was young, it may have seemed as if I might become another Swede myself. I was bigger and stronger than most of the kids, and I could be quite dominant in basketball games, in Little League baseball, and in the swimming races at Shadybrook Swim Club (our summer playground). For instance, in my last year of Little League, I pitched a no-hitter and hit two home runs in a 3-0 win. I also pitched in the all-star game against Nutley's all-stars, and in six innings struck out fifteen batters, who were literally afraid to bat against me because of the speed of my pitches.

The reason I was doing so well at this age is simply that I had matured more quickly than my peers. I was 5' 7" by the time I was eleven years old, and physically stronger than the other kids. However, nearly fifty years later, I am still 5' 7"; my only growth since sixth grade has been in width, not height. In a funny bit of irony, Swede's kid—the one who overpowered the other kids at a young age—was described as "tiny Bob Masin," the junior point guard, in a newspaper preview of Columbia High School's basketball team. Tiny!! I thought that was a bit excessive. But it helped make me realize I was never going to be another Swede by any stretch of the imagination.

After Little League I rarely played baseball, and truthfully I even found the sport a little boring. But just before beginning my first year at Columbia High School, Jack Fletcher, our very colorful varsity baseball coach, visited our home. I suppose he had heard I had been pretty good in baseball in my younger years, and wanted to encourage me to try out for his team. And my being Swede Masin's son may have led him to assume that I would be a star athlete like my father. However, I was planning to try out for the track team—figuring I would do exactly as my father had done: put the shot, throw the discus, etc. After all, I was Swede Masin's kid.

So, it was an interesting conversation with Coach Fletcher; I wanted to be respectful, but I had already lost interest in baseball and was planning on track. The coach suggested my lack of size did not bode well for my chances in the shot and discus. Swede was present for the conversation, but said little. He would have been supportive of whatever sport I wanted to go out for; but as always he was hesitant to push me in any direction. So when Coach

Fletcher asked Swede for his opinion, he tended to agree with the coach: that it didn't look like my size (or lack thereof) would be in my favor for the track events in which I was interested. That is how, with my father's gentle nudge, I ended up playing baseball for Jack Fletcher, and did much better than I ever would have done in track. At the same time I also avoided another direct comparison with Swede, in which I would have, once again, paled.

In doing the research for this book, I have spoken to many people. One of the more amazing revelations for me was discovering how well known my father was. It seemed as if he was known and respected by *everyone*: from famed author Philip Roth mentioning in a letter that he knew of my father's legendary athletic prowess; to Alvin Attles, another Weequahic legend, joking that he got tired of hearing his coaches rave about Swede Masin; to Phil Yourish, executive director of the Weequahic High School Alumni Association, casually mentioning that "everyone" in his group (class of 1964) knew of Swede; to Mike Cohen, class of 1960, a great Weequahic player and eventually a big-time college head coach, saying matter-of-factly "we *all* knew of Swede Masin." In fact, Mike remembers being a little nervous when he finally was to meet my father—though the nervousness quickly dissipated when he realized how down-to-earth Swede was.

The anecdotes go on and on, and are amazingly consistent: "Of course I knew of your father. He was a legend."

Many of the above conversations were with people who knew *of* my father but never actually knew him as a person. The accolades from those who did know him are my favorites. He genuinely touched many people during his life, and the love and respect in their voices and in their comments were wonderful. To those who knew him well he was a big teddy bear.

So, take it from my siblings and me, being asked if we were Swede Masin's kid always made us smile and gave us pride. It made us feel special. I can not wait for the next time it happens—just so long as the follow-up question isn't "and what the heck happened to *you?*"

Max, Leo, Seymour, and Sonia Masin, ca. 1926.

Seymour Masin, age 4

CHAPTER TWO:
SEYMOUR'S FAMILY

MAX AND SONIA

My father's parents were Russian immigrants. Both were born in the 1890s and arrived in the United States in the early twentieth century. My grandmother, Sonia, was from a family of musicians. Based on the information available to me (mostly Aunt Shirley's memories), Sonia's family was well educated and did not suffer the hardships of immigration any better or worse than the endless newcomers to this country at the time.

My grandfather, Max, was not as fortunate. When he was a child, his mother and father were murdered, shot execution-style, during a Cossack raid on their village. These government-sanctioned raids, pogroms, were not an uncommon occurrence in Russia. Being Jewish came with more than a little peril in that time and place. My grandfather virtually never talked about this in the presence of the grandkids.

As Pop Pop Max related, he was sent by relatives to escape the conditions in Russia at age fifteen to the United States, the land of promise. Like countless others, the immigration officials mistakenly misspelled his name. Max Mazin (pronounced Mozzin) was now officially Max Masin. As my grandfather related, he arrived with two rubles in his pocket and the address of a distant uncle living in the tenements of Manhattan.

He got a job as an ironworker at a factory that manufactured fire escapes. In his thick Russian accent, he told us kids on numerous occasions that the work was "veddy veddy" hard but was a small price to pay for the "rewards." He worked sixty hours per week (ten hours per day, six days a week). He was compensated ten cents an hour (six dollars per week). Every week, when he received his pay, he was so overwhelmed with all that money, he gripped it as hard as he could and ran home as fast as he could.

Like many of his peers, Max was a relentlessly hard worker, and in this great new land of opportunity, it paid off. By his early twenties he had become an independent building contractor, with a terrific reputation for quality, honesty, and reliability. He also gained a reputation of solicitously looking after his workers, doing his fair share of the heavy lifting as well as handling chores that might be deemed dangerous. He'd rather take these on than ask his men to do so.

Along with numerous other immigrants, many of them Jewish, my future grandparents eventually settled in Newark, New Jersey. They raised two sons, Leo and Seymour, in pleasant but modest dwellings in a wonderful time and place.

My grandparents—along with a few aunts and uncles—were practically the only people who never abandoned my father's given name of Seymour. To everyone else it was always Swede, a nickname suggested by my father's lifelong friend, Tim Lesnick while they were seven-year-old campers.

One day when I was young, maybe ten or eleven, my grandfather Max called. After a few pleasantries, I called for my father, who picked up the other extension. Unbeknownst to Swede, I stayed on the line. Soon the two elders said their good-byes. Being the clever wit that I (thought I) was, I tried to pull a fast one. Just as Pop Pop Max was hanging up, but just before Swede did, I lowered my voice as far as possible, went to my best attempt at a Russian accent and said strongly "Seymour!" Swede, who was in the process of hanging up, heard his name and said "Yes?" He later told me he thought his father had forgotten something and was trying to catch him before he hung up. So I advised him, "Seymour, your son Bobby is a veddy, veddy good boy. You should raise his allowance." As perfect as my impersonation was of a seventy-year-old Russian Jewish immigrant, my father miraculously was on to me. Result: no allowance increase. I would still be stuck at the current rate of about ten cents per month, or whatever it was. But at least I had the pleasure of hearing my father's laughter. He got a kick out of my (failed) effort.

Max and Sonia were incredibly gentle people—with the possible exception of when Sonia threatened to murder a thuggish truck driver; more on that in a minute. For themselves, they were incomparably frugal. As far as they were concerned, they never needed anything. Their focus was on the health, happiness, and well-being of their loved ones. Like many grandparents, they fawned over their grandkids. Pop Pop Max could be shy and stoic, but not around the little ones. Nanny Sonia was very outgoing and funny, and she loved to laugh.

Mel Brooks and Carl Reiner had a routine on their album, "The 2012-Year Old Man," in which Brooks, the old man, complains about his Jewish parents. When it would be pouring rain and thundering and lightning outside, the Brooks character would urge, "Ma, Pa, there's rain and thunder! Come, come in out of the rain!" His parents, getting soaked, would insist,

"No, that's ahriiiight. We're fine. We'll stay out here in the rain." Reiner, the "interviewer," asks "Why do you think your parents would rather stay outside than come in?" To which Brooks' 2012-year-old man replies, "Who the hell knows? Jews are nuts."

Well, my grandparents weren't nuts. They were wonderful, generous people. But the old Jewish couple in the Brooks/Reiner routine *did* remind me of Max and Sonia.

On my first job out of college, I worked within ten minutes of my grandparents and would try to visit during lunch as often as I could. Sonia would usually make one of my favorite dishes: matzoh brei (fried matzohs and eggs) and I would sit down to a platter the size of Mount Kilimanjaro of this stuff. Often, while eating, the conversation would turn to my need to get married:

Sonia: "So, Bobby, ven are you getting married? I vant to go to a vedding."

(Frankly, I really didn't think I was ready, considering I wasn't dating anyone).

Bobby (with a straight face): "Nanny, there is no one good enough for me."

Sonia (first staring at me, waiting for me to let on that I was joking, and then): "Believe me, you're not such a bargain."

(Me, not a bargain??!!).

The Weequahic section of Newark changed significantly over time. The next generations of Jews had started to migrate to the suburbs as early as the 1940s and 1950s. The culmination of this migration was the violence that erupted in Newark during the summer of 1967.

My grandparents, who had lived on Grumman Avenue in Newark for many years, were the last white family on their street at the time the riots occurred. But even they left the home they loved and settled about four miles away in Elizabeth. One day, I accompanied Sonia and my Aunt Shirley to City Hall, where my grandparents needed to register in their new city. The drive over was scary. Aunt Shirley drove, and she didn't appear to notice (or particularly care) that there were other vehicles on the road.

As I sat in the back seat, cowering, I counted four separate drivers flashing their middle fingers at us. Perhaps Shirley thought they were telling her, "You're Number One!" Eventually, a big lug of a truck driver (middle-finger flasher number five), in the lane to our right, started barking criticisms, with plenty of expletives. Sweet, gentle Sonia responded by leaning out the passenger side window, shaking her fist at the untoward trucker, and screaming, *"I'll kill you!! I'll kill you!!"* She then pulled herself back into the car, turned toward Shirley and me, and burst out laughing. She had really impressed herself. The truck driver, probably not wanting to engage in fisticuffs with my seventy-five-year-old grandmother, drove off.

We arrived at City Hall and met with one of the clerks who began asking routine questions.

Clerk: "Have you lived in the United States for six months?"

Sonia (incredulous): "Six months??!! We lived in Newark for 30 years!!" And then, turning to Aunt Shirley …

Sonia: "Six months!" (she said in a mocking way to suggest the clerk was a bozo).

At this point I took the liberty of explaining what the clerk meant with his question, after which Sonia's trash talking subsided. But getting through the registration process was waaaaay more complicated than I expected. We finally made our way home, Shirley Knievel behind the wheel, with several more "You're Number One" gestures along the way.

Sonia was a hoot. Once, when she visited us in South Orange, my father's pants had a slight case of wardrobe malfunction; the flap that covers his fly had unraveled and was open. His fly wasn't open, but his pants were an eyesore. My grandmother, who as a young lady had been a seamstress, had her trusty needle and thread in her pocketbook. She took them out and told my father to stand still while she fixed it. Swede was not about to let his mother sew his pants in the area of the fly. So as she walked after him, he kept walking away. As Sonia escalated, so did Swede. Faster and faster they went, running throughout the house, my father exclaiming, "Ma, I don't need it fixed!!" Meanwhile, Sonia was laughing harder and harder as she pleaded with her son to slow down so she could fix his pants. In fact, Sonia showed such good speed that she may have been the source of Swede's quickness! In the end, he conceded by changing his pants and letting his mother do the mending.

Another Sonia anecdote I remember well was a conversation between her and … Swede, the Dancin' Fool.

Every two years, Weequahic High graduates hold a reunion for the athletes who have played for the school. It is highly popular, very well attended, and attracts men from many different eras. I know my father always loved going.

On a Sunday morning after one such event, we were visiting Max and Sonia. They were getting on in years and both were losing some of their sharpness. The following Swede/Sonia exchange was entertaining to watch. Paraphrasing from memory:

Swede: "We had our Weequahic sports reunion last night. It was a lot of fun and we had a great turnout."

Sonia: "So you mean to say you vuz dencing?" (dancing)

Swede: "No. Ma. It was our *sports* reunion. It was all men."

Sonia: "Ohhhh, it vuz all men, and you mean to say they vuz dencing?!"

Swede (slowly): "Ma. This was our sports reunion. We have it every two years, and only men go. There were no women."

Sonia: "Ohhh, it was only men. I see. But you mean to say they vuz dencing?!"

By now we were all laughing, including my grandmother, although I don't think she knew why. She was just not getting it, and when she saw us kids laughing, and Swede laughing, she joined in. Even today, when I picture in my mind the Weequahic sports reunion, I see several hundred ex-athletes … dencing.

While Sonia was the cut up, Pop Pop Max was the quiet leader of the Masin clan. No one ever wanted to disappoint him, and everyone treated him with respect. In fact, my siblings and I were the exact same way with my father, not wanting to disappoint him in any way. I used to observe that my father and Uncle Leo would occasionally challenge their mother (though respectfully), but virtually never their father. When Max took a strong position on something, there was rarely a challenge or debate. He was on the quiet side, and did not often impose his will. But when he did, the issue was settled.

My grandfather was always considered a very gentle person. Whereas my grandmother had tons of personality and a little bit of mischief about her, Max spoke quietly, infrequently, and soothingly. Except once—when Pop Pop somehow got into some story telling. This was a little unusual, because he did not often talk about himself. So, when he got to describing the various skirmishes he'd had in his life, we were all shocked, no one more than my father. *Fights*?! As far as we knew, Max Masin, though strong as Hercules, was way too gentle a man to fight. So we were amazed and entertained by *how many* incidents Max described. Each story was similar in that Max would be walking along, minding his business, when one or more bullies would challenge him, try to rob him, and so on. The funniest part, or at least the part that amused my father the most, was the commonality of the "punchline" (no pun intended) of every incident. Every story ended with Max proclaiming, matter of factly, while throwing an imaginary backhand in a dismissive way, "And then … I laid 'em right out." There must have been ten different episodes, and in each one Pop Pop laid 'em right out. The best part was watching my father, who was absolutely astonished by these stories. He burst out laughing after each one.

In 2000, Patty took it upon herself to film individual interviews of my mother and father. It was a great idea, one that I would recommend to virtually everyone. My father was eighty at the time, my mother seventy-five. The results yielded superb nuggets of information, stories, and opinions, and, more importantly, timeless reminders of my parent's personalities.

In the video, Patty asked Swede about his father. He clearly adored his father, and he always wanted to do the right thing, but Swede (wincing) admitted that you never wanted to cross him. Similarly, my Aunt Shirley told me that she was somewhat intimidated by her father-in-law. I don't think she ever wanted to cross him either. Personally, growing up I viewed Max as a strong, quiet guy, and I never considered or worried about crossing him.

However, the irony is that Swede did "cross" his father on the two biggest loves in his life: his constant participation in sports and his wife, Estelle. Big Max had no knowledge of or interest in sports, and he was jolted by his son marrying a gentile.

Looking through my father's scrapbook, there are numerous articles about him dealing with the parental objections to him playing sports, particularly football. Actually, early on, my grandparents knew nothing about the nature of the game of football. For all they knew, football was no worse than tiddlywinks. But after finally attending one of Swede's football games, one in which Swede was knocked unconscious, Gentle Max's position on his son playing football was simple: he wasn't going to play. Period. The coach, Art Lustig, visited their home; other fathers tried to convince them; and more. But more on that later.

Decades later, when I was a senior in high school, I injured my knee early in the football season. I had surgery the next day, and remained in the hospital for fourteen days. Today, for the same injury I would probably be in the hospital for one day. But this was 1965.

One week into my stay, my grandparents came to visit me. They sat there looking at me, terribly pained expressions on their faces. They felt so badly for me! In the meantime, my leg was truly hurting. As uncomfortable as I was, I didn't want to admit that I was in pain; that would *really* upset them. All I needed was a little pain medication, but I was too young and too stupid to call the nurse and ask for some. So for two hours, Max and Sonia pretty much sat there, shaking their heads, frowning. I remember thinking they were undoubtedly furious with my father for letting this happen to me. At least they could rationalize that there would be no more of that horrible game of football.

But the following year, at the University of Delaware, unbeknownst to Max and Sonia, I was playing football again. During the final game of my freshman year, while wearing a leather helmet (which might be a great story for a future book), I got banged up. Somehow the running back's rear cleats got in between my helmet and face mask as I was tackling him. The result was a nasty kick in the face, below my right eye, causing a deep gash. This was going to be a problem, because in several days I would be heading home for Thanksgiving break and visiting my grandparents, whom I had not seen for three months.

I'll never forget my grandfather's reaction. We arrived at their house on Grumman Avenue, and there was Max, greeting us at the door with a big smile. But the moment he saw my injured face, his face fell instantly. He didn't have to ask what had happened; somehow he knew right away how I'd been hurt. Particularly after my serious knee injury the previous year, Max and Sonia could not believe my father would let me play football again. Most of our visit that day consisted of watching my grandfather lecture my father, who was sitting in a chair in the kitchen, looking down at the floor. It was the angriest, *by far*, that I would ever see Pop Pop Max. And Sonia? She stood next to Max, her arms folded, nodding her head, agreeing with everything my grandfather said. "He's right, Seymour. That's right, Seymour." Fortunately, they directed their anger at my father; I still got my platter of matzoh brei.

So there you have it: my stereotypical Russian-Jewish immigrant grandparents, gentle as could be. Unless you messed with them. In which case Max would "lay you right out" or Sonia would simply "kill you."

UNCLE LEO

My father and his older brother, Leo, never had a cross word between them. The one possible exception may have been the earth-shattering incident of 1926, when my father, six years old at the time, ate all six bananas that Sonia had brought home from the produce wagon. The ten-year-old Leo, apparently wanting a banana, took exception and sat on Seymour's stomach, trying to push them out. No luck.

Other than that episode, they loved and respected each other. In fact, the way my father spoke of Leo, he practically idolized him. In our video of Swede, he talks about always wanting to tag along with his older brother and his friends. Leo was usually patient about it, but sometimes pesky Seymour was, well, a pest. Once, Leo warned his little brother not to follow him and his buddies. My father agreed, but the moment the group left the house he climbed out the window to follow them. Unbeknownst to little Swede, the ground level doors to the underground cellar, directly below the window, had been left open, and he took a nice, long tumble down the steps.

Both brothers were big, strong guys. Both were natural athletes. They were wonderful sons to Max and Sonia, virtually never giving them any trouble. Both brothers had great senses of humor. But the fellows were not totally alike. Leo spent money. He enjoyed the finer things. My father was a very generous person, but as my Aunt Shirley (Leo's wife) said, "your father was tight. He spent nothing." And Uncle Leo was a very nice dresser. He appreciated nice clothes. Swede? Not. The only nice clothes my father wore tended to be Leo's hand-me-downs, of which he had a steady flow for more than eighty years.

Shirley and Leo came to my wedding near Susie's hometown in very rural (*very* rural) southern Delaware. It was a four-hour drive from North Jersey, so virtually all the Jersey guests stayed overnight. Their options on where to stay were very limited—only a few small roadway motels with tiny rooms. My buddy, Steve Samich, claimed that when he put the room key into the door keyhole, it broke the back window. Now that's a small room. And I remember Uncle Leo opening the door to his room after checking in. He gazed inside, turned and faced Aunt Shirley, who was heading his way, and announced with a straight face, "I found *my* bed Shirley." Funny.

I was always impressed with the unconditional love and support Leo and Swede had for each other. My father said endless times that Leo was the true star athlete of the family, and I think he genuinely believed it. They were so similar in many ways, though in other ways they were quite the opposites. Most importantly, when the chips were down they were always there for each other.

THE MASIN COUSINS

Leo and Shirley had two daughters, Barbara and Judy, and one son, Richard. Barbara, the eldest, was always viewed as an adult by the rest of us. She always stayed "above the fray," if you know what I mean. She was ahead of her time and age. She was/is very bright and was probably more sophisticated than the other six Masin kids combined. Although she has always loved sports and being among athletes, she did not participate much herself—unlike her siblings and her cousins. You know, all that sweating and stuff. One hundred years ago or so, Barbara married her high school sweetheart, Arthur Bartner. Cousin Artie, a family favorite, has been the director of the University of Southern California marching band since 1970. The famous USC band, loved by the home crowd, pretty much despised by the other side. I tease Artie, calling it the world's most hated band, and I think that's just the way he wants it.

Barbara's brother, Richard (four years my senior), and I have always been close, even sharing a house for two years in Laguna Beach, California. It was there that I had one of my finest moments as a competitor. One evening we were having a dart gun fight—you know, the ones that would shoot the plastic darts with the rubber-suction tips. I believe they have since been outlawed, or at least I hope so. Well, I had only one dart left and Richard decided to charge. I retreated through the living room and into the kitchen. The aggressor was not far behind me. I had my back against the far wall with no cover. My yellow-bellied cousin was protected, perched behind the side of the refrigerator. I was doomed. As Richard, laughing with glee, prepared to put me out of my misery, I took my only desperate chance. In one quick motion I raised my gun and fired. Well, not only did I hit Richard in the nose, *but it stuck!!! Right on Richard's nose*!! Being a good sport, and recognizing that history had been made, my cousin left the dart attached to his nose so we could savor the moment. Boy, did we howl at my improbable shot. Although in retrospect, the target was quite generous. But I digress.

Richard, like his Uncle Swede and his father Leo, was outstanding in any sport he tried. He was big, strong, and fast. After he graduated from Gettysburg College, he was invited two years in a row to try out as a free agent with the Philadelphia Eagles. He was 6' 2", 220 pounds, and played tight end. Although he didn't make the Eagles team, he got some very good press for his training camp performance, particularly during his first year.

During the spring and summers prior to his leaving for Eagles pre-season camp, he and I worked out every night, without fail, at the park in South Orange. Most of the workout consisted of us running pass patterns. Richard would run ten patterns at a time, then I would run a few to give him a breather. We actually became a heckuva pass/catch combination, reaching a point where Richard didn't drop anything, making one-handed catches, shoe-string catches, leaping catches, and so on. He was on fire, and the continual sprinting was getting him in great shape.

But was he ready mentally? At the end of our last workout before he would have to leave for training camp, Richard was about to run his very last pattern: a deep fly pattern right down the sideline. To make it interesting, I set up the scenario: "Okay, Rich, here's the situation. The Eagles are about to make their final roster cut after today's exhibition game. You are right on the bubble of making the team or being cut. It's late in the game, and they call your number. They want you going long down the sideline. If you make the catch, you'll make the team; if not, you won't. This is it."

With this set-up, Richard ran his last pattern of the summer. He was at full sprint. I unleashed a long bomb, and it was on the money. As my cousin was in full stride, the ball touched down perfectly in his outstretched hands and ... he *dropped* it!! After several months of daily workouts, thousands of passes thrown and caught to perfection, Richard demonstrating great hands, and then this? Obviously, it had no bearing on anything, but to this day it's a great memory. Actually, we both loved those workouts. We put a lot into them, we got a lot out of them, and they were a blast.

THE PRESSURE OF THE FOUR QUESTIONS

One of our great family traditions was Passover Seder at my grandparents' Newark house on Grumman Avenue. We have great home movies of one such get-together: Pop Pop Max giving the blessing over the wine and the bread; Max, Leo, and Swede getting the correct bills together to give to the grandkids after we searched for the matzoh; the actual calamitous search for the matzoh or afikomen, which had been hidden somewhere in my grandparents small house; and more.

My cousin Barbara always found the matzoh. *Always* darn it! In the home movies you can see her strutting around, holding the matzoh, taunting and trash-talking her siblings and cousins. My cousin Richard, always fiercely competitive, had trouble handling his yearly also-ran status, and still broods over it.

Years later, I asked Barbara what her secret was for always finding it before the rest of all the other Masin kids. She said it was very simple: the rest of us were just incredibly *stupid.*

Personally, I have other ideas. I think Aunt Shirley may have helped Barbara a tad with a hint or two. You know, subtle information, like where the darn thing was hidden! There, I've finally gotten that off my chest.

Jewish tradition has it that the youngest (capable) child asks the Four Questions. In my early teens I was enrolled in Hebrew School, and was thus the designated Four-Questions Asker. Richard, after several years of singing (with a very unfortunate singing voice), was finally off the hook. I was supposed to sing the Four Questions in Hebrew, and my grandfather Max (the eldest) was supposed to answer in English. Sounds simple, right? Enter my cousin Judy—my age, and consistently one of the all-time great cut-ups, with a very infectious laugh.

The very first Seder in which I did my thing, something—perhaps my inability to hit some of the notes, perhaps my mispronunciation of some or all of the words—tickled Judy's funny bone. She tried to suppress her laughter, and she succeeded ... for all of a half-second. Then she burst out laughing. But I suppose everyone rationalized that it was merely a case of opening-night jitters, so it was pretty much forgotten, until 365 days later. Once again I started singing "Ma Nish Tah Na Halilah Hazeh," at which point Judy again burst out laughing. Even worse was that her laughter infected others at the table. It spread to my sisters, my brother (who was too young to know what he was laughing at), Richard, my mother, my Aunt Shirley, my grandmother Sonia, and of course me. We all had a bad case of laughing gas—all except some at the table who did not have our same sophisticated sense of humor: my father, Uncle Leo, and Pop Pop Max all sat there unsmiling, shaking their heads, quite disgusted with our pathetic lack of self-control. Actually, my guess is that if my grandfather had not been there, Leo and Swede would have joined in on the levity as well. But they generally deferred to their father, and if he was not laughing, they would not laugh either.

It gets worse. The next year, even though it went unsaid, foremost in our minds was if we could maintain our dignity, refrain from losing our self-control, and demonstrate our maturity. Patty claims she would be anticipating the Seder for days, coaching herself not to laugh when I'd make a fool of myself. That question was answered sooner than we had imagined. When my cousins arrived and walked through the door to my grandparents place, Judy and I made eye contact. What a surprise ... she burst out laughing with that infectious cackle of hers. Of course, within five seconds, my mother, my grandmother, my aunt, my sisters, my brother (who still didn't know why we were laughing), Richard, Judy, and I were howling, doubled over. Swede, Leo, and Max? Disgusted.

Even though the Seder was still half an hour away, we knew we were doomed. "Ma Nish Ta Na Halilah Hazeh-eh, Me-kol Haleh lo-ote." The "ote" got me every time.

The annual Passover Seder remains an important part of Masin family lore. I am so happy we have portions of one on film. The strongest memory is of the family laughing uncontrollably at me. But recalling our wild searches for the Afikomen, of Barbara's dominance in finding it (I won't say she cheated, because she told me she'd kill me if I did, but ... she cheated), of Pop Pop Max quietly presiding over the evening's events, of Judy's beaming face, and most of all, my grandparents simple, tidy home at 123 Grumman Avenue.

I loved going to their home and can still remember all the great food and rummaging through the attic with my siblings, fascinated with some of the old and unusual stuff we might find. The Seders, the frequent Sunday breakfasts, my grandfather's quiet yet firm demeanor, my grandmother's mischievousness and sense of humor, my grandparents' Russian accents, their Jewish expressions, the old, classic furnishings, the framed pictures of my great grandparents, whom my siblings and cousins and I never knew, and more. All of these are great memories etched forever in our minds. And I suspect the majority of the other homes in the Weequahic section provided many similar memories.

CHAPTER THREE:
GROWING UP WEEQUAHIC

Leaving aside all the wonderful—but very general—stories I've always heard about growing up in the Weequahic section of Newark, I have trouble figuring out exactly what my parents did as kids. They were never very specific about their early years, other than that they trudged five miles back and forth to school every day, barefoot in the snow. Maybe that's what they spent most of their childhood doing ... walking back and forth to the Maple Avenue and Chancellor Avenue Schools. Fortunately, Patty's video interviews offer a few clues as to their day-to-day lives.

My mother was *extremely* close to her family: father Jack, mother Helen, brother Horace, and her Aunts Irene and Stella. And not unusual for the times, Estelle spent some of her teenage years sharing a room with her grandmother.

My mother related that when she would come home from a date, her grandmother would question her about the boy. After going through the question-and-answer period, grandma would finish with a warning in her broken English: "No lettum a touch a you!"

Listening to my mother, it was the age of innocence. She would *never* cause trouble, she was respectful and well-behaved. It sounded almost corny as she described how terrific the times were. Socially, the kids hung together, went to the ice cream parlor, went to the movies, etc.

In the video, my mother tells the story of going to a local carnival one evening as a youth, and riding on the Ferris wheel, which got stuck just as the ride concluded. Estelle was in her seat, virtually at the top, waiting for a long time. She was somewhat terrified—though not of the Ferris wheel being broken and not of it falling apart. No, she was beside herself because she had told her mother she would be home by nine p.m. Well, zero hour was approaching, and there was no end of the ordeal in sight. So she's yelling as loud as she can to the ride operator on the ground: "My mother's expecting me home by nine!! She's going to be very worried!!" I'm sure the ride operator was quite moved.

The Lepores frequented the Jersey Shore. They spent many summers there, and moved to Long Branch once my mother graduated from Weequahic. She loved the beach as a youth, the one exception being when she was swimming at age five and got caught in a bad undertow. She was helpless and was sure she was drowning, but luckily the lifeguard spotted her and saved the day. She remembered him putting her on a barrel on her stomach, rolling her back and forth to push the water out.

Based on what information I could glean over the years, my mother was very popular in school. She always had a friendly, outgoing personality, and being a total knockout probably helped her make friends and influence people. And it was interesting observing her talk on the video, almost longing for the simple, innocent life of her youth.

Like my father's family, the Lepores lived on a handful of streets at various times, including two-story homes on Keer Avenue, Aldeen Street, Grumman Avenue, and others. Coincidentally, the Masins lived on those same three streets as well as homes on Lehigh Avenue, 18th Street, and Maple Avenue. Several of those homes were built by my grandfather Max. I have no idea why people moved so much. If memory serves, many of those homes were quite similar, so I don't understand this "musical homes" phenomenon. Perhaps they were trying to stay one step ahead of the law.

My mother and her life-long friend, Dotty (Doyle) Blackstone, started playing together when they were two, and they remained close until my mother passed away. When I called to reminisce with Dotty, the first thing she said was how much she missed my mother and her contagious personality. They were particularly tight at Weequahic High. There were apparently no disadvantages to not being Jewish, as they were both very popular and had many friends. The fact that Dotty and my mother were extremely attractive probably didn't hurt. Admittedly, I am biased, but will say that my mother was always strikingly beautiful, which when added to her personality, garnered her plenty of attention. In paging through her high school yearbook, it appeared every kid in the school wrote well-wishes to her.

Estelle, Dotty, and other friends loved the Jersey Shore and went there often. My mother had a dark complexion to begin with, and during the summer, after spending many days at the beach she would turn even darker, resulting in her nickname, "Blackie."

My mother told me that while of high school age one day she was crossing Ocean Avenue in Asbury Park when the driver of a large Cadillac convertible stopped to ask directions. The driver was Buddy Baer, 6' 7" heavyweight championship boxing contender (and brother of one-time heavyweight champ Max Baer). He asked my mother if she would like to join him. She respectfully declined.

Sometimes they would go to the Deal Casino, a very popular beach club not far from Long Branch. Dotty said one time while there, Swede, who was back stateside from the war and was courting my mother, showed up in his Navy uniform. "When he walked in, all the girls swooned."

Estelle Lepore, Weequahic's captain of the cheerleaders, had it made growing up in the Weequahic section.

* * * *

As for my father, getting him to fill in some details about his youth was, uh, challenging.

Bob: "So dad, what did you do as a youth growing up in the Weequahic section?"

Swede: "Well, we used to play all the time."

Bob: "Were you serious about your schoolwork?"

Swede: "Unfortunately, not really. We were too busy playing."

Bob: "What did you play?"

Swede: "All kinds of games."

Talk about a conversation going nowhere! But I do know that my father was always very active, that the Masin family spent parts of the summers at the shore (Bradley Beach) as well as at resorts in the Catskills, that young Swede went to camp during some summers, and that he was a proud member of the "Bay View Flashes," a social and athletic club, starting when he was ten. But as I ponder my father's doings as a youth, whether at the beach, at Weequahic Park, at Maple Avenue School, or as a member of the "Flashes," he mostly just played.

The big guy did like to talk about his gang, er, club, the Bay View Flashes (named for the members' proximity to Bay View Avenue). The group stayed intact for at least ten years, as we have a great photograph taken in 1940 commemorating the ten-year anniversary. So what did this group do for those ten years? Based on Swede's comments on the video, not much. They played some sandlot football against some of the other neighborhood clubs, and they had "meetings" where they played penny poker. Other than that, the video suggests, they could have used a little more variety of activities.

Patty: "So dad, what did you do at these high-level meetings besides play penny poker?"

Swede (struggling to think of anything): "Eh, we'd discuss things."

Patty (laughing): What did you discuss?"

Swede (looking unsure of himself): "I dunno, different stuff."

Patty and Swede: Laughter

Patty: "Did the Bay View Flashes have officers?"

Swede: "I don't remember having any officers."

Patty: "Did you play sports against the other local clubs?"

Swede: "Yeah, sometimes. The other clubs had the good athletes. We were the … you know, the sissy club.

Patty: More laughter.

I wonder if my father ever suggested to his fellow gang members a name change to the Bay View Sissies?

I used to wonder about my parents growing up in the 1920s and 1930s. No television, no video games, no DVDs, no computers, no little league, etc. But even back then the days were still twenty-four hours long, and those hours needed to be filled. Did Swede and Estelle and their families sit around and listen to the radio a lot? I don't remember them talking about it, but I'm sure they did. Did they read all the time? They both liked to read as adults, so I suppose so. Did my father go to Hebrew School? Probably, but he never mentioned it. Did my mother frequent church? She never said. Did they take frequent trips to visit relatives? Who knows? Other than summers at the Jersey Shore, I am quite positive there was little family travel. Sure Saturday movie matinees were popular, but I have always been curious about what kids in those days did to pass the time. I guess, as Swede said, they just played.

My father's Bar Mitzvah, certainly by today's standards and probably by the standards of the day, was unusual. For instance, my brother Doug and I had large receptions in beautiful venues following the services. Swede? After his Bar Mitzvah ceremony, his pre-planned celebration was to take four friends by bus to swim at Olympic Park, a huge, popular amusement park on Newark's border. Given the option, Doug and I would have followed Swede's precedent in a heartbeat. Estelle made sure we were not given that option.

Moving to the teenage years, there did not seem to be much dating. Based on conversations with many of my parents' contemporaries, there was a lot of group socializing. One social event my father did *not* want to attend was when he turned sixteen. As a gag Swede's buddies arranged for a surprise "Sweet Sixteen" party at his house. Since Sweet Sixteen parties tend to be female celebrations, my father was shocked and embarrassed when he was greeted at his house. His reaction? He bolted out the door of the house, bounded down the front steps, and went into hiding for three hours. End of party.

SWEDE THE CHEATER

My siblings and I are so lucky and thankful that Patty thought to film individual interviews with our parents. They were getting on in years, so their recall was not perfect, but they provided lots of family history, insights, feelings, and a terrific record of their great personalities.

For instance, Swede, told Patty a story we had not heard before. He reminded us that in high school many kids tended to socialize together in groups. Formal dating was not prevalent, at least among my father's friends. But one particular New Year's Eve, they were attending a social function that would require pairing up. So the fellows agreed to put the names of the girls in a hat and to draw blindly to establish the couples.

Well, Swede recalled how he had his eye on one particular girl, Ruth "Bibi" Yurow, so he rigged the event. He made sure he held the hat, and he "volunteered" to go first. Unbeknownst to the rest, Swede the cheater had moistened the small piece of paper with the object of his desire's name, so it was easy for him to "blindly" choose Bibi's name as his date. It worked like a charm. And sixty-plus years later we finally heard the truth. So much for my father being an advocate of fair play, good sportsmanship, etc., especially when a pretty girl was the issue. And in relating this anecdote, did Swede show any remorse for his deceitful act? Not really. But it *was* entertaining to watch my father on tape, acting so sheepishly as he told this story.

In a recent conversation with Stan Gilbert, my father's oldest and dearest friend, he laughed about this revelation of Swede's, and said my father never admitted this sneaky ploy to his buddies until many, many years later. But the part Stan remembers best is how disgusted the gals were when they found out how the pairings took place.

Stan: "They didn't talk to us for a while. Here they thought after three years of group socializing, the guys finally wanted to pair up with specific individuals. Instead they were treated as objects, little pieces of paper in a hat." And in Bibi's case, a little damp piece of paper.

* * * *

One of my father's favorite claims to fame was that he was not only a member of the Weequahic High School Glee Club, but was also elected president of the club by his fellow members ... as a freshman. Sounds impressive, but apparently he was appointed to this lofty position because no one else wanted the job. As it turns out he did not have to deal with the responsibility very long.

Once again Stan Gilbert played an important part in Swede's short-lived reign. The two freshmen nightingales were horsing around during one club singing session, and as Swede "gleefully" reported in the video, he threw Stan out of the classroom window. Twice. Hopefully Stan had it coming—perhaps he was singing off-key. After all, my sweet, gentle father would never do such a thing without a good reason. I'm *sure* of it. And Stan did confirm that Swede threw him out the window "gently." At first, while telling this story, my father joked (with a straight face) that it was "only" a twenty-foot fall to the ground. But he quickly admitted it was a first-floor window, and that Stan's freefall was only a few feet.

Recently, Stan got a kick out of remembering some of the details, especially Swede's expression when Stan returned to the room after the first "fling." Swede (looking pleasantly surprised): "Stan? What are *you* doing back here?" Followed by "fling" number two.

The incident ended not only Swede's brief tenure as president, it ended his tenure as member of the WHS Glee Club. Oh well, the Glee Club's loss was the world's gain.

* * * *

How about the Big Apple? In his youth, my grandfather Lepore frequently went there with his buddies to dance. It was the place to go. But I doubt my mother ever went into the city; she preferred it closer to home. Swede told of the time, when he was at Weequahic High, that basketball coach Art Lustig took the team to the old Madison Square Garden to watch a college basketball game. Stanford had traveled east, and their All-American, Hank Luisetti, had perfected an effective but curious shot ... one-handed! Well, my father said he and his teammates were astounded by this star player shooting with just one hand! Imagine!

Sherm Harmelin was one of my father's favorites. They were boyhood pals and had played together at Weequahic. I called Sherm, looking for any tidbits he might share—even though I had heard many of them before. Sherm reminded me that Swede's mother Sonia would leave dozens of carrots in a big jar on the kitchen table, and Swede devoured them every day. He had heard carrots were good for the eyes, so he not only liked the taste, but also liked the health benefits. When reminded that he needed glasses most of his adult life, Swede always responded, "Can you imagine how bad my eyes would have been if I hadn't eaten all those carrots!?"

Sherm also recalled the time another Weequahic buddy, Sid Zimmy, had just gotten a car and decided to drive with some other guys to the red-light district in Scranton, Pennsylvania, to "end their virginity." (I kid you not). Laughing the whole time he told this story, Sherm said they invited Swede along to "participate." Apparently, my father declined—though he did offer to go and pay fifty cents to watch. In any event, the car broke down on the way, and the guys wasted most of the day in Philadelphia as it was being repaired. When it was fixed, the gang drove back to Newark. Mission: Unaccomplished. But at least Swede saved half a buck.

Speaking of travel adventures, Stan Gilbert provided several other childhood anecdotes about Swede that I had not heard: for instance, going to a place where you could drink all the orange juice you could for fifty cents. Stan was amazed that Swede set the record, drinking eleven large glasses. Besides his taste for orange juice and carrots, Swede also loved hot dogs. Stan said he and my father probably set a few world records eating Millman's, and eventually Syd's dogs.

As youngsters, they played all kinds of ball games virtually every day, including pick-up basketball, touch football, and occasionally tackle football without pads. Stan remembered preparing for a tackle football game with a group of boys from another neighborhood, when, just before the kickoff, they pointed at young, strapping Swede and announced, "We don't want him to play." Apparently Swede's size and muscular build could be intimidating, even at an early age. Stan said my father was disappointed and angry that the other team would not play with him in the game.

One of the other disadvantages of Swede's size as a youth was when he and his buddies went to the Saturday matinee movies. Stan said the ticket taker refused to believe my father was younger than twelve, which would qualify him for the youth ticket price. Every time my father had to plead his case for the lower price; but if I know Swede, there was no way he was going to pay as an adult if he wasn't one!

Stan also reminisced about the seltzer fights he and my father had in my grandparents' basement (where there was always a crate or two of seltzer), and how they would both be soaking wet when it was over. And the makeshift "basketball" games that Swede, Stan, Abe Golum, and Marty Goldstein (who sadly died at Iwo Jima) played in my father's bedroom. After a struggle for a loose ball, all four fell simultaneously onto my father's bed, breaking it. These Weequahic kids, what are you gonna do with them!?

Laughing, Stan also remembered a college basketball game in which he played against my father. It was late in a one-sided game, and the two buddies were lined up next to each other on the foul lane, waiting for a player to shoot a free throw. Just as the shot was to be launched, Stan grabbed the back of Swede's shorts at the belt, and my father retaliated by stepping on Stan's foot. It's safe to say that neither of the wise guys got the rebound.

While talking to Stan, I got the impression he could have reminisced for hours about growing up in the Weequahic section with my father and their other buddies. The more we talked, the more anecdotes he remembered. I could have listened all night.

So there you have it: Swede's youth in the Weequahic section. It was all about penny poker, high-level meetings where they discussed all kinds of "stuff," a short-lived Sweet Sixteen party, a Bar Mitzvah celebration at Olympic Park, carrots, hot dogs, orange juice consumption, seltzer fights, group socializing, getting de-throned as president of the Glee Club, Saturday matinees, and games games games. Oh, and one fruitless trip to Scranton. Regardless, as both my parents attested many, many times, growing up in Newark's South Ward was like heaven on earth.

A smiling stunning Estelle, ca. 1963.

CHAPTER FOUR:
ESTELLE, STELLA, ESTELLOOCH

Stellaahh! That's the way Swede would occasionally address my mother, as Marlon Brando did to his wife in *A Streetcar Named Desire*. He was also fond of calling her Estellooch. In any case, my mother, Estelle, was stunning. Admittedly, I'm biased, but most people thought she was drop-dead gorgeous. I can't tell you how many times people would say to me, "Your parents are so good-looking. What happened to you?"

My mother was quite vivacious and had a great personality. Though she loved to laugh, she also enjoyed a good healthy argument. You usually knew where my mother stood on most subjects, and more often than not her positions were to the right of Attila the Hun. Interestingly, she had a kinder, gentler side that would show itself as well, demonstrating her sympathy toward the underdog.

MY MOTHER'S SIDE

My mother's ancestors, originally from the Naples area of Italy, had quite a few vowels and syllables in their names. My grandfather was born Antonio Lepore, and his parents were Orazio and Giuseppina (Cotugno) Lepore. He had a favorite uncle, the dashing Umberto Cotugno.

My grandmother was born Pasqualina Cuozzo, and her parents were Caesar and Esterina Cuozzo. Esterina's maiden name was Chichizola (pronounced Keekeezola). She also had a favorite uncle: Antipasta Fontomboppoppoppalone. Okay, I made the last one up. But even without the fictitious Uncle Antipasta, it's fun to say my mothers' ancestors' names, as long as I don't have to spell them.

Great-grandfather Orazio owned and operated, at one time or another, some excellent restaurants in New Jersey. The one in Long Branch, known as Lepore's, looks like a mansion in a beautiful setting, with a huge porch in front. He also had restaurants in Newark, Morristown, and Elizabeth.

Unfortunately, great-grandpappy Orazio had something else: a gambling problem, and he gambled his way out of owning his restaurants.

Great-grandfather Caesar was a barber in New York for many years. One of his customers was the Italian giant, Primo Carnera, one-time heavyweight boxing champion of the world. Hopefully, if he knew what was good for him, he gave Primo good haircuts.

My mother was born in 1925, and her younger brother Horace (named after his grandfather Orazio) was born eight years later. Uncle Horace never cared for his name. He preferred his boyhood nickname, "Ace" (Horace without the "Hor"), and later in life used his middle name, Bruce. My uncle was an athletic fun-loving guy, who spent much of his childhood pestering his older sister, Estelle.

There was really nothing extraordinary about the Lepores and the Cuozzos; they were similar to many other Italian families who made their way to the New York metropolitan area around the turn of the century. Like many of their peers, they maintained strong family connections, worked hard, and assimilated well to become American citizens.

My mother's side of the family was very colorful—outspoken, loved to laugh, loved to eat, feisty as could be. My grandmother Helen Lepore was quite opinionated; so were her two sisters, Irene and Stella. When the three sisters got together, look out, there was going to be fireworks. They were not shy, retiring types. Watching them argue was a sight to behold, and invariably they'd drag others into their rhubarbs.

One day, some of the family was in my parent's small living room. Swede and Estelle, my grandmother Helen, and Aunt Irene were there. Then my buddy Dave Fargnoli (aka The Ghoul) and I showed up. Dave is an original. Picture James Gandolfini, Danny DeVito, Howard Cosell, and a Martian, mix them together, and you have Dave. There was a political argument in progress, and I could see the twinkle in Dave's eye that this was a great opportunity for him to stir up trouble. At one point, my aunt started bashing hippies.

This was Dave's chance. He stood up and announced, "Ya ready for this?! I will not get *one* hair cut on my head until *every* soldier comes back from Vietnam!" Naturally, all hell broke loose. My grandmother and Irene went on the attack, targeting hippies, long hair, liberals, etc. But every few minutes, when there was a lull, Dave would re-announce, "*I repeat!*" (Then a pause for effect). "I re*fuse* to cut *one* hair on my head until they're *all* back!" On and on, Dave baiting Helen and Irene, which would once again ignite them.

Finally, my grandmother raised the bar, attacking Dave personally, calling him something like jackass or dummy. With that, Dave stood up, and feigning rage, shouted "*Mrs. Lepore*," then charged across our crowded living room, grabbed my grandmother by her shoulders, and started shaking her violently. (Okay, maybe not violently, but the crazed look on Dave's face was hilarious). Well, with that we all started howling with laughter, especially Helen and Irene. I'll never forget the expression on my grandmother's face. She was helplessly laughing uncontrollably. Her body had gone limp. The only one not laughing was Dave, who continued to feign rage. He was right in Helen's face, shouting that he *"couldn't take it anymore!"*

That episode epitomized my grandmother, my Aunt Irene, and Dave. They all thrived on high-brow verbal engagement and the sophisticated exchanges of well thought out points of view. Translation: they loved yelling at people in order to win their arguments. For the rest of us it was quite entertaining—though not for Swede; during these episodes, he would typically sit in his chair with a slight frown, slowly shaking his head in disbelief, wondering what the world was coming to.

* * * *

The three sisters—Nanny, Aunt Irene, and Aunt Stella—were always entertaining guests. One day my sister Patty drove to the Jersey shore to visit the aging sisters at my grandmother's house. Helen and Irene apologized to Patty the minute she arrived, explaining that they could not visit with her yet, because they did not want to miss their favorite soap opera, which was just coming on. Patty understood, but Aunt Stella was not happy with them. She was mortified at her sisters' rudeness, and she was fuming. Here Patty had driven close to an hour to visit them, and they could not tear themselves away from the tube because of a dumb soap opera?!

So Aunt Stella kept making snide remarks to Helen and Irene. They were "selfish, rude, mean," etc. And she kept it up. She kept needling. Finally, my Aunt Irene had had enough. "Get a load of who's talkin!" she shouted to everybody and nobody. "God forbid somebody should interrupt *you* when *The Flintstones* are on."

Funny stuff. We still laugh about it today. In retrospect, it would have been interesting if Patty timed her next visit so that she arrived just as *The Flintstones* was coming on. What would Aunt Stella have done?

* * * *

In her early eighties, Aunt Irene's health failed her. She was in the hospital—actually on her death bed. Her son Michael was in the room, attending to her. But, with tubes attached seemingly everywhere, she was mostly just laying on her back, unconscious, as weak as could be.

The phone rang, and it was a nephew calling. He asked Michael about Irene, and then told him to tell her he would be in to see her on Saturday. (This conversation took place on a Wednesday).

Michael leaned over next to his mother's ear and relayed the news: her nephew would be in to see her on Saturday. Michael wasn't sure if his mother could hear him or not. But it did not take too long for him to find out. For as soon as he was finished delivering the message, my Aunt practically jumped out of the bed. She sat up, looked at Michael and said in disbelief: "*Saturday! The flowers on my grave will be dead by Saturday!*" Then she disgustedly mumbled "Saturday!" again to herself, and lay back down. She passed away the next day. That was my Aunt Irene.

* * * *

My mother's father, Anthony "Jack" Lepore, and I share many physical traits: short, bald, and a big nose. He was less outspoken than my grandmother, possibly because he couldn't get a word in edgewise. He was clearly the dapper dresser of the family, as evidenced by our home movies. His dapperness rubbed off only on my mother, who was also a very nice dresser. The non-dapperness of the Masin side of the family clearly outweighed the example set by Anthony. Remember, we kids would dress up as bums every Halloween merely by wearing Swede's clothes.

Anthony Lepore was a wise ass, a great story-teller, and loved to tease us kids. He would occasionally speak Italian, but mostly just swear words. He frequently used a swear word to describe me, but since the kids and future grandkids might read this, I'll leave it up to their imagination.

For the Masin kids, our "vacations" consisted almost solely of day trips to my grandparents' house in Long Branch on the Jersey shore. The Lepores lived on Dunbar Avenue, a couple of blocks from the beach. Those days on the beach in Long Branch, which are well documented in our home movies, are terrific memories for all of us kids; sometimes the simplest things can create the most lasting of memories. For us, playing at the beach, swimming in the waves with my father, hamming it up for the home movies with our parents, eating a picnic lunch, made for an ideal day. The negative was that these day-trips necessitated incredibly long journeys in both directions … as much as a whole hour's drive! For some reason the Masins as a whole, and particularly the kids, detested long car rides. They seemed to go on forever. I think we invented the tortured question "Are we halfway there yet?!" Dale, Patty, and Doug were particularly impatient naggers. On the other hand, I typically sat quietly, hands folded in my lap, being as polite as a nice young man could be among the whining and complaining of my spoiled siblings. And if they remember it differently, let *them* write a book.

But our day trips to Long Branch were the best—making for some of the greatest memories of my life—all kept very much alive by the home movies Swede took. When we were really little, my mother would hold our hands and walk us to the water's edge. As the wave would roll in, I'd run from the water toward the camera, a goofy smile on my face. As we got a little older, my father would take us, one at a time, into the surf. How we loved it! He made it so much fun, even if some of those movies are embarrassing today: the ones showing Swede carry me into the surf when I was well into my forties.

We would finish the day with a feast of my grandmother's spaghetti and meatballs. That was the drill, time after time: drive to Long Branch in the morning, play at the beach late morning until late afternoon, spaghetti and meatballs for dinner, drive home in the evening. Our perfect "vacations."

Once my parents took a rare, one-week vacation; a cruise. The Lepores stayed at our house in South Orange for the week. Now, most kids would do anything to have their grandparents baby-sit them for a week. Seven days of being spoiled; what could top that? But for us it was hell. "Benito Mussolini" Lepore was worse than any sadistic drill sergeant ever depicted in any war movie. He would put up this obnoxious chart, with all the required chores for each of us for the entire week, and he glued a little star in the box that corresponded to the chore, once it was finished. We all felt as though we should be wearing uniforms and saluting as we passed them. Helen was the drill sergeant's faithful assistant, and was almost as strict as he was. Picture an Italian, shorter version of Nurse Ratchet.

I remember hearing the same stern suggestions all week long from Drill Sergeant Lepore: "Don't do that! Don't touch that! Stop picking your nose! Keep it down! Do your homework! Clean your plate!" Boy, was he strict! Admittedly, the passage of time may cause me to exaggerate just a tad. But ask my sisters; they remember it the way I do … as hell on earth. On the other hand, Doug—who was still very young at the time—was always spoiled anyway and got a free pass, as usual. Bottom line: we could not wait for our parents to get back, so we could return to our natural state of laziness and misbehavior.

Anthony Lepore was quite a story teller and once admitted that he had tried joining the bootlegging trade. He was driving a small, open truck, with booze hidden under crates of tomatoes, but got stopped by a cop, who uncovered the "loot." According to Anthony, in those days the way to bribe a cop was to say, "You look like you could use a new hat," or "How would you like a new hat." Anthony gave it a shot. The cop replied, "Sure, but the hat will cost fifty bucks." Remember, this was probably seventy-five years ago or more. "*Fifty bucks!? What the hell kind of hats do you wear?!*" That was my grandfather's first and last day in the bootlegging business.

When my grandfather was young he would get all dressed up and go to New York dance clubs, occasionally with George Raft, who would become a well-known actor. George Raft, himself very dapper, was known to (allegedly) hobnob with some notorious organized crime figures. And for years Anthony Lepore worked in Newark's City Hall, during the Hugh Addonizio administration. Mayor Addonizio (a World War II hero) got himself in trouble and spent years in jail for corruption. Anthony saw some interesting things in interesting times.

After retiring from City Hall, my grandfather worked as a teller at Monmouth Race Track. One day I went to the track with my friends Eric and Judy Perlmutter. As bettors we were total novices. We kept going to bet at the window where Anthony was working, and we kept nagging him for tips. He said he had none, but even if he did he would be uncomfortable passing them along. Finally, prior to the last race, he caved under the pressure and relented. He'd heard some comments about a horse that we might consider betting on.

We three novices placed our bets. In fact, between the three of us, we had five different horses covered to win, place, or show in a race that had eight total entrants. Sure enough, the other three horses finished 1-2-3. Pathetic.

Another funny story my grandfather told me is that decades earlier he and the family had gone to a local college basketball game. They knew some of the players on one of the teams, but their team lost because "a big lug" on the other team totally dominated the game—getting every rebound, scoring most of the points, all quite effortlessly. Anthony rooted aggressively against this guy, who turned out to be his future son-in-law, Swede Masin, playing for Panzer College.

Anthony had various names and sayings for us. I won't mention what he called me on the grounds it might incriminate me, but he referred to Patty as Madame Fifi and Mary Pickford. He'd pinch Dale and Patty and Doug's cheeks and say "Quanto sei bella" (You are so beautiful), and then he'd pinch my cheek and say "Quanto sei bruto" (You are so ugly). Are you sensing a pattern here? I always came out on the bottom of his Italian barbs.

My grandfather, Anthony "Jack" Lepore, like the rest of the Lepore side of the family, exuded personality. If you happen to meet up with him in heaven some day, don't ask him for any hot race tips.

ESTELLE

Perhaps one anecdote best describes my mother: she is in her seventies, a petite woman, walking home to her apartment. In her path was a large group of teenage boys (perhaps twenty or thirty); they had just gotten out of South Orange Middle School for the day. Like most teenage boys, they were rowdy and loud, happy their school day was over.

As my mother approached, she was somewhat uneasy around so many rambunctious kids. As she was literally walking through the crowd, two of the boys started wrestling with each other, very close to where Estelle was walking. She was concerned about being accidentally trampled or knocked over. She stopped short, faced the mob and shouted, "*Hey, cut it out!*"

This got everyone's attention, and all the boys froze as they turned and silently stared at my mother. She maintained her angry glare. After a few awkward seconds, one and then several and then the rest of the boys burst out laughing. And then so did my mother. Everyone present had a good time with that one. She continued her walk home, laughing all the way. That was Estelle … in your face, feisty, and loved to laugh.

Estelle Lepore, captain of the Weequahic cheerleaders, 1942.

A young Estelle, just out of high school, impressed the judges at a beauty pageant on the New Jersey Shore, 1943.

My mother graduated from Weequahic High School in 1943 and was captain of the cheerleaders. You can tell by viewing the photos of my mother and the squad that she was having a blast. For instance, one day there was an altercation at the Barringer-Weequahic football game and the cheerleaders on both teams got involved. My mother claimed she hit one of the male Barringer cheerleaders over the head with her megaphone. Come to think of it, in one of the old photos it appears my mother's megaphone has a dent in it. Estelle never used the megaphone at home with the kids; her weapon of choice there was her spatula.

It must have looked funny as my mother, furious with her kids for one reason or another, made her way to the kitchen drawer, which concealed her weapon, the spatula. The kids would bolt the scene as if someone had dropped a stink bomb. By the time I was nine or ten, it dawned on me that on the very few occasions my mother caught up with me and swatted my tush with her weapon, something was missing. There was no pain. From that point on, when Estelle headed for the spatula drawer, I laughed, knowing how lame the consequences would be. That's when my mother went to Plan B, the weapon we kids would always fear: Swede. "Wait til I tell your father!" That quickly wiped the smile off my face. Playing the "Swede card" never failed.

My mother was somewhat of a homebody. She was not very adventurous, she was not particularly fond of traveling, and she had a genuine fear of flying. What my mother loved more than anything else was her family. From when we were little kids until her final years, Estelle pushed all of us towards family get-togethers.

For instance, when Susie, Julie, Max, and I would travel back to South Orange from the West Coast, my mother wanted to know what our schedule was to the minute. Where were we going to be each day? Each evening? When are you going to visit with your friends? Where are we meeting for dinner? Who's cooking? What day are we all going to the South Orange pool? She was so demanding about this stuff! Estelle was a very organized person, and she wanted the rest of us to have a specific game-plan and schedule.

And then there was the family photo. It became traditional that every summer when Susie, Julie, Max, and I traveled home (I will always refer to South Orange as home), we *had* to make sure we were all together for the family picture, which my mother would use for her upcoming holiday greeting cards. She would fret about it, not wanting to risk *not* taking care of this yearly tradition of recording family history. She nagged us until it was done. Patty, the family photographer, would set up her camera on a tripod, usually in Swede's back yard. Then the hard part: getting everyone in position, dressed properly, facing the camera, hopefully smiling, etc. This was easier said than done, especially with the little ones. Patty used her ten-second timer, and more often than not the toddlers would be distracted by something, or they were hot, or they didn't want to be held, or they were whining, or they were picking their nose, etc. We needed many takes, which tried the little ones' patience. But ultimately, when all was said and done, we ended up with a terrific family photo that we loved sending out during the holidays.

One year Patty brought a bunch of those fake noses and glasses for all of us to wear for a joke photo. Secretly, I took the fake nose off and just wore the glasses. Everyone else had both. I wanted to see if anyone would notice. Unfortunately, when the photo was developed, no one picked up on it, which tells you something about the size of my nose.

Today all of us covet the resulting family pictures; they are priceless. All thanks to my mother… and photographer Patty.

It may be an Italian thing, but my mother was very demonstrative with her affection. She loved to hug her kids and grandkids. She was *so* excited to see the little ones. Max used to joke upon arriving in South Orange, "I hope Nanny doesn't hug me too hard again!"

Max reminded me that invariably, after Estelle's bear hugs, she would lightly pinch some skin on his arms and admonish him, "Max, you're too thin!" At which point I'd ask, hopefully, "Am I too thin?" Estelle's reply: "No, not you tubsy." Okay, I admit it … I made the "tubsy" part up.

* * * *

Estelle prided herself on making the holidays wonderful for her family. She was *big* on tradition. She was not an expert on prepping for the Jewish holidays, so Swede and his family took care of that in their low-key manner—though my mother was always an interested participant in our Passover Seders, the lighting of the Hanukah candles, and she even did most of the planning for Doug's and my Bar Mitzvah receptions. However, when it came to Christmas, Easter and, of course, birthdays, Estelle was on top of her game. Even though our Christmas tree was tiny, fake, and white, it was well decorated. We each had a stocking, and every year we'd find in them an orange, popcorn balls, walnuts, etc. We'd always have our Easter egg hunt—often we'd find all but one of the eggs, which would show up about six months later—and we'd have little baskets with chocolate bunnies.

In reminiscing with Dale, Patty, and Doug, we all agreed there was somewhat of a "good cop, bad cop" dynamic with my parents. Estelle, the "good cop," was usually more tolerant than the big guy. "Bad cop" Swede had little patience for bad, inconsiderate, or mean behavior. He expected us to be excellent citizens, good students, honest, and more. Estellooch (as Swede liked to call my mother) was more understanding.

Whenever my siblings had a problem, they were usually more comfortable going to my mother than to my father. None of us ever wanted him to worry about us or to upset him. Estelle was better at dealing with her kids' screw-ups. I wasn't comfortable going to either of them, but of course I can't remember ever doing anything wrong.

When I asked Doug about this, he recalled, "It was easier to talk to mommy about problems without her freaking out. Daddy wanted us to be perfect. Luckily, we *were* for the most part." So there you have it. For the most part, we were perfect. Except when we weren't.

My mother took tremendous pride in making a great home for her family. She was extremely organized; we used to tease her because she made lists her whole life: to-do lists, food-shopping lists, holiday-shopping lists, etc.

We very rarely went out to eat and when we did, it was usually going to local eateries, such as Gruning's or Don's, for burgers. Because when it came to preparing meals, my mother was the best. While attending Montrose Elementary School, which was right next to our house, we went home for lunch every day, and every day Estelle was ready for us with soup, sandwiches, etc. Dinners were healthy, well-rounded, and delicious. We always had an appetizer and we always had multiple food groups. There was always a main course, a vegetable, often potatoes, and always a salad. In fact, Estelle made the *greatest* salads, loaded with all kinds of fresh stuff, and with her own dressing concoction, often making this my favorite part of the meal. She'd make chicken or fish or beef or veal, and of course a variety of Italian dishes which we *loved*.

On special occasions, my mother often went overboard on the number of different dishes she prepared: filet mignon, delicious salads, baked ziti with the best marinara sauce ever, sautéed broccoli with lots of lemon and garlic, antipasti consisting of roasted peppers, prosciutto, cheeses, olives, etc. And I'm telling you it was *all* terrific! My father would always say the same thing, shaking his head as my sisters paraded all these platters to the table: "There must be ten thousand items here!" But, in fact, no one loved my mother's cooking more than my father. On these occasions, he would always lament the amount of delicious food he consumed.

Like other great chefs, Estelle never measured ingredients. She had a real gift when it came to making food appealing to the eye, the smell, and the taste buds. Virtually every Sunday we ate spaghetti and meatballs, and it was nothing less than world class.

The lasting impression we all have is that the meals, besides being delicious and healthy, were so well mentally and physically prepared. Estelle worked hard at this, and it certainly paid off. She was not fancy, but she was a terrific cook.

* * * *

My mother could be very traditional, even old-fashioned. She expected good behavior and high moral values, and she could be very outspoken (even preachy) about such things. So it was very curious and amusing when Estelle told us that a young cousin called her for some advice. This cousin is very attractive, and was offered an opportunity to pose nude for *Playboy* magazine. Guess who she called for advice on the matter? And my mother's advice? It was something along the lines of "*Are you out of your mind?! Don't you even think about it!*" Typical Estelle. I always loved this story, both because of my mother's very predictable reaction, and because our cousin went to Estelle for an opinion on the matter. Well, she got a very clear opinion.

* * * *

Whereas my father loved the outdoors, my mother was more of a city person—actually an indoor person (other than the beach). She could not relate to the pleasures of nature as much as others do, as illustrated by the following story:

In my long career with Columbia Sportswear Company (based in Portland, Oregon), we would take customers to Montana for several days of fly-fishing and upland bird hunting. We stayed at a terrific lodge, not far from where Custer fought his final battle. The fishing took place on the Little Big Horn River, where the trout fishing was great.

Most attendees were experienced fly fisherman and hunters. Not me. As a hunter, I was Barney Fife. As a fisherman, I was, well, Barney Fife. One of my first times on the river, a guide took another Columbia associate, Mike Egeck (Barney Fife Jr.), and me to a spot on the river for some introductory lessons. After watching us for a few minutes, the guide stated that his record of never having one of his clients shut out (meaning not catching *any* fish in a day) was in jeopardy with us. Yes, we were that bad.

I remember thinking that the guide had positioned us too close together as we were practicing our casting. I was thinking it was a good thing I was wearing sunglasses since I preferred not getting hooked in the eye. As I was thinking this, Egeck, on the backswing of his cast, hooked my lower lip. I'll never forget the look on his face when he realized he'd hooked a 200-plus pounder. (That would be me). Actually, it was no big deal. The guide carefully removed the hook, there was some blood, but within minutes we were back fishing … albeit much further apart.

Not surprisingly, news of this incident spread eastward to my family: I mentioned it in passing to Susie, who mentioned it to Patty back in Jersey, and in the retelling the details were somewhat exaggerated. So, after Patty told my mother, Estelle was on the phone to Portland in a New Jersey minute. Her reaction was pure Estelle. The phone conversation was funny:

Estelle: "*Bobby, what happened?!*" (in a tone suggesting I might not pull through).

Me: "What do you mean?"

Estelle: "You know what I mean! What happened to your lip?! And don't you lie to me!"

Me: "Ma, it's nothing."

Estelle: "What do you mean it's nothing? It's *not* nothing!"

Me: "Ma, you can't even see a mark anymore!" (A slight fib).

Estelle: "I don't believe it! Did you go to the hospital?!"

Me: "Ma, you can't even see a mark!"

Estelle (and this is classic Estelle): "*What the hell do you have to go fishing with those morons for anyway?!*"

Me: Helpless laughter

Estelle: "I'm serious! Why don't you stick to playing basketball, like you used to?!"

Ah, where to begin? First, my mother went on the attack without knowing the facts. She suggested I play basketball instead of fishing. At my age basketball is much more risky than fishing, especially considering the thugs I play with. But the worst thing is that she referred to all of the guides, Columbia management, sales reps, as well as tens of millions of other Americans who enjoy fishing … as *morons*!! That was Estelle. Shoot first and don't bother asking any questions later.

Some years, Columbia President and CEO Tim Boyle would invite sports celebrities to join us in Montana. Steve Bartkowski, Ed Marinaro, John Havlicek and Bob Knight all joined us on one or more occasions. My mother was a *huge* college basketball fan; she loved March Madness. Because Coach Knight was her favorite, she asked me to get a picture of the famous coach.

I had brought my video camera and one morning asked Knight and Havlicek if they would send some greetings to my mother for the camera. They said they'd be happy to do so.

Coach Knight: "What's your mom's name?"

Me: "Estelle."

Coach Knight: "Turn that thing on."

Me: "You're on the air."

Coach Knight: "Estelle, we're out here hunting and fishing in beautiful Montana, having a great time. But we found out your son is the kingpin for some damned pornography ring out here. We're gonna get a rope and string the son of a bitch up from the nearest tree." He kept up his dialogue with more of the same. He must have mentioned my mother's name four times.

Then John Havlicek greeted my mother in his typically gentlemanly way. Like Knight, he made sure to mention my mother's name. These two basketball legends, the best of friends, seem to have opposite personalities.

Estelle *loved* the video. She got such a kick out of Bob Knight's brash style and coarse sense of humor. But for her the best part was that both celebrities were talking directly to her. Calling her by name throughout the recording made the tape a prize possession for my mother. She showed it with pride to all her friends.

* * * *

My mother was an excellent athlete. Clearly a bit of a tomboy., my mother was very coordinated and excelled at any sport she tried: softball, tennis, ice-skating, volleyball, swimming, even throwing snow balls—which was evident in the home movies taken during snow storms; Estelle would invariably throw them at the man behind the camera. My father claimed that my mother even taught him how to throw a spiral with a football; certainly not so, but a story he always told. All in all, my mother was remarkably graceful. Considering her era, when there were so few opportunities for women in sports, Estelle's athletic prowess was very impressive. If the times had been different, my *mother* might have been the one remembered as Weequahic's legendary athlete.

In the 1970s, my mother joined the South Orange Rescue Squad with which she was associated for twenty years. She was a very gung-ho, dedicated member of the squad, and she eventually became president. During her career there, my mother worked closely with the fire and police departments and was a staunch supporter of both. During this time, Estelle's political stance veered to the right. She was going to be on the side of law and order, period. She was a point person in getting funding for bullet proof vests for the cops, which was very much appreciated by the men in blue. In the early 1990s my mother was named "Woman of the Year" by the Lion's Club, most notably for her efforts on behalf of the South Orange Police Department.

My mother loved South Orange. She patronized the retailers and the restaurants, and she worked proudly for the rescue squad. And she was easy to love back. Her energy, sense of humor, and fearlessness were fun to be around. Although my mother was not shy about speaking her mind and could be less than patient with anyone who disagreed, her feistiness was beloved by her friends and was clearly a part of her incomparable personality.

THE LETTER

My mother was more than a high-spirited person and a world-class cook; she had a softer side as well. Perhaps the best way for me to describe it is to share a remarkable letter written to Patty by a New York doctor who had grown up in South Orange. She received it in early December 2005, three months after my father passed away:

Dear Patty,

I don't think we ever met. My older brother attended Columbia High School with you. As a kid (I was born in 1960) I remember hearing your name and the name of your brother Bob. A strange sequence brought me to write you.

I was flying home from Paris last month and reading the book *American Pastoral.* All the references to Newark were so amazingly familiar to me. When I got home, I called my brother and told him about the book. He then told me he had read it and said that the character "Swede" was very loosely based on your father. He then went on to tell me that he recently read that your father had passed away.

Actually, the member of your family I knew was your mother because I rode on the South Orange Rescue Squad. I did meet your father a few times at Squad parties and such. When I looked at your dad's obituary, I learned for the first time that your mother had also passed away. Since, I've been thinking about your mother and wanted to pass on my thoughts to you.

I rode on the Squad my junior and senior years at Columbia. I was utterly miserable and unhappy at home and at school and couldn't wait to graduate and leave. During a great part of my senior year, I cut school as much as possible, perhaps one to two days a week. In retrospect, I don't know how I graduated! Since my parents couldn't know I was cutting school, I rode on the ambulance during the day and therefore spent a huge amount of time with your mom.

I was obviously taken by how pretty she was—dark hair, blue eyes (am I remembering correctly?). But as a gay man, trust me that her looks were not what drew me to her. She was so full of life, funny and charming. You should know that she spoke about all of you (her children) very often, beaming with pride.

But the reason I'm writing you is to tell you about her inner kindness to me. She was clearly very sensitive and most definitely picked up on the fact that I wasn't very happy and was spending so much time at the Squad to avoid school and home. The other riders gave me the impression that I was somehow intruding on their turf and wanted this pesky high-schooler to go back to school. But your mother looked beyond the surface and I'm sure understood that I was having trouble. She responded to me with generous kindness, warmth, interest and understanding. I felt a special connection with her.

We didn't stay in touch after I left in 1978. Although I've thought about her often to this day, it just felt a little strange having contact with her outside the "Squad." But I wanted you to know that I've continuously thought of her as one of those rare and special people in our lives who touch us in a most special place; and this makes them unforgettable.

So I suppose it's somewhat out of the ordinary for you to receive a condolence letter about your mother at the very time you are grieving your father. And I am so sorry about his passing. Yet I still wanted you to know that your mother left her mark on people and in ways you never knew. I so wish I could have had the opportunity to tell your mom how much her kindness meant to me. I hope you don't mind me telling you.

I told my brother I was going to write you and he told me to say hi to you. He's a doctor, with four kids.

I hope you are doing well and again, I'm so sorry for your loss of both your dad and mom.

Sincerely,

Every time I read his letter (and I do so quite often) I get emotional, amazed at how it was written out of the blue. The letter describes a side of my mother we rarely saw and provides a very tangible example of how sensitive she really was. I loved hearing such sweet comments about my mother (from someone I didn't know) four years after her death. It was like finding treasure.

I took the liberty of writing back to the doctor, thanking him for his wonderful letter, and how much it meant to my siblings and me. I also asked his permission to use some of it in the book. He encouraged me to use whatever part of the letter I wanted to, and went into more detail about his appreciation for Estelle. There is nothing quite so nice as hearing someone say nice things about my loved ones. This generous man gave the Masin family a great gift, which we will always cherish.

* * * *

I often regret that my parents did not stay with us a little longer. It would have been wonderful for Max and Julie to have had more time to bond with their grandparents, both of whom were great with kids and were always so entertaining to be with. Everyone would have benefited so much. Hopefully this book will bring them a little bit closer.

CHAPTER FIVE:
THE SCRAPBOOK

SWEDE AND HIS GAMES

To know my father was to love him. But many people knew of him only due to his success in sports. Since he provided few details to his kids, we had to rely mostly on anecdotes we heard from Swede's friends. Luckily, the many articles about my father in his scrapbook, mostly from the three major Newark daily newspapers at the time, provide excellent documentation of what (to some people) defines my father: his extraordinary all-around athleticism. It is what generated the "legend" label.

My Aunt Shirley has always been a huge sports fan. Even before she married my Uncle Leo, she was an avid follower of my father's sports career. Luckily for us, she kept a scrapbook of Swede's exploits, and for that we are forever grateful. Like our home movies, the numerous newspaper articles provide a vivid reminder of events that happened many decades ago.

I viewed my father's scrapbook recently for the first time in more than thirty years. I had forgotten so much, and there was also so much I had never appreciated--comments about his athletic stardom I had never noticed before.

It was interesting to follow the scrapbook's story line, beginning with pre-season football write-ups in the fall of his freshman year in high school, and ending with his post-World War II stint with the Newark Bobcats in the American Basketball League (a precursor to the National Basketball Association). It's the story of how he grew from a very raw, strapping fourteen-year-old, who barely knew the rules of the various sports, to a twenty-six-year-old United States Navy vet, playing professional basketball against the likes of George Mikan (a 6' 10" center who was named one of the top fifty players of all time).

Right from the start, my father had all the tools. The pre-season football articles (his freshman year) in 1934 describe this big, strong, kid with tremendous potential. He ends up the all-around star of the newly formed team. He passes, runs, punts, defends, etc., and, barely fourteen, is mentioned on the all-city team.

He moves on to basketball where he must have been an intriguing challenge for his highly respected coach, Art Lustig. Here was this young, impressive-looking athlete who didn't know what he was doing on a basketball court. Early in the season Swede learned the game playing for the junior varsity. Very quickly he was brought up to the varsity, and by the end of the season he was a starter. In the season finale, Swede led all scorers with fifteen points.

In the spring it was on to track and field. In the Newark City Meet, still not fifteen, with virtually no training, he won the shot put event with a throw of almost fifty-eight feet, shattering the city record by well over a foot. This record stood for more than forty-five years, at which time the meet was discontinued. He put the shot, threw the discus, ran hurdles, sprinted, high-jumped and broad-jumped. He really was a natural, and he absolutely loved to compete.

My father used to tell us that he spent his youth playing—playing anything. It was informal, playground activities without any supervision. A favorite story of his was describing his very first "organized" basketball game, in the seventh grade. They were playing the eighth grade. The opening tip went to my father, and he dribbled down court for a lay-up. Unfortunately he shot at the wrong basket. Luckily, he missed, but his teammate followed up and put it in.

Both Swede and my father's lifelong friend, Sherm Harmelin, remembered this game. Because Sherm's older brothers played basketball, he knew the rules and carefully explained them to Swede before the game: "I told your father to pass me the ball, and I'll shoot." Apparently, Sherm didn't bother to tell my father which basket to shoot at. Sherm also said that the Weequahic section's Allie Stoltz, world champion caliber boxer and Newark sports hall of famer, played in that game as well.

My father's sophomore year was spotted with bouts of parental objections, according to several articles in the scrapbook. Max and Sonia didn't want their son Seymour to practice every day all year long, and of course they were worried about potential injuries. In their minds, sports were purely frivolous without any apparent benefits.

At times I wonder how much of this was "a Jewish thing." It was common for Jewish immigrants not to show interest in nor appreciate sports. The conventional wisdom (at least from my perspective) has always been that the Jewish community was far more interested in stressing education and the arts more than sports, particularly the "barbaric" ones like football. My father never mentioned it, but I wonder if he was disappointed that Max and

Sonia rarely saw him compete, especially considering his success in sports. I'm sure it helped that both my Uncle Leo, Swede's older brother and perhaps something of a father figure, and my Aunt Shirley were very supportive of my father and attended many of his games, both in high school and college.

The only way my father was able to convince his parents to allow him to play football his sophomore year in 1935 was by committing *not* to play basketball. He figured he would deal with that when the time came. But everything changed in the game against Hillside High School on Thanksgiving Day when Swede was knocked out cold. This proved to be a turning point in my father's high school sports career. Swede was returning a kick-off (teammate Milton Luria recalled it was a ninety-yard return) when he was gang-tackled. After that the details get sketchy, as time seems to have blurred people's memories about that day. Some who were present swore the Hillside team "went after" Swede, actually *trying* to knock him out of the contest. Some claim my grandmother, Sonia, was present, and she ran onto the field to tend to her son, and actually helped pull him off the muddy turf. My father only remembers returning a kick-off. He was never aware of the other details, other than he knew, after the fact, that his football playing days were doomed with his father there to witness the brutality of the game. I suspect my Aunt Shirley's version is the most accurate. She remembers that she, Max, and Leo—but not Sonia—were at the game, and that when Max saw his son lying unconscious in the mud, he was beside himself. Leo ran onto the field, although he was just as worried about Max as he was about my father.

Naturally, despite his pleading, begging, crying, nagging, and arguing, the football kayo would kayo football for Swede for two years. Who knows, if my father had not been knocked cold that day, or if Max had not attended the game to see firsthand what football was like, and if he had not seen his motionless son on the muddy field, Swede might have ended up playing pro football. Looking back, my father felt it was his best sport.

Not surprisingly, my father did not honor his commitment not to play basketball. He begged, nagged, pleaded, cried, and relentlessly pestered Max and Sonia. There were even numerous newspaper articles regarding coaches, parents, and even the athletic director working on my grandparents. But they wanted their Seymour to rest and be safe.

Years later it was amusing to hear Swede describe his frequent "crying" to his parents to let him play. I would have loved seeing this big, burly teenager "crying" to his gentle but steadfast immigrant parents—especially because in our presence Swede virtually never cried. The one exception, of course, was that the big guy got teary-eyed at the conclusion of every *Father Knows Best* episode; but then who didn't?

When it came to playing sports, however, shedding tears was Swede's key strategy with Max and Sonia and finally Swede the nudge wore his parents down. He returned to the court, steadily improved, and started becoming a noticeable force near the basket. At this time, Weequahic also had Irv Keller, a true star on the team. He was the top shooter, scorer, and playmaker—and an all-around great basketball player. With Irv and the constantly improving Swede, Weequahic kept getting more dominant.

Weequahic's most intense rivalry was with nearby South Side High School. Both were great teams with star-laden rosters, including Irv Keller, Swede Masin, Mike Purzycki, and Willie Hurst—all among the leaders in Essex County scoring. Typically Weequahic and South Side played each other three times a year; the games attracted such huge followings that they had to be moved to the Newark Armory, which would be filled to capacity with nearly 5,000 boisterous fans—a huge crowd for a high school basketball game in *any* era. The Newark newspapers previewed each game with generous coverage and the post-game reports were long and detailed. Even to this day, Weequahic and South Side alumni remember this intense rivalry well.

In the scrapbook—there in black and white—Swede's steady progress, becoming an athletic phenomenon, is clear. By his senior year, he received the most votes of any player in New Jersey on the all-state basketball team. It was also in his senior year that (with the help of others, especially his brother Leo, his strongest and most influential "lobbyist") Swede miraculously talked his parents into letting him play the last four football games of the season. I *love* the write-ups of those games. My father had the potential to be a monster of a football player. There were few if any athletes in his era with his combination of size, speed, strength, explosiveness, smarts, and athleticism. Dr. Milton Luria, class of 1939 and a lineman on Weequahic's football team, observed this remarkable combination in Swede's running style while carrying the ball: "Your father was a slashing, power runner. He rarely juked, and didn't run around defenders; he ran *through* people. And he was a great hurdler. He jumped over a lot of would-be tacklers. As big and strong as he was, he was incredibly fast." Most of the game write-ups refer to Swede's outstanding exploits in every aspect of the game. They describe his running, passing, receiving, and his dominating defensive prowess. What a linebacker he must have been! And if the articles are to be believed, he must have been the greatest punter of all time. In fact, I remember fielding punts with my father when I was a kid. Every punt was a boomer: long, high, and a perfect spiral. He was incredible: the best punter I ever saw.

One article, in assessing my father's ability, suggested he could go on to become one of the best college athletes in the country in all three sports: football, basketball, and track. This is a remarkable prediction, since I would

Swede, back row center, on the 1937 Weequahic High School football team.

be hard-pressed to think of many other athletes who might be called one of the best in the *country* in three sports. And the amazing thing is that Swede eventually *did* become a college superstar in soccer, basketball, and track, even being named to the Coaches All-American team in soccer.

Something else I noticed in the scrapbook were accolades that did not show up in the box scores (which at the time did not record very many statistics). For instance, the articles frequently mentioned Swede's defense (in both basketball and football), his all- around play at the basket (rebounds, tip-ins, blocks), his cleverness, his great passing, and of course his domination on the center jump. (Remember that through 1938 there was a center jump after every basket and successful foul shot. Swede was terrific in this facet of the game).

The scrapbook articles also frequently praised the way my father conducted himself on the court, mentioning his good sportsmanship, his enthusiasm, and his effort. I shouldn't be surprised. My father was always a good sport. He loved the games and the competition. He was clearly happy when he was competing. He was surely in his element.

"Your father always tried *so hard!*" That's what Stan Gilbert, my father's dear friend, remembered most about Swede competing in all sports. Stan Levy, another Weequahic graduate and longtime manager of the Shadybrook Swim Club, recalled that my father did not dwell on his sports accomplishments and exploits. But when he was competing, he *clearly* wanted to win. That was Swede. From the time he was a young kid, he just loved to play games. And win at them.

MIGHTY PANZER

Then came Panzer, a small teachers' college in East Orange (now part of Montclair State University), which has a fascinating college basketball story from the late 1930s to the 1940s. During his first fall season in 1938, my father knew he would not be allowed to play football, so he tried soccer and ended up becoming captain of the team his senior season. Once again he was in a position where he was somewhat freakish-looking on a soccer field. There were not many 6' 1", 200-plus pound musclemen with great speed, playing soccer.

His basketball experience at Panzer was nothing less than phenomenal. The East Orange school was tiny; less than 200 students. But they almost *always* won. They had a fourteen-game winning streak broken by Long Island University at their court in December 1938, my father's freshman year. The final score was 41-36 and Swede, who virtually never expressed sour grapes, felt Panzer got a raw deal from the referees that day. Panzer's excellent center, 6'7" Herman Knupple, got into very early foul trouble that day and my father believed the calls were very questionable. That year LIU won the National Invitation Tournament, and was considered the best college team in the country. However, after that game, LIU would not schedule Panzer. This was probably a good idea, because Panzer went on to win their next forty-four games (over two-plus seasons), which at the time was a college basketball all-time record.

Coincidentally, Seton Hall University had its own winning streak going at the same time. Led by All-American Bob Davies, who would go on to star in the NBA, they won forty-three games straight. With two long winning streaks at colleges only a few miles apart, a game between these two schools would have been natural, a David vs. Goliath contest. But despite a lot of talk, an official game never happened. Swede, surely biased, felt Seton Hall had little interest in scheduling a game that would have been a "little to gain, lots to lose" scenario for them.

On this topic, Sid Dorfman, the *Star-Ledger's* great sports writer, wrote in March 2002, "At their height the neighboring Essex schools generated a fierce rivalry that developed cultish followers throughout the state." His article proceeded to speculate why the two teams never met in a regular season game. However, the two teams *did* play a scrimmage once. Frank Chenitz, Swede's friend and Panzer teammate, remembered many of the details: that Seton Hall had trouble (as every team did) dealing with the combined size, strength, and athleticism of big Herman Knupple and Swede near the basket; that Honey Russell, Seton Hall's famous coach, became unhappy with what he considered a lackluster effort by superstar Bob Davies, first shouting at him and finally taking him out of the game; and that the game subsequently became one-sided in Panzer's favor. It was no surprise that many top rated teams had little interest risking a loss to little Panzer College.

One team that did schedule a game with Panzer was New York University, which when they met had won fifty of their previous fifty-one home games. Talk about home court dominance! Panzer traveled to NYU, and clobbered them. It wasn't even close; the game was decided in the first half. Based on the write-up in the scrapbook, Swede had a great game. He was all over the court: scoring, stealing, rebounding, passing, and blocking shots. The unfortunate result of this game was one more school unwilling to schedule Panzer again.

During his first two years at Panzer my father played on the wing. Big, strong Knupple was very effective near the basket, and with these two players Panzer was a major force inside. After Knupple departed, Swede went back to his favorite place: the middle. According to the write-ups, being under-sized at center didn't slow my father's game one bit. Reading between the scrapbook lines, it was obvious that the raw talent at Weequahic High School, the one who as a freshman barely knew the rules of the game and could hardly shoot or dribble, had now become a seasoned veteran who had mastered every aspect of the game of basketball.

Frank Chenitz, Swede's Panzer teammate and a regular in the backcourt, remembered many details of playing on those great teams, especially my father's leaping ability: "God he could jump! There'd be a crowd under the basket, and suddenly only his hand would emerge well above the rest. He could out jump the 6' 7" Knupple. Your father was the first white guy that could jump like that … I would lob alley-oop passes to him. He was the first guy I ever saw who could catch the ball above the rim with two hands and drop it in." Frank also talked about my father's improbable strength: "We were required to take a course in wrestling. He was *by far* the best wrestler in the school. The coach wanted to make a professional wrestler of Swede due to his agility and strength. One time at practice I got into a scrape with the 250-pound Knupple. He came after me. Well, Swede grabbed him and put him on the floor like he was a toy, until he finally calmed down."

The Panzer team was often referred to as the "Iron Men" because the five starters regularly played the entire game. Such a small school was not bound to have much depth. In the scrapbook clippings, the players most frequently mentioned in Swede's four years there were Knupple, Chenitz, "Bibby" Martens, Moe Berger, Jerry Kampf, and "Happy" Lieder. Sid Dorfman said they could beat *anybody*, and was amazed at the way they could move the ball. I suspect these guys from almost seventy years ago could teach a few things about fundamentals to today's players.

Swede's coach, Al Gorton, raved about him—but so did many of the opposing coaches. For instance, Matty Begovich, coach of rival John Marshall

The big guy, Swede, was a great leaper, as demonstrated by this jump ball at Panzer College, ca. 1940.

College in Jersey City (which would eventually stop Panzer's winning streak at forty-four games) saw my father play up close over four seasons. He claimed Swede was as good as or better than All-American (and future NBA All-Pro) Bob Davies. The only difference was that "Masin was not a Fancy Dan." In 1970 *Sport Magazine* rated the top pro basketball players of the first half of the twentieth century. The great George Mikan was number one. Bob Davies was number six. I don't know what these subjective ratings mean, but it is not often that one can be favorably compared to an all-pro and hall of fame basketball player. Being compared to Bob Davies, and being compared to South Side High's remarkable Lonnie Wright (for all-out athleticism) were the two scrapbook items of which Swede was most proud.

I fervently wish that Panzer College and its unprecedented success would become much more visible on college basketball's history map and appreciated by more people today. Their story reminds me of the movie *Hoosiers*, though at the college level. Hal "Peanuts" Lefcourt, a top player for Panzer just after World War II, is the long time president of the Panzer Hall of Fame, which unfortunately, in spite of his efforts, has not yet been officially recognized by Montclair State University. (Panzer merged with Montclair State in 1958). Panzer College's fascinating basketball legacy underscores the fact that nothing in sports is impossible.

* * * *

Each spring my father continued to excel for the track team. He captained the team his senior year, as he did the soccer and basketball teams. He competed in some major meets, including the Penn Relays and AAU meets, and virtually always won. For instance, he was state AAU champ in the shot put and discus. And if he didn't win, as in the Penn Relays, it was because the incomparable Alfred Blozis, the Hoya Hercules, was competing. In the early 1940s, there was no one on the planet who could top him in the shot. He must have been as extraordinary an athlete as there ever was, and should be the subject of a movie, if only they could find someone to play his character credibly. More on him in the next chapter.

MASIN DEFERRED

In 1941, the fall of his senior year, my father was notified by the draft board to report for active duty in the Army. When he arrived at Fort Dix he was sent home due to a pending action that would permit college seniors to finish their last year before reporting. So while there were questions regarding Swede's availability, Panzer Coach Al Gorton was very direct about Panzer's chances without him: "We should have a good season if the Army doesn't snatch Swede Masin. As he goes, so will Panzer. If we lose Swede, the bottom will be struck." He added, "If Swede dons the khaki, we may as well forget about this season."

The Newark *Star-Ledger* agreed, in an article by Jim Ogle (who later would become the beat writer for the Yankees). Describing Panzer's chances for the upcoming season, Ogle observed, "Panzer received an unexpected boost when Swede Masin, rated by many the equal of Davies, received a deferment from his draft board. Just how long he will be around is uncertain, but he will start the season with the Panthers."

Ogle's feature story on Swede in February 1941, "A Basketball Star Was Born Because Weequahic Had No Swimming Pool," is one of my favorites: "For want of a swimming pool, Seymour (Swede) Masin, the latest college sensation, became one of the greatest collegian players to ever perform on a local court." The article goes on to report that my father loved to swim, and that if Weequahic had a swimming pool he would have gone out for that sport instead of basketball. Instead, he tried out for the basketball team, and "When he first appeared on the court it looked as if he would never make it as a cager. He couldn't handle the ball, couldn't shoot and knew very little about the game." The article goes on to cover his rapid improvement in basketball as well as his successes in track and football.

The article is accompanied by two photos of my father: one posed shot in his basketball uniform; the other in a suit and tie, sitting at a desk (with his feet on the desk), studying. We loved the content of the article, but the picture of Swede in his suit and tie was particularly amusing.

The big guy must have been a load of a basketball player at Panzer. Their success against all competitors was truly remarkable. This little East Orange school could play anyone in the country and teach them a lesson in effort, smarts, teamwork, and talent. And Swede, all four years, was the man.

As I keep re-visiting my father's scrapbook and being reminded and stunned by his athletic versatility, I love the reverential tones in the way he is described: "Big Swede Masin" (heck, I think the sportswriters viewed him the same way I did as a kid, as the biggest man on Earth. In reality, he wasn't that big), "Swede Masin, the great center," "sensational Swede Masin," etc. As the NBA's Al Attles remarked to me, "Your father sure impressed a lot of people."

Roughly twenty-five years after Swede, Lonnie Wright came on the Newark scene and made his mark as an athletic legend. To this day I hear people claim that Swede and Lonnie were the two best all-around athletes to come out of Newark. One of the things about Lonnie Wright and my father is that they not only starred in virtually any sport they tried; they also excelled at every aspect of those games. In basketball, both could play any position, and were great offensively and defensively. In football, they could pass, run, defend, etc. They succeeded at any track and field event, whether it was running, weights, or jumping events. Their combination of size, speed, smarts, strength, agility, explosiveness, leaping ability, and competitiveness is obviously very rare. They were different than the rest of us.

Reflecting back on his basketball skills, my father felt the best part of his game was his defense and his jumping ability. He prided himself on shutting his man down. He boxed out better than anyone I've ever seen—another talent that does not show up in the box score. He realized early on that a basketball player spends half his time on the court playing defense, and that shutting your man down won games just as much as scoring points does. He must have been an extraordinary defender, and an extraordinary leaper, as evidenced by his rebounding, shot-blocking, tap-ins, and domination in the center jump.

Some game summaries describe how my father dominated the center tap against Willie Hurst and Ernie Young, the two reigning all-state centers while Swede was still an underclassman. These were star players, taller than Swede, and were known to be excellent jumpers. Swede consistently won the center taps throughout these games, and was considered a critical factor in Weequahic victories.

His inside scoring (follow-ups to missed shots, tap-ins, etc.) is mentioned constantly in the scrapbook. As my old friend and neighbor, and current Big Ten Commissioner, Jim Delany observed: "Your father had great bounce. And he'd keep jumping, relentlessly."

Even in games in which Swede scored very few points—and as a general rule the games had much lower scoring than today—the write-ups suggested that he totally dominated the game. For instance, in a game against a great Trenton team, and their outstanding center, the aforementioned Ernie Young, my father scored only one point. Yet he was described as having dominated the game, shutting down the 6' 2½" Young (who totaled two points on a hook from the corner), "winning every center tap," and dominating under the basket. He was the so-called key to the 20-15 victory. Make no mistake, Swede scored plenty in other games. His junior and senior years, in both Weequahic and Panzer, he was his team's leading scorer and always among the leaders in Essex County (high school) and New Jersey (college).

Here is a sampling of some of the words, phrases, comments, opinions, and stories I found especially interesting in my father's scrapbook:
- "Throughout the regular season 'Swede' carried the Weequahic team on his shoulders."

- "A big fellow, packing 200 pounds, Masin outmatched most schoolboys physically. Actually he is only 17 years old. The chief of the Indians will fold his tent at Weequahic in June and then will take to the warpath in the college ranks. Which college? Right now he has a hankering to go to Michigan." (This was part of his write-up upon being named all-state in basketball).
- "Swede Masin, who invariably gained the tap in the battle with Hurst at center" (against arch rival South Side and their great 6' 4" center, Willie Hurst).
- "Although Swede Masin, pudgy 14 year old freshman halfback" (I only wish I was aware of the "pudgy" moniker while my father was still with us. I would have had some fun with it. However, based on the pictures I've seen of my father as a youth, I'd say describing him as "pudgy" was a stretch).

Some representative headlines and commentary from newspaper articles dealing with parental objections from Max and Sonia:
- "Parental Objections May Keep Star Out Of Line-Up"
- "Indian Whoops Turn To Groans As Masin Again Bucks Parental Grid Objection"
- "Masin May Quit Grid; Blow Seen To Indians"
- "Many believe that if he continues on to college he will be one of the outstanding stars in the country in football, basketball, and track, providing he gets the consent of his parents"
- "Seymour 'Swede' Masin, triple threat fullback sensation will return to action this week. Masin was out for more than a week on account of parental objections. Charles Schneider, newly appointed AD [Athletic Director], had a talk with Masin's parents." I'll bet my grandparents, as young immigrants to the U.S., never would have foreseen receiving so much ink in the sports section of the Newark newspapers. And I find it remarkable how much coverage was given to the "parental objections" issue.

A few more accolades from his Weequahic years:
- "Twice getting off punts of 65 yards that found the coffin corner on each occasion." (He was a world-class punter).
- "Time and time again he took the ball off the backboard and never once was he outjumped." (A common theme in his basketball career. Swede's jumping ability must have been extraordinary).
- "Masin Directs Attack"

- "Masin's sterling exhibition. The curly haired football star was in the middle of every play, fought like a bearcat, and mustered a passing attack which many times caught South Side flat-footed."
- "Most of Masin's damage was accomplished from under the basket with sensational over-hand, off-balance shots that found their mark with amazing consistency."
- "With husky Swede Masin setting a furious scoring pace ..." (Another important basketball game against rival South Side).
- "Harmelin and Masin both had 8, and scintillated on defense." (My father's buddy Sherman did it all too).
- "Swede Masin, sensational 15 year old star, smashed the previous record ..." (Breaking the city shot put record by over a foot).
- "A bear under either basket ..."
- "Swede Masin, Weequahic's great center ... "
- "The Indians, with big Swede Masin in the starring role again . . " (Yet another huge performance versus South Side).
- "On the tap Weequahic's pivot, for all his bulk, consistently out-jumped the Negro ace, thereby throwing the rival offense out of gear before it had started." (Against Trenton's all-state center, Ernie Young. And the use of the term "Negro ace" certainly reflects the different times).
- "There is no question that he made an all-state candidate of Swede Masin, husky center, who two years ago was one of the most awkward performers in the state and tripped over his own feet." (I love this one, discussing Art Lustig's mentorship of Swede. My father adored Lustig. I hope the "tripping over his own feet" comment was an exaggeration.)
- "I can't understand why so many pupils are walking around half dead, and mumbling something about exams. Before I thought they cried because they had unmanly chests, but when Swede Masin started to do the same, my theory went up in a fog. (Yes diary, I was in the same hall with him today, and as he walked by, I actually brushed against him!)" (This was a tongue-in-cheek entry in the school paper. I guess Swede was a big man on campus).

And then on to Panzer:
- "Swede Masin, former Weequahic star and a freshman at Panzer also delivered the goods. Masin was in almost every play, fighting for the ball and was invaluable with his floor work." (In a close loss to Long Island University, the best college team in the country at the time).

- " ... and at one point leaped high over the basket to knock out a Brooklyn goal." (Goal tending!).
- "Right now Masin is rated one of the best basketball players of all time in local circles." (Part of the great feature article about Panzer's Swede by Jim Ogle).
- "Begovich Rates Masin As Davies Equal"
- "Matty Begovich, coach of Jersey City's John Marshall, thinks Swede Masin of Panzer College is 'the equal of Bob Davies of Seton Hall, as an all-around ballplayer. The only thing about Masin is that he isn't a fancy Dan, but he's every bit as good as Bob.'" (Matty Begovich coached in numerous games against Swede and Panzer, and he officiated in many of Seton Hall's games. Naturally, I think he was a great judge of talent!).
- "Panzer received an unexpected boost when Swede Masin, believed by many to be the equal of Davies, received a deferment from his draft board."
- "Swede Masin went on a one man rampage by dropping in 12 field goals and a foul for 25 points to pace the Panthers to their 21st consecutive triumph over a 2-year period." (25 was a lot of points in those days. Also, did Panzer *ever* lose?!).
- "In presenting the team trophy, the John Marshall coach paid a special tribute to Seymour "Swede" Masin, Panzer captain, as 'one of the greatest players he'd ever seen.' (This again from Begovich, someone who had starred as a player for the best team in the country [St. John's "Wonder 5"], was a very successful college coach, and a highly rated college basketball official. He'd seen plenty of great players in his day).
- "Masin The Panther Strong Man"
- "Panzer Star Whole Show In Title Win"
- "John Marshall Can't Stop Him In Loop Play-Off"
- " ... and Panzer rooters can thank—more than anyone else—the husky, good-natured "Swedeheart" of the East Orange cagers, Seymour (Swede) Masin." (How often, in a game write-up, is an athlete's "good nature" mentioned? I got a kick out of that. As hard as he tried in his various sports, Swede still kept a good perspective on the games he played. I think comments like that are what separate my father from most great athletes. As hard as he tried, he never forgot it was about playing games).
- "The 36-31 score in favor of Panzer was directly a result of Masin's superiority."
- "The entire attack was built around Swede."

- "And he was indirectly responsible for many other counters from his astute passing." (This commentary came after a crucial win for the conference championship against their always tough rival, John Marshall. The article goes on to describe two incredible field goals my father scored in the second half. Both were with his back to the basket, at some distance, and were very acrobatic. The second basket came at a crucial point at the end of a close game. The first shot was described as "amazing," the second shot was described as "impossible").

- "Several well qualified basketball experts have long rated Masin the equal of Davies in everything except showmanship." (An article about Swede's inclusion on the all-time Panzer team).

- "Matty Begovich remarked the other night that he is glad his team doesn't have to see any more of Swede. 'He is the best player in our conference,' said Matty. 'In fact he is so superior to all the others that there isn't any comparison.'" (More raving about Swede by his rival coach).

- "Masin's collegiate track exploits included the gaining of both the shot put and discus records in the North Jersey Intercollegiate Conference. He was state AAU and Metropolitan College Champion in both events." (An article about Swede joining the Navy, highlighting his track and field accomplishments).

- "Masin played a sterling brand of ball against the Philadelphia Sphas Sunday and will be an asset to the Bobcats in play under the basket." (An article about his first pro game for the Newark Bobcats, soon after returning from the Navy).

- "Masin was voted the best soccer center half in the country by the coaches association and a little All-American in basketball. In 1941 he was the state AAU champion in the discus and shot put. (Part of the summary of his accomplishments mentioned upon his induction with the first group of the Newark Sports Hall of Fame).

* * * *

It was so much fun revisiting his scrapbook after so many years. I knew my father was a great athlete, but some of the superlatives about him blew me away. I loved the talk about his effort and sportsmanship, which was like icing on the cake. Seeing all the names from my father's sports life was also a treat: Sherm Harmelin, Irv Keller, Art Lustig, David Fast, Herman Knupple, Willie Hurst, Ernie Young, Mike Purzycki, Bob Davies, LIU Coach Clair Bee, Al Blozis, Matty Begovich, Al Gorton, George Mikan, and others. I especially enjoyed the references to "pudgy" and "tripped over his own feet," as well as the numerous pictures of my father, his teammates, and his competitors, from Weequahic to Panzer to the Newark Bobcats.

Perhaps the most astounding thing to me was Swede's versatility: his scoring, defending, passing, or rebounding in basketball; his running, receiving, defending, and punting in football; his prowess in the shot put, discus, hurdles, sprints, or the jumps in track and field; his being named to the Coaches All-American team in soccer, a game he picked up in college because it was there. Swede excelled in all of it.

Perhaps most importantly, I could read between the lines to see that my father viewed sports in a very healthy manner. He loved to compete and to try his best, and he hated to lose; but he was also a great team player, he played fair, and when the game was over it was over. He never changed from when he was a young kid, in that he simply loved to play the games. We should all have such a healthy perspective.

* * * *

I have contemplated how my father would fare as an athlete today, in an age of specialization. Athletes who are considered good in a sport, say basketball or soccer, are under great pressure to make it a year-round focus, even at an early age. Weight training has become much more scientific and much more important, and even performance-enhancing drugs are being used by athletes at many levels. Swede would have nothing to do with any of the above. Specialization? When I used to ask him his favorite sport to play, he always answered "whatever sport was in season."

So, for better or worse, athletes and the games they play have changed. And Swede? If he grew up today he would certainly buck the specialization trend. He loved too many activities too much not to participate in them. With today's training techniques (assuming he would have the patience to endure them), he would most likely be bigger, stronger, and faster than he was—and he would need to be to compete against today's bigger, stronger, faster athletes. His versatility in track and field would have drawn the attention of good coaches; he would have made a world-class decathlete. There was no event for which he did not have the right physical tools.

Today my father would be a guard in basketball. But with his phenomenal leaping ability, his body strength, and his freakishly strong hands he'd still be a beast around the basket. Today's game is all about speed and athleticism, some of his greatest attributes. He would certainly thrive in today's "up tempo" style of play. Not that he ever complained, but Swede probably would prefer today's NBA player's compensation compared to the thirty dollars per game he was paid while playing for the Newark Bobcats in what was a precursor of the NBA.

Assuming he could somehow overcome the objections of Max and Sonia, his anti-football parents, Swede would be a monster at almost any position on the gridiron. He never dwelt on this stuff, but I know my father wished he could have pursued football. He felt he was best suited for that sport.

Finally, Swede would be aghast at the drug use (cheating), which has infected virtually every sport today. He had such a wholesome, natural approach to competition that I can't even imagine his disenchantment by such blatant loss of perspective on how athletes should conduct themselves. Perhaps his time and place in sports was the perfect fit for my father. He surely had no complaints.

CHAPTER SIX:
SWEDE'S CONTEMPORARIES

THE COMMON THREAD

During the process of researching this book, a common thought kept recurring. Even allowing for my bias, my father's contemporaries, cronies, and competitors, as well as his institutions of higher learning, all seemed so very interesting, and so original, and in most cases, so forgotten. To cite just a few examples:

- At one time, **Weequahic High School** was labeled the best high school, academically, in the United States. This rating, though very subjective and probably biased, suggests how highly regarded the school was. Back in the day it's safe to say Weequahic did have an inordinate number of great, respected, demanding teachers, and a student body that was, as a whole, brilliant. That, as well as the school's incomparable alumni association, makes it special. Also, the school's most famous alumnus, novelist Philip Roth, often uses Weequahic section locales in his widely read novels. There is clearly something special about the school. Just ask the alumni. They'll be happy to explain what is so unique about their magical alma mater.
- When people ask where my father played college basketball, and I respond **Panzer College**, the blank stares are comical. Virtually no one has ever heard of it. And yet the tiny Cinderella story school in 1939-1941 won forty-four straight games (then a collegiate record) as well as eighty out of eighty-five. They played against much bigger schools and manhandled them. Many top teams refused to schedule them; those that did regretted it. Tiny Panzer College, the giant killers: Spectacular, wildly successful ... and forgotten.
- In his time, Newark's **Longy Zwillman** was as powerful as any organized crime figure. And although he was reportedly the brains behind the so-called crime syndicate that included the likes of Bugsy

Siegel, Meyer Lansky, and Lucky Luciano, his name is far less known. That is just the way he wanted it. The country's biggest bootlegger during Prohibition, he worked at cultivating an image of refinement, generosity, and civility. Longy Zwilman was a true, one of a kind, original. And compared to many of his peers, mostly forgotten.

- Super-human yet forgotten, **Al Blozis** will someday emerge as one of the sports world's most amazing athletes. It's just a matter of time; he was too special to be so anonymous.

- **Bob Davies**, a college All-American and perennial NBA all-pro, is remembered only by the most astute basketball fans and historians. He was Bob Cousy before Bob Cousy. With unprecedented flair on the court, the "Harrisburg Houdini" was the inspiration for the main character in the hugely popular Chip Hilton book series. A true original, yet barely remembered.

- **Monte Irvin** is in the Baseball Hall of Fame ... a very select group. So he is not, nor will he be forgotten. But he came *this* close to being another Mays or Aaron or Mantle. Or Jackie Robinson. Monte was considered a strong candidate (by Branch Rickey) to break the "color line" of Major League Baseball. But recently discharged after a long stint in the Army, he wanted some time to hone his skills. In the meantime, Jackie Robinson made history. With just a little different timing, Monte Irvin would be a household name everywhere. It already is in my household.

- **"Iron Mike" Purzycki** is perhaps the least known of Swede's peers mentioned in this book. But if you ever met him you'd never forget him. Gruff, fearless, and witty, Iron Mike has inspired countless stories. As an athlete he did it all; as a personality, he was unmatched. I would tell you more about this fierce competitor and total original, but as he used to growl, "familiarity breeds contempt."

And then there's Swede Masin. Like most of the people above, he didn't perform before television cameras. Millions of people didn't see him play on the small screen the way college and pro stars are today. His shot-blocking wasn't highlighted on ESPN. He wasn't interviewed by reporters after every game. His exposure to the public was regional. He might have become a nationally known athlete if he had pursued football or the decathlon, but playing basketball and soccer for a small college in New Jersey was not the path to fame. However, for Swede, this wasn't the point. Like the other athletes discussed in this chapter, he was both special and original.

In their own way, all of the above should have a movie made about them. In the meantime, I am delighted to use this book to introduce some of my readers to these colorful, accomplished men and institutions.

LONGY ZWILLMAN

My father's name was sometimes mentioned in the same breath as a contemporary of his who, so far as I know, he never met. This man was similar to Swede in many ways: he lived in the Weequahic section of Newark, was tall and handsome, Jewish and generous, the son of Russian immigrants, and made his living primarily in the liquor business. Both were very beloved by friends and neighbors.

In a *Star-Ledger* column featuring Swede, in 1999, columnist John McLaughlin described the Weequahic section of Newark's reigning celebrities: "Abner (Longy) Zwillman, the gangster-politician-philanthropist, and Seymour Masin, a wondrous athlete of extraordinary versatility."

Funny, I've heard Swede and Longy lumped together before, in the context of people describing the Newark "celebrities" of the time. But I knew very little about this man whose name seemed to pop up alongside my father's from time to time. In reading about him, he certainly was a larger than life character. And most of the comments I've heard or read from people who somehow knew him were very respectful and even reverential.

Because there are so many legends about the tall (6' 2", hence the "Longy" nickname), notorious Zwillman, it's challenging to know what is true and what is not. Part saint and part sinner, he has been called the "Al Capone of New Jersey." He was said to be North America's most prolific bootlegger during Prohibition. He has been credited with being the "brains" behind the so-called "Big Six," the crime syndicate that included Meyer Lansky, Joe Adonis, Frank Costello, Lucky Luciano, and Bugsy Siegel. He has been linked to an attack on one of his bootlegging rivals, Richie "The Boot" Boiardo, in which Boiardo was shot no less than twelve times … and survived! According to lore, Al Capone came to New Jersey to help broker a truce and end the violence.

Clearly Zwillman was extremely shrewd, wealthy, and influential. He was a true criminal mastermind. And yet he is not remembered in the same notorious manner as Capone, Luciano, Dutch Schultz, and others of his time. He had a knack and a desire for distancing himself from the seedy side of his "profession."

Vita Holtz Orenstein is the mother of a good friend, and the daughter of Lou Holtz, an associate of Zwillman both during and after Prohibition. Vita recalled occasional business meetings at their house, when she and her sisters were shielded from the conversations and not even allowed downstairs. Of Zwillman, she recalls: "He was a gentleman, not a hood. He didn't want notoriety as some of his peers did. He was different than the others. And supposedly he was good to his mother." I chuckled at Vita's last comment, because there was a book written about Jewish gangsters by Robert Rockaway. The title: *But He Was Good to His Mother.*

Zwillman was a huge protector of local Jews, whether it was street peddlers being targeted by local street thugs, or organizing and funding the "Minutemen." The Minutemen were crusading ex-prizefighters, mostly Jewish, and other assorted "muscle" men, led by Nat Arno. Their mission was to disrupt totally (with their fists and clubs) Nazi Party rallies in and around Newark in the 1930s. Moreover, Zwillman's generosity was legendary. He gave huge amounts of money to Catholic churches, soup kitchens, and Jewish temples. He reportedly gave $250,000 to a Newark slum-clearing project, and he was said to have offered a large reward for the safe return of Charles Lindbergh's infant son. Of course, he also was generous with cops, judges, prosecutors, politicians, and the press. For this particular generosity he most certainly expected something in return.

In 1959, Zwillman was found hanging in the basement of his West Orange home. There remain questions as to whether he took his own life or was murdered. Apparently his health was failing, and at the same time he was being forced to testify to federal authorities about his many ties to organized crime. So there was plenty of motive to go around.

Love him or not, Longy Zwillman was a remarkable character. His life story would make a terrific movie.

Regarding similarities between Swede and Longy, admittedly there are some. But the differences are glaring. They each have their own distinct version of legendary status of a long-ago Newark. And they *both* were good to their mothers.

BIG BERTHA

Have you ever heard of the Hoya Hercules? The Human Howitzer? The Georgetown Colossus? The athlete of whom Pulitzer Prize-winning sportswriter Arthur Daley of the *New York Times* once wrote, "He was the most magnificent physical specimen these eyes have ever beheld."

That would be Al Blozis. Ever hear of him? If you are like most people the answer is no, which is too bad. He deserves to be recognized. Because Al Blozis, besides his freakishly incredible athletic accomplishments, was a courageous war hero as well as a warm, gentle guy. Like Swede, another gentle giant.

Of all the athletes my father competed with or against, none impressed him more than Blozis. He loved talking about his legendary strength and ability. They competed against each other in numerous East Coast track meets. There were many outstanding athletes competing, but according to Swede, none compared to the chiseled giant. And as legend has it, as dominant a performer as he was in track, he may have been even better in his first love, football.

In September 2001, on the sixtieth anniversary of the New York Giants drafting Blozis to play for their NFL team, the *Star-Ledger's* great columnist, Jerry Izenberg wrote about the forgotten star: "You could barely block him head-on. Teams would try to trap him at the line of scrimmage and Blozis would heave the trapper into the ball carrier. Case closed; no gain."

And how about this: In 1941 United Press International named three men the American Athletes of the Year. One was the great golfer, Ben Hogan. Another was considered by some to be the greatest heavyweight boxer ever, Joe Louis. Both are household names (at least in many households). The third was Al Blozis. Based on his accomplishments he certainly deserved the award. It amazes me that *his* is not a household name.

In his prime (when he graduated from Georgetown in 1942) Al Blozis certainly stood out physically. He was a perfectly proportioned 6' 6", 256 pounds. His accomplishments include:

* Five world records in the shot put
* Twenty-eight records broken
* All-American tackle
* NFL All-Pro tackle for the NY Giants
* Member of National Football Hall of Fame
* National shot put champ, 1941, 1942
* Although playing only two years, named to the NFL's all-decade team of the 1940s
* Decorated war hero

In the spring of 1940, Blozis competed in an indoor meet at Madison Square Garden. He lofted the sixteen-pound ball and broke the previous world indoor record by two and a half feet. Next, with the twelve-pound ball, he broke the existing record by three feet. Then he heaved the eight-pound ball more than seventy-eight feet, thus adding eight feet to the world record! Remember, shot put records, when broken, are typically eclipsed by a matter of an inch or less. He was breaking world indoor records by multiple feet!

Upon graduation from Georgetown, he was recruited by boxing promoters who were convinced they could make him the next heavyweight champion of the world. He wasn't interested, saying he didn't like to hurt people. (Thank God).

He was rejected from military service because of his height, but after constant hounding, he joined the service in late 1943. While training at Fort Benning, Georgia, he broke the Army's two-pound grenade-throwing record with a heave of ninety-four yards! He had obliterated the previous record by thirty yards!!

In 1945, while he and his platoon were fighting pockets of German resistance, some of his men went missing. Refusing to delegate, Blozis went searching for the soldiers himself, in a blinding snowstorm. A fellow soldier claimed to have seen the fatal blast from a German machine gun which took the Hoya Hercules's life. He was awarded the Bronze Star posthumously .

Swede liked to remember his teammates, coaches, and competitors. But he clearly viewed some of them as very special. Al Blozis was one of them. My father was an outstanding track athlete in high school and college, specializing in the shot and discus. He competed against Blozis in some major Eastern meets and observed how physically imposing he was: huge shoulders, no fat on him. But Swede didn't just admire his size, strength, and athleticism. He remarked about his nature.

Swede got to know this amazing competitor when Blozis actually spent time giving my father some much-needed pointers on how to improve his technique. Because Swede had never really been coached in the shot put and discus, he felt disadvantaged in these events and was greatly impressed that his competitor would graciously take the time to help him. It's probably the main reason he would talk about Blozis so often, who was an original for his time and place.

What a shame Al Blozis died so young. I wish I had met him. He was an extraordinary, special athlete, and it sounds like he was an extraordinary, special man. From what I've read and heard about him, he reminds me of my father, only bigger. Al Blozis, another contemporary and competitor of Swede's, and another one of a kind and true original.

BOB DAVIES

The New York Metropolitan area has always been a hotbed for the game of basketball. But at the college level, 1939 must have been special. The nation's best team, and winner of the NIT, was Long Island University. They were in the midst of a forty-three-game winning streak. Right across the river, in the Oranges of New Jersey, other teams were making news as well. Seton Hall University began its own winning streak, which also happened to reach forty-three games. And minutes away, tiny Panzer College outdid everyone, beginning a forty-four-game winning streak, which at the time would be the longest *ever* in college.

The star player for Seton Hall was Bob Davies. He was a two-time all-American, but he was more than just outstanding. He was, like other contemporaries and competitors of my father, a true original. Known as the "Harrison [Pennsylvania] Houdini," he was the first player to master the art of dribbling and passing behind his back, demonstrating a flair for the game which had not been seen before. His college coach, Honey Russell, appreciated his player's artistry: "He had such uncanny control of the ball behind his back that it never concerned me. He made it look as easy as the conventional dribble."

Davies was the main attraction for what at the time was the largest crowd in basketball history, some 18,400 at Madison Square Garden in an NIT tournament game against Rhode Island State College (now the University of Rhode Island) on March 19, 1941.

But make no mistake, Davies was more than just fancy with the basketball. He was first team all-American in 1941 and 1942. He played and starred in pro basketball for ten years, including being a first team all-star four straight years (1949 through 1952). He led the league in assists in the 1948-49 season. He set a then NBA record of twenty assists in one game. In 1946-47, he was the league MVP. In 1970, *Sport Magazine* named its top players in the first fifty years of the century. Bob Davies was number six. He was one of ten players named to the NBA's Silver Anniversary team (the first twenty-five years of the league) in 1971.

And to top it all off, he was the inspiration for the title character in a sports fiction book series called Chip Hilton. The Hilton character was a "golden boy" athlete who would always lead his team, regardless of the sport, to the championship with last-minute heroics. The author of the series was Clair Bee, who had been the coach of Long Island University during its sports heyday. (I wish he'd used my father for the inspiration of his title character. I would have loved reading the "Seymour Hilton" sports series). Today, copies of the Chip Hilton series have become collector's items.

The genuine high-profile superstar was Davies. And he was the player that certain coaches and sportswriters compared my father to quite favorably. Swede always said it was "crazy" for them to make such claims; after all, Davies is an all-time great. But if the articles and quotes are to be believed, my father sure had some credible advocates of his abilities. To be compared to an original legend like Bob Davies is the ultimate compliment.

MONTE IRVIN

My father often spoke about a terrific all-around athlete he competed against in high school, who lived in Orange, New Jersey, and who starred in football, basketball, baseball, and track. This was Monte Irvin. When the *Star Ledger* of Newark published their picks for Jersey's greatest high school all-around athletes of the twentieth century, Irvin was number nine.

When Swede was a junior at Weequahic, he competed against Irvin, a senior at Orange High, in basketball. Two excellent teams, and two all-around star athletes, who guarded each other. They had similar attributes … big, strong, fast, and athletic.

It was a close game, with Weequahic clinging to a one-point lead as time was running out. With seconds to go, Irvin put up an outside shot, which rebounded long, back to the shooter, who then hit a long shot from the corner as time expired. Orange won, 18-17, or 17-16, or 15-14. You see, many years later Monte and Swede saw each other at a social function. They greeted each other like old friends, not competitors. Naturally they commiserated about that great basketball game many years earlier.

But Swede was sure the final score was 18-17. Monte was positive it was 17-16. So they joked on and on about who had it right. As the evening ended they agreed to disagree on the final score. They didn't really care one bit. They just enjoyed catching up that night.

Fast forward a decade or so. I attended a sports banquet in Wilmington, Delaware, and one of the celebrities at the head table was Monte Irvin. After the festivities, some of the guests of honor made themselves available for signing autographs, shaking hands, and so on. When Irvin was free, I introduced myself. "Hi Monte, I'm Swede Masin's son." The Hall of Famer seemed genuinely happy to meet Swede's kid, and he howled when I said "My father sends his best and asked me to remind you that the final score of your game was 18-17." And then he responded with certainty that the score was 16-15. (He had lowered it from the previous decade). He even suggested it might have been 15-14. In any event, I really enjoyed meeting him that night. He was a very impressive man. In particular, I'll never forget the way he beamed when I mentioned I was Swede's son (not just another boring guy wanting an autograph). And he was extremely animated talking about that game of long ago, which he won with his last-second heroics.

Monte Irvin is now in his late eighties, living in Florida. Based on a recent phone conversation with him, he continues to impress and has amazing recall. He still remembers the Weequahic-Orange game vividly; his game-winning shot from the corner, how he and my father battled each other the whole game (he referred to Swede as a "horse" inside). He also remembered the names of other players in the game, most notably Weequahic's other star, Irv Keller.

And the moment I brought up the issue of the correct final score, he didn't even let me finish the sentence; he remembered his conversation with Swede from many years earlier. "It was 14-13!" he said. I laughed, because there was no way I was going to win the debate, and also because the score continues to creep down!

Irvin clearly remembered the match-up with my father. He said they had great respect for each other, both for their talent and otherwise. Swede certainly never forgot this impressive guy, and he had plenty of opportunity to root for him in the following years. Because Monte Irvin, later on, was a monster of a baseball star.

Since the mid-1950s I have been a big baseball fan, and especially a Willie Mays fanatic. I was a little too young to know a lot about Monte Irvin. But in researching his accomplishments, I was amazed at how good he must have been. A small sampling:

    * Five time all-star in the Negro League, playing for the Newark Eagles

    * Triple Crown winner of the Mexican League as well as MVP

    * MVP in the Puerto Rican Winter League

    * Inducted in the Baseball Hall of Fame in 1973

    * Led the Giants in their miraculous comeback to win the pennant in 1951. Third in the National League MVP voting

    * The perfect mentor for the Giants' young phenomenon, Willie Mays

Some felt Monte Irvin was the ideal choice to break baseball's "color" barrier. After serving in World War II, he had a conversation with the Dodgers' Branch Rickey, who believed Irvin had "the right stuff" to be the first black player in the Major Leagues. But Irvin didn't think he was ready to play at that level after his long stint in the service; he needed some time to get rid of the rust. Not long after, Jackie Robinson made history.

One more thought about Monte Irvin. The more I've learned about him, the more impressed I am. There is the sports stuff; he was one of the best ever. Like other stars of the Negro Leagues, there was limited exposure to his talents (he could hit, run, field, throw, and hit for power as well as just about any player ever), and so he is not quite the household name as a Mays, Mantle, Aaron, Robinson, Clemente, Musial, DiMaggio, Ruth, and Gehrig. But from what I can tell, he was every bit as good.

No wonder my father, after "battling the whole game" with Monte Irvin, always spoke so admiringly about him. He's a legendary athlete, a terrific man, and a true original.

IRON MIKE

Then there was Iron Mike.

When I was in high school my father told me stories about Mike Purzycki. He had been an all-around star athlete during the same era as Swede. Both are members of the Newark Sports Hall of Fame, and both were named to the all-decade basketball team in New Jersey for the 1930s. He went to Newark's South Side High School, Weequahic's direct rival. Legend had it that Mike was ejected from a football game against Bloomfield High, the perennial power in the state at the time. Apparently Mike took exception to an ethnic slur directed his way by an opposing lineman, and the punches started flying. Both players were kicked out of the game.

After the game, still fuming, Mike decided to visit the Bloomfield locker room *by himself*, to mete out justice. Another brawl ensued. The lopsided odds apparently didn't bother Mike. As the story goes, Mike landed one hell of a sucker punch before he was subdued. In any event, this story was my first introduction to "Iron Mike" Purzycki and his family.

For many years, Weequahic versus South Side was *the* rivalry in Newark and beyond, particularly in basketball. And in the mid to late 1930s, both teams had star players. Besides Purzycki, South Side had a great center, Willie Hurst, and Weequahic had Swede and Irv Keller, also one of the school's all-time greats. Fan interest was extremely high, so the games were played in the Newark Armory, allowing for nearly 5,000 spectators. And in virtually every heated game, South Side's high scorer was Mike Purzycki.

This was one keen rivalry. There was much familiarity among the fans and the players, and there was always much at stake, especially city and county superiority.

Swede and Iron Mike remembered those games with fondness. The games were played at the highest level, and they were always competitive and entertaining. Nevertheless, in those days they were competitors, not friends.

After high school, Swede went to Panzer College, Mike went to Villanova. They didn't see each other again for almost thirty years.

* * * *

In the summer of 1966, right after graduating from Columbia High School, I was at a friend's party and saw a guy wearing a University of Delaware t-shirt. I would be attending Delaware that fall, so I approached him. It turned out to be Joe Purzycki, Iron Mike's son. We hit it off right away, and we've been lifelong buddies ever since. I soon learned that Iron Mike had two sons—Joe and his older brother Mike—and my close friendship with the Purzycki brothers would bring Swede and Iron Mike together again, but this time as friends, not as competitors.

Both Joe and Mike were "Big Men on Campus" at the University of Delaware and record-setting football stars, Mike as a receiver, Joe as a cornerback. Both had rugged, movie-star looks and strong personalities. And they could take care of themselves. Like father, like sons. No one messed with the Purzyckis.

But the true original in the family was the patriarch. Marion "Mike" Purzycki was a bull of a man. In his days of competing in sports he was 5' 11", 220 pounds of muscle. By the time I met him, well into his fifties, he was in the 300-pound range, built like a barrel. He had hands like catchers' mitts. He clearly had a hard-nosed side to him, but he had a very soft side as well. And he was incredibly funny, with a sharp wit. Marie Purzycki, "Mrs. P.," was a saint. I'm sure it was interesting trying to keep up with the big guy. She was very petite, and she was one of my all-time favorite people. She was like a second mother to me.

Iron Mike was the stereotypical used car salesman. Picture Tony Soprano, plus a great sense of humor, but minus the rap sheet. For a time he had multiple car lots in and around Newark. Business etiquette, rules and regulations were not his highest priorities. He tended to conduct his business on a cash-only basis. And as Mike and Joe remember, the lot locations changed frequently. It seems Mr. P. was trying to stay a few steps ahead of someone.

Once when Joe was home from college, his father wasn't feeling great, so he asked Joe to drive over to the lot and pick up the day's receipts. Since the lot location had recently changed for the umpteenth time, Joe couldn't find it. He stopped at a pay phone and called the manager for directions:

Joe: "Hello, is Vito there?"

Vito: "No. Who's this?"

Joe: "This is Joe Purzycki. Who's this?"

Vito: "Oh, okay. This is Vito."

Joe loved to relate this story to demonstrate the caliber of Iron Mike's "business associates." He always referred to them as outlaws.

On another occasion, one of Joe's "uncles," Uncle Tony, was visiting. He was going on and on about what a "dear, sweet man" a certain organized crime kingpin was. Joe naively became inquisitive:

Joe: "But Uncle Tony, I thought he killed, like, one hundred people or more."

Uncle Tony: "*They had it comin'!*" he shot back angrily (as Iron Mike roared with laughter).

I guess perspective is everything.

* * * *

The boys were raised in the Vailsburg section of Newark, but the family later moved to Point Pleasant Beach on the Jersey Shore .The Purzyckis loved having Mike and Joe and their buddies at their place. The beach town was a great venue and the location, right along the boardwalk, was ideal for beach access and people watching. There was always lots of action there, and it was always a bunch of rowdy, macho wise-asses. This crowd was not for the faint of heart. The digs, mocking, insults, arguing, and more were non-stop. And no one loved it (and promoted it) more than Iron Mike.

There was a hoop out back, and on occasion Mr. P. would come out and shoot around with one or more of us. He was nothing short of amazing to watch. He was automatic! From any angle or distance he was an incomparable shooter. Here's this tank of a man, years from being in shape, with his huge mitts, swishing two-handed set shots from every angle, with ease. Iron Mike must have been an incredible scorer during his South Side days.

Mr. Purzycki was the first to admit that when he was playing, he was never shy about shooting. He never met a shot he didn't like, and years later, when Joe was playing at Vailsburg, his father's recommended strategy was "If you're hot, keep shootin'. If you're not, keep shootin' til you get hot."

In football, Iron Mike must have been quite the fearsome lineman. He used to chuckle when relating how, on the first play from scrimmage in every game, he would greet the opposing lineman across from him by growling, "I'm gonna *kill* you!" And with his size, strength, athleticism, and especially his disposition, it must have been incredibly unpleasant to be lined up against him. If I were to define "mayhem," I would use a picture of Iron Mike as an illustration.

Iron Mike was also a fire-balling pitcher in baseball, even though (as he himself has admitted) his control left something to be desired. He said he'd occasionally feel obligated to shout to an opposing batter, as he feigned frustration: "I have *no* idea where this ball is going!" That must have been quite encouraging for the poor batter to hear.

* * * *

Often, weather permitting, Mr. P. would sit outside on the deck of his house, which abutted the Point Pleasant Beach boardwalk. One day two teenage boys on bikes rode past and were being very loud and obnoxious as they rode back and forth. Finally, Mr. P. had taken enough of the racket they were making, and barked at the boys to cut it out. The two unruly cyclists were taken aback, and both stopped and stared at the complaining deck-sitter. They quickly assessed that their adversary, while a massive guy, was over the hill and overweight. They started taunting. "What are you going to do, chase us down?" and "Hey old man, are you going to run after us?" and "Come on fatso, why don't you catch us?!" (If only those two dummies knew with whom they were dealing).

As the boys were talking trash, Iron Mike planned his move. He was sitting next to the screen door, and nonchalantly, in his trademark gruff, low-pitched growl, called Casey, the family's large, high-strung (vicious) German Shepherd. Casey immediately bolted to the door, ready to slay for his master, and began making a low, guttural growl of a noise. Casey was anxious to keep his world title—the meanest dog that ever lived.

While the cocky troublemakers were in mid taunt, Mr. P. flung open the door and at the top of his lungs growled "*Get 'em!!*" The mighty Casey charged. Mr. P.'s fondest recollection of the event, as he told the story, was the "blood-curdling screams" emitted by the panic-stricken, petrified taunters. Both had a couple of seconds to gather themselves and take off. No use. They both veered off the boardwalk, onto the sand. Fortunately, Casey was more bark than bite, and he was intimidated by Mr. P., who got him back before any damage was done to the teenagers, both of whom were begging for mercy.

In some ways, Casey was the canine equivalent of Mr. P.—albeit without the same sense of humor. A good example of this occurred every time that Dave Fargnoli, a good friend of the Purzycki family, came to visit. Normally very brash, Dave utterly feared Casey, and became uncharacteristically uncomfortable and extremely nervous whenever Casey was present. But Mr. P. showed no sympathy whatsoever toward Dave's plight. His advice to Dave—delivered in a flat, foreboding, monotone growl—was simply, "No sudden movements." So there Dave would sit, motionless and petrified, avoiding direct eye contact with Casey.

* * * *

Mr. Purzycki was a world-class beer drinker. He loved it ice cold, he drank it fast, and he drank a lot of it. Schaefer beer, in cans, was his favorite. Sometimes one or more of us would sit at the kitchen table in the Point Pleasant house and chew the fat. Once in a while it was just Iron Mike and me. Naturally I wouldn't nor couldn't keep up with the beer consumption. Mr. P. could down four beers in the time I'd drink just one. So if I had three or four or five beers in the evening ... well, do the math. And you could never tell he had consumed so much beer. What I remember most was that whenever I'd get up from the table to get a beer, Mr. P. would say in his gruff voice: "Bobby, put a few more up top." Up top of course was the freezer. He loved 'em ice cold.

Once, suffering from some health problems, Mr. P. was hospitalized for a few days and Swede went to visit. Iron Mike related a conversation he had that morning with the doctor as he made his rounds:

Doctor: "Mr. Purzycki, are you a big beer drinker?"

Iron Mike: "I guess."

Doctor: "How much beer do you drink?"

Iron Mike: "I don't want to tell you."

Doctor: "Go ahead. Impress me."

Iron Mike: "Maybe a case a night." (And I'm sure they were all ice cold).

For Swede, this was unthinkable. A liquor salesman for fifty years, my father rarely drank any alcohol. If he did, it was one drink. He was shocked to hear how much beer Mr. P. consumed. He gave Iron Mike a mild pep talk about how he should try to take better care of himself, but he didn't think it was going to stick. The two superstar athletes from Newark, from the same era, were so similar and yet so different. Funny, but both men disliked their given names. Here were these two big, strong, strapping all-around athletes, and their real names were Marion and Seymour. No wonder they preferred Iron Mike and Swede.

On a Sunday morning one summer, Mr. P. slept in. Even by his standards he may have had one or two too many ice cold ones the night before. Finally, late morning, he made his way to the kitchen. Mrs. P., her two sons, Joe's wife Sharon, and I were sitting around the table, talking. Iron Mike took his normal spot, at the head of the table. He was a little grumpy, not saying much. Mrs. P. was up and about, cooking for the gang, and while doing so uncharacteristically went into a diatribe at her husband. "I'm tired of you drinking too much, getting up late and in a foul mood, not raising a helping hand," etc. She stayed after him for a couple of minutes; all the while Mr. P. sat motionless at the head of the table, his huge hands and arms resting gently in front of him. He stared straight ahead, saying nothing. The whole time he had quite the mean scowl on his face. When Mrs. P. finally finished, an uneasy silence filled the room. We were all waiting for a response. Finally, Iron Mike spoke. With his monstrous right fist he pounded once on the table, looked up and growled, *"Coffee!"* Now, know that he did this for effect (based on the twinkle in his eye) and it *was* hilarious. Although I'm not sure Mrs. P. would agree.

* * * *

In 1976, Mr. P.'s son, Mike, and I hatched a plan to row a boat in the ocean from Lewes, Delaware, across Delaware Bay to Cape May, New Jersey, and then follow the coast north to Point Pleasant Beach. The total distance was approximately 130 miles. Every weekend that summer Mike and I trained, rowing in the waters near Point Pleasant. We took the boat out every Saturday and Sunday, each week going a little longer and getting in better rowing shape.

One weekend my parents came down to visit with the Purzyckis. As Mike and I returned from a training row, we needed some help lugging that boat through the sand back to the Purzyckis' driveway. Swede came over to lend us a hand. As he walked towards us on the beach, Mike was taken by the extraordinary shape my father was in. A very well-built guy, Mike is not easily impressed, but he was in this case. So was I. Swede looked like Charles Atlas, only more muscular.

Mike and I were not especially worried about our upcoming trip, but guess who was: two of the toughest, strongest guys of their generation, Iron Mike and Swede. Neither wanted us to take this journey, and neither was shy about trying to talk us out of it. They both warned about us not having control of our destiny (bad weather, rough seas, etc.), and they couldn't understand why we wanted to risk this "adventure." In particular, Mr. P. appealed to my common sense on numerous occasions to convince his son we should abort the mission. In retrospect it's interesting that these two fearless guys were fretting more than anyone.

Finally, in the late summer, we took the journey. The five-day trip was hard but great. When we arrived at Point Pleasant Beach, Mrs. Purzycki was our welcoming committee. Mr. P. had made an anonymous phone call to the *Asbury Park Press* newspaper, alerting them to the arrival of two remarkable adventurers. Shockingly, they opted not to send a team of reporters and photographers.

You may have heard the huge sighs of relief from the two burly sports icons when we arrived safely. Swede and Iron Mike were more relieved than anyone.

* * * *

My parents and the Purzyckis traveled together to watch their sons play in the Boston University versus Delaware football game in Boston. They went to the hotel bar and ordered drinks, and Swede was taken aback by how much beer Iron Mike consumed, and how fast he consumed it. (Mr. P. could be a little impatient at times, so he ordered two beers at a time).

Mr. P. also frequently attended football games at the University of Delaware Stadium, which was (and still is) a great venue for spectators. The grandstand is very close to the field (there is no track in between). Large green hedges separate the fans from the players, and sideline security is always tight. The sideline was for players, coaches, trainers, cheerleaders, and perhaps a newspaper photographer. Oh, and also Mr. Purzycki. Somehow he'd talk his way onto the sidelines for every game. Once, during a close game, while watching from his normal spot on the sideline, Mr. P.'s view of the field was somewhat blocked. He growled "*Down in front*!!" to the Delaware cheerleaders.

* * * *

Joe Purcyzki was like his father in many ways. He went into coaching after graduating from the University of Delaware in 1970, and was itching to be a head coach at the college level, when an opportunity suddenly opened up at Delaware State University, a historically African American college. Against the advice of almost everyone, Joe threw his hat in the ring—and to everyone's surprise was given the coaching job in 1981 over two strong African American candidates. What ensued was a fascinating four-year odyssey that included many emotional highs and lows, disappointment and success, press coverage that was at times wonderful and at times brutal, and a lesson for just about everyone.

At first, shock waves pulsed throughout the campus. Many students, players, and staff were furious with the decision. How was this white coach from New Jersey going to relate to an all-black roster at a predominately black college? There was a death threat, various organized protests, and even some players who were anxious to see their coach fail. But Joe's fortitude and charisma prevailed.

When he interviewed for the job, Joe had projected ahead four seasons, and had set goals of winning two, four, six, and then eight games over that span. They ended up winning two, four, seven, and eight. There would be articles in the *New York Times* and *Sports Illustrated* (which referred to Joe as the "White Shadow").

Approximately twenty years later, Joe was inducted into the Delaware *Black* Sports Hall of Fame. In attendance at the ceremony were many of Joe's former players. At the conclusion there were plenty of hugs and tears. Some day there will be a great movie and/or book about the Purzycki era at Delaware State. This is one terrific human interest story.

* * * *

My father always preached the fundamentals to his four kids. Do the right thing, be good citizens, live a healthy life, practice the golden rule, treat everyone respectfully, etc. I'm sure he felt if we did these fundamental things, we'd end up okay. He clearly tried hard to live his life that way.

Iron Mike? He preached three things to his beloved sons, Mike and Joe. Just three things.

1) Always keep an arm's length away (so as not to get sucker-punched).

2) Don't panic.

3) Trust no one.

Pretty simple, and a tad more cynical than Swede's preachings.

Once, after Mr. P. had reminded Joe of his three rules for life, Joe felt he needed a little more clarification.

Joe: "Dad, when you say trust no one, do you really mean *no one*?"

Mr. P.: "Trust no one"

Joe: "But what about Grandpa Babci?" (Iron Mike's Polish-immigrant father)

Mr. P.: "Yeah, okay, you can trust Babci."

Joe: What about Aunt Kitty?" (Mrs. P.'s sister)

Mr. P.: "Trust no one"

Joe and I still laugh today about Iron Mike's selective approach to abiding by his three rules for life. But reading through the lines, Mr. Purzycki, in his gruff manner, was just trying to prevent his sons from getting hurt.

One of my family's closest friends in Portland is Peter Hunt, a.k.a. "Big Pete." We play sports together (he is unstoppable on the basketball court), argue politics, hike together, etc., but one of his favorite pastimes is listening to Iron Mike stories. He is very familiar with Mr. P's three basic rules for life. Not long ago, while working in a food distribution warehouse at night, Pete heard that a suspicious guy was in the parking lot. Pete went out to investigate, and confronted the surly-looking lug who was snooping around, up to no good. Pete asked him what he was doing there, and the guy responded with a punch to my buddy's jaw. Pete, a terrific heavyweight wrestler and football star in high school and not someone to mess with, quickly brought the guy down and subdued him. He kept him wrapped up until an associate called the police, who took the guy away. But Pete did come away with a fat lip. Naturally, I got all over him for not abiding by Mr. P's tenets, especially "trust no one" and "always keep an arm's length." He agreed and now has new-found respect for Iron Mike.

Yes, Marion "Iron Mike" Purzycki, Seymour "Swede" Masin's contemporary, competitor, and eventually his friend, was a true character in every sense of the word. He could be a little rough at times, but beneath the roughness was a very loving husband and father. As colorful as his sons are, there will never be another Iron Mike. He was truly an original.

CHAPTER SEVEN:
OFF TO WAR

My father spent four years in the United States Navy, but his military career started unusually. In early November 1941, one month before the attack on Pearl Harbor, when Swede was a senior at Panzer College, he was drafted by the Army and instructed to report. He said his good-byes, and with a group of fellow inductees took a train to Fort Dix, New Jersey. Once there, he sat and waited for a long time, eating a "dried out cheese sandwich they gave us," when finally a soldier called his name and told him to "go home."

So Swede rode the train back to Newark, went home to Grumman Avenue, and ate the fresh-baked cookies his mother had waiting for him. It seems the draft board had decided that college seniors would be allowed to finish their final year before reporting and called her to say my father would be getting a temporary deferment. My father never expressed what a relief it must have been. *But what a relief it must have been*! He was undoubtedly looking forward to his senior year at Panzer, and now he could experience it. But like millions of other young Americans, he knew what lay ahead. My father's generation, often described as our country's greatest, would soon be put to the test.

Swede had so much going for him at the time. He was still living in the wonderful Weequahic section, he was a highly respected and talked-about athlete at the college level, and he even had become a great student. Knowing that anything could happen while at war, most of it bad, must have been like a huge, black cloud hanging over the heads of my father and so many of his contemporaries.

So Swede finished his senior year. The college grad was accepted into Officer's Candidate School by the U.S. Navy. He spent two months at Cornell University for an indoctrination program, where he learned about all things Navy.

Upon completion, my father reported to Guantanamo Bay, Cuba, where he would spend the next twenty-two months. After some training in mine warfare, he became the commanding officer of a mine sweeper, the *USS Endurance*, patrolling the waters in strategic shipping lanes.

From Cuba my father went to Yorktown, Virginia, where for twelve weeks he attended the Naval Mine Warfare School. From there Swede traveled by ship across the Atlantic along with almost 25,000 other military personnel. It was a converted luxury liner, which was now a troop transport ship, carrying personnel from varied branches of the service. It was a very fast ship, so it went unescorted until it approached its destination. Speaking for myself, considering the constant threat of U-boats, I would have been *real* happy when that ship reached its destination. I don't care *how* fast it was.

In Swede's later years, he had difficulty remembering the exact sequence of the various places he was stationed. He spent time in and around Algiers and North Africa, all around Italy, including Sicily and Sardinia, and the south coast of France.

For the next seven months, my father once again piloted a mine sweeper, the *YMS 16*, patrolling and escorting in the waters between North Africa and Italy. They took enemy fire on two occasions, but there were no casualties.

For millions of parents, these were perilous times, and my own grandparents were no exception. Max and Sonia, who enjoyed vacationing in and around Bradley Beach, New Jersey, told me that during the war years, they would sit on a bench on the boardwalk, look out at the ocean (knowing their son was out there somewhere), and pray he was safe.

During his time across the Atlantic, my father wrote the lyrics and music for a love song. So many young people, worldwide, were in harm's way, in places they heretofore had never heard of, risking their lives. So many loved ones were torn apart. The scary times, plus his own feelings, inspired his song. Here is a sampling of some of the lyrics:

> "They say that parting is such sweet sorrow
> The sorrow I see easily
> But when it comes to the sweet part
> It hasn't appeared to me"

> "The touch of your lips so dear
> The sound of your sigh
> That moment I held you near
> Then whispered good-bye"

> "The tears welling in your eyes
> Your effort to smile
> Our visions of paradise
> Delayed for a while"

These and the rest of the lyrics, as well as the music, are not the normal fare from big, strong jocks. Swede was very shy about it, and never tried to publish it later, despite plenty of encouragement. But on several occasions, with extended family around, my grandmother Helen (who would accompany on the piano) talked my father into singing his song. It was another clear example of Swede's softer side.

One day, while patrolling waters off the North African Coast, my father climbed down into "the hole" of the ship. He descended the hatch ladder, steadying himself with his right hand holding the ledge above. The open hatch cover, which was extremely heavy, had been left unsecured. The seas were rough, and the tilt of the ship knocked over the hatch cover. It landed in a thud, smashing the three middle fingers on Swede's right hand, almost severing the three digits. My father always felt fortunate his head was lower than the hatch opening; if it had landed on his head he might have been killed. His fingers needed over 100 stitches, but they were saved. Then an infection set in, complicating his recovery. He was sent to a hospital in Algiers, and was ultimately flown with other injured military personnel to a naval hospital on Long Island. He recovered, but the middle finger on his right hand had some irreparable damage. The upper knuckle was intentionally set in a bent position. (It would have been problematic for many reasons to have his middle finger sticking up!) And the nail, which always continued to grow and needed clipping, was very badly misshapen and remained discolored the rest of his life.

Stateside, Swede was a Battalion Commander of the Ammunition Depot at Earle, New Jersey. While there he was able to get back to his beloved Weequahic section of Newark quite often, commuting by train. By this time, my mother had graduated from Weequahic High School and had moved with her family to Long Branch. But she commuted back and forth to Newark regularly to work in a munitions factory, helping the war effort. As fate would have it, Estelle and Swede met on one of their train commutes. Although they knew of each other, they had never formally met before. In fact, several years earlier while seniors in college, my father and his buddy Stan Gilbert had gone to a Weequahic basketball game. Stan vividly remembers my father pointing out this beautiful cheerleader, who really attracted Swede's attention. Who would have guessed she would be his future wife? And coincidentally, when Estelle was in high school, she noticed my father walking past the Lepore home. She ran to tell her parents that Swede Masin, "that great athlete," was walking by.

After meeting several times on the train during the war, Estelle invited Swede to her parents' house for spaghetti dinner, and the rest is history. He

Swede, home from the war, courting Estelle at the Jersey Shore, 1945.

and my future mother began seeing each other often, both in and around Newark and the Jersey shore. Eventually they started making wedding plans.

As the war was nearing a close, my father was transferred to Bremerton, Washington, where he was a Barracks Commander. The war ended, and in very late December 1945, my mother journeyed to the Pacific Northwest, arriving on the final day of the year. The next day—the first day of the new year—with a talking parrot as their witness, they married. And in April 1946, my father was honorably discharged from the U.S. Navy. From there they took a honeymoon trip down the West Coast, and then to 123 Grumman Avenue, Newark, New Jersey.Like so many of his contemporaries, Swede did not talk about his stint in the military very often. Occasionally he would share a few details, but he never talked about what it was like, after growing up in the sheltered Weequahic section, to contemplate having to kill anonymous enemies. Or to contemplate being killed by anonymous enemies. I think Swede wanted to shield us from the combination of anxiety, drudgery, longing, homesickness, apprehension and fear that comes with four years in the military, especially during a time of war.

But there is no doubt about the fear of war that this generation experienced. As Stan Gilbert explained to me, "It was a sinking feeling. We knew we [the U.S.] would end up involved." Along with many others, Stan participated in a peace march in and around Broad and Market Streets in Newark, ca. 1940. But soon afterwards, while in college, he got his draft number. "It was always hanging over our heads while we were in college. It was just an awful feeling when we had to go off to war." I can only imagine, and wish that my father had shared more of his feelings and memories of those frightening times.

Stan served as a spotter for an artillery unit, so he often had to position himself far forward, approaching German lines. He told me, "Because I was forward of my unit, I was more vulnerable to capture. And if you were Jewish and were captured by the Germans … "

Once, in 1944, Stan and his unit had a brief stopover in Naples, Italy. In the harbor he saw a number of mine sweepers, all in a row. They were the YMS class of sweepers, and Stan knew that was the type my father was on. Swede's oldest friend, who at one time lived two doors away on Maple Avenue in the Weequahic section, excitedly hustled up and down the Naples harbor, looking for my father's vessel. But to Stan's disappointment, he was informed that *YMS 16*, Swede's mine sweeper, was out, patrolling off the coast of Sicily.

It would have been a wonderful, albeit brief reunion for the boyhood friends—a short respite from what must have been a constant, all-consuming feeling of homesickness and foreboding. I can't help but wonder how often our service people asked themselves "When will my number be up?"

Swede and Estelle, soon after their wedding, stationed in Bremerton, Washington, 1946.

Today there are plenty of people who maintain that we never should have dropped the atomic bomb(s) on Japan. I remember my father wondering out loud if it was necessary to drop the second one. I asked Stan his opinion. His response was clear. "We thought it was great! It ended the war!" I doubt many of the servicemen felt differently.

On several occasions throughout his life, I remember my father lamenting how the German people could so wildly endorse and salute their mad leader, Adolf Hitler. How could a demented person like that win over the masses? I thought of that after talking to Stan about his memories of the war. The last thing he said, as his voice tailed off: "I still can't figure out how the German people … "

In his nearly four-year stint, my father saw a lot of the world. He met people from all walks of life (some of whom became lifelong, cherished friends), he protected fellow service people, and he was most certainly protected by others while in harm's way. Most importantly, our side won and he survived. Many brave people were not so lucky.

CHAPTER EIGHT:
SWEDE AND RELIGION

My father's parents, Max and Sonia, were religious people. They were members of Temple B'nai Abraham in Newark, one of the better known Conservative temples in the area. (Today it is a mosque). They practiced their Jewish religion, well, religiously. Like many other Jewish immigrants from Europe and Russia, they had been persecuted for their beliefs in their homelands. Newark, particularly the Weequahic section, offered a safe haven for my grandparents and their religious freedom.

My father, in some ways, was a very religious man. He had a strong belief in God; he always acted very protectively of his Jewish religion; and he was very sensitive to anti-Semitism.

With his blond hair and blue eyes, and the non-Jewish sounding name Swede Masin, it was not uncommon for my father to hear anti-Semitic remarks by people who didn't realize his faith. As tolerant a person as he was, these incidents really tore at him.

But as proud as he was of his own religion, my father felt strongly that religion should be a personal thing. The more organized and "group think" it became, the less comfortable he became. And he always used to remind us of what he and his peers were told in the Navy: "Never argue about politics or religion. No one could ever win those arguments."

So here's this nice Jewish boy, living in a wonderful Jewish neighborhood, with kind Jewish parents, and mostly Jewish friends. And then in 1946, towards the end of a four-year stint in the Navy, he marries my mother … a nice Italian Catholic girl. Of course, today this is not uncommon. But in 1946 it was much more attention-getting. Remember, my father was probably about as wonderful a son as any parents could have. He was loving, respectful, and hardly ever got in any trouble.

When asked about his youth, my father used to tell us what a problem child he was for his parents. You know what his two horrendous examples were? One, when he was about four, he started walking back and forth under a big horse that was stopped along the curb. It was pulling a cart that was used for collecting garbage from the row houses. My grandmother was beside herself when she realized what her toddler was doing. And two, the "famous" incident when, at age six, little Seymour ate all six bananas my grandmother had brought home, and brother Leo unsuccessfully tried to push them out by sitting on his little brother's stomach. That's it! Those were his two big examples of how he made life so miserable for his poor, suffering parents. Drinking? Never. Carousing? Never. Fighting? Never. Causing trouble in school? Never. (Well, throwing his buddy Stan Gilbert out the window might qualify. It cost him the presidency of the Glee Club. But heck, it was a ground-level window. No harm, no foul). Being disrespectful? Never. (Of course there could be no excuse for eating all those bananas. What a rotten kid).

But marrying a *shiksa*, well, that was devastating to his parents. Even my Uncle Leo and Aunt Shirley, who adored Estelle, tried hard to talk Swede out of marrying her. They felt there was going to be too much angst for the family. My father was always very close to Leo and Shirley, and often relied on their advice. But in this case, the more they urged, the more stubborn my father became. He had already made up his mind.

I regret that I never asked my father about when and how he broke the news to Max and Sonia that he'd be marrying a Gentile. I suspect it had to be *very* unpleasant, especially since my father was always so respectful to his parents. Perhaps Swede never mentioned it to us because he didn't want to portray my grandparents in a negative light.

In any case, my mother flew to Seattle to marry my father, who was stationed in nearby Bremerton. Estelle was always a very nervous flyer, and this trip was a horror story for her. The weather was terrible. There was tons of bad turbulence, cancelled connecting flights, etc. It took her three days to finally get to Bremerton, and she was a wreck. The only bright spot was that there were mostly servicemen on her journey, and they kind of adopted her and looked after her. (I'll bet).

But she recovered, and my parents married on New Year's Day 1946. Swede and Estelle told us the witness to their wedding was a talking parrot. They lived in a small apartment on or near the base for a few months until my father was discharged. Swede, an officer, liked to bring some of the enlisted sailors home for my mother's delicious spaghetti and meatballs. What a treat for them!

Upon his discharge, my parents took a long honeymoon vacation down the West Coast. Upon arriving in Los Angeles, they were having trouble finding a room until a man in one hotel lobby overheard their plight and offered to help. He made one phone call and got my parents a terrific room at the Miramar Hotel in Santa Monica. The good Samaritan was none other

Swede and Estelle on their West Coast honeymoon, 1946.

than Jack Warner of Warner Bros. fame. (I'm guessing he took one look at my parents and envisioned them as potential Hollywood stars, but of course I'm biased). Another memorable honeymoon moment occurred when my parents went dancing one night in a nightclub in Westwood (Swede and Estelle were great dancers), and Gary Cooper and Clark Gable were there. While dancing on the crowded dance floor, my father intentionally maneuvered my mother (without her knowing) so that her rear end lightly bumped up against Cooper's rear end. How many people can brag that they rubbed tushes with the great Gary Cooper?!

Back in Newark, Max and Sonia were in mourning; it would take a while for them to get over this. As wonderful as they were, my grandparents were old school, and very dedicated to their faith and its traditions. They expected their two sons to marry Jewish girls. It was expected, it was assumed, and it was what nearly all Jewish children did. Of course these sentiments were not limited to Jewish families only. Estelle's parents also had some concerns about the "mixed marriage," but because they had lived for many years in a predominantly Jewish area, with predominantly Jewish friends, it was much less traumatic for them.

Perhaps this is the reason my mother later downplayed the controversy of her joining the Masin family. She recalled that the first time her parents and Swede's parents got together was "pleasant." She even claimed her parents "impressed Max and Sonia" with their use of Jewish expressions. I always felt that my mother came across as being "more" Jewish than my father. My mother also mentioned how much she appreciated the help she received from Uncle Leo and Aunt Shirley. They were very supportive of Estelle and Swede, and helped convince my grandparents that the world would not end because of a Gentile joining the family. In particular, my mother relied on Shirley to "hold her hand" throughout the "process" of becoming a Masin.

As the saying goes, time heals all wounds, and the fact that my father married out of the faith became a non-issue. My parents returned to Newark, and actually lived with Max and Sonia for several months until my father could save enough money to get their own place. Similarly, they also spent part of the time with my mother's parents at their house in Long Branch.

In retrospect, my parents must have consciously avoided making much of their religious "controversy" to their kids. But it must have been touchy for a while. Over the years my siblings and I heard comments from my parents' friends about how upset Max and Sonia were at the time. Max reportedly sat *shiva* after my parents wed. And Swede's best childhood buddy, Stan Gilbert, said my grandmother Sonia asked him to try and talk her son out of marrying "the pretty Italian girl." Stan passed along my grandmother's sentiments to

Swede and Estelle proudly show off their first car, 1946, in Long Branch, New Jersey.

Swede, who took it in but seemed disinclined to talk about it. At that point Stan felt he had done his job and dropped the subject forever.

Frank Chenitz was another of Swede's buddies who was asked by Max to talk Swede into not marrying Estelle. Dutifully, Frank broached the subject with my father. Apparently Swede was losing patience with the issue, because he was quite abrupt with his response: "Frank, don't ask that question any more. I don't want to hear it. I'm going to marry her." Like Stan Gilbert, Frank had done his duty and wanted no more part of it.

Once Swede and Estelle were married, they raised all four of us kids in the Jewish faith. We were members of Temple Israel, a Reform synagogue in South Orange, where Doug and I were Bar Mitzvahed. We celebrated all the Jewish holidays, but we also celebrated Christmas. We had a Christmas tree, albeit a fake one, about three feet high and white, which we placed on a lamp table. We also painted and hid Easter eggs. We followed these customs from a traditional standpoint, not a religious one.

Swede was conflicted about his religious beliefs. As proud as he was of his faith, he was quite careful not to impose his beliefs on others. To his four kids, he always preached the Golden Rule. He'd instill in us that if we "did the right thing," God would be on our side. That was about it: do the right thing, be considerate, and be good citizens.

There were times when my father wanted to go to our temple to pray, usually for an ailing friend or relative, and on some of these occasions he could not get into the temple because it was locked. Regrettably the temple had been vandalized and was often kept locked during the day. So instead he went one mile away to Our Lady of Sorrows Catholic Church. My father felt that if God would listen to his prayers, it would be regardless of the venue.

Similarly, when Swede went to the large, beautiful community pool in South Orange, he often would sit with some nuns who frequented the pool. Swede didn't view them as Catholic nuns; he viewed them as nice, personable women with whom he enjoyed visiting with and from whom he often received tips on cooking. The community pool, by the way, is named for Peter Connor, who was posthumously awarded the Congressional Medal of Honor for his bravery in Vietnam. Peter's twin sister was Mary Connor, a lifelong resident of South Orange, and one of my mother's best friends.

Mary observed, "Swede liked to be with women, period." I used to notice that as well. Not that he was a womanizer; he was the furthest thing from it. But I always sensed he was more comfortable bantering with women, due to the non-macho nature of the dialog. And in retrospect it seems his closest lifelong friends were very sweet, gentle un-macho guys without a mean bone in them: Saul Berkowitz, Donny Kurtz, Eddie Denholtz, and Stan Gilbert.

Another of my father's favorites was Monsignor Michael Kelly of Seton Hall Preparatory School. After Swede retired in 1995, he enjoyed watching high school sports: soccer, football, basketball, lacrosse, you name it. Besides Columbia High School games, he went to many events at Seton Hall Prep, which is not only a great school academically but also a powerhouse in many sports each year. Swede got to know Monsignor Kelly and they really hit it off; they had much mutual respect for each other. Over time, Monsignor Kelly gave Swede a pass to Seton Hall Prep sporting events. My father *really* loved that. Middle-class Swede, by then retired with limited income, not to mention alimony payments to my mother, totally appreciated the gesture. As Swede and the other thrifty guy, Ben Franklin, used to say: "A penny saved is a penny earned."

Sometimes my father's stance on religion was difficult to figure. He seemed uneasy about organized religion, but at the same time he was a very spiritual guy, who tried to keep an open line of communication with God. He was proud of his own religion, but he never let religion be a barrier to friends or, for that matter, even to his spouse! So he was every bit as comfortable hanging with the nuns at the pool, or bonding with Monsignor Kelly as he was with his endless Jewish friends. He was both color-blind and religion-blind.

So that was Swede. No barriers. Elderly people, young people, any color, any gender, any religion, any sexual preference, rich or poor, popular or not;

with Swede it did not matter. In fact, if there was any bias on his part, he probably leaned toward the "underdog."

After college, my buddies and I played in a softball league in South Orange. Often Swede would walk to the park and watch our games. During this time a shabby-looking man with some physical and mental disabilities also watched the games. He usually stood by himself with his cane down the left-field line in foul territory. Swede, instead of standing close to the diamond where everyone else watched the game, would sometimes stroll over and watch with the other man, just to keep him company. I used to glance over and watch the two men chatting. My father was terrific that way. He treated everybody the same way, with respect. This small anecdote made a very lasting impression on me. Swede had such a wonderful, giving nature. It was the part about my father that I loved the most. I can still remember thinking to myself how proud I was of him, being so kind to this man who probably didn't have many friends.

Swede was such a sweet guy, and so darn unassuming, that it can be very difficult for me to always follow my father's example. My favorite poem is Rudyard Kipling's "If," which contains the following passage:

> If you can talk with crowds and keep your virtue,
> Or walk with kings—nor lose the common touch; ...
> Yours is the Earth and everything that's in it,
> And—which is more—you'll be a Man my son!

I think Rudyard was talking about Swede!

On the occasion of Bob's Bar Mitzvah, 1961: Swede, Bob, and Dale (back row);
Doug, Estelle, Patty.

CHAPTER NINE:
THE DIRTY ROTTEN STINKING
MASIN KIDS

Truth be told, the four Masin kids were easy to raise. Other than when I was setting fire to toilet seats (more on that later), we rarely gave my parents trouble. Dale, the oldest, was born December 1946. I arrived August 1948. Patty showed up July 1951. And Doug landed, via alien spacecraft, August 1957.

My sisters, Dale and Patty, must have been a dream for my parents. Both were good, conscientious students, respectful non-trouble-makers, etc. You know … squares.

They were also both very athletic, like our parents. However, in the 1950s and 1960s there were very few opportunities for girls in sports. Dale was more like my mother, very coordinated and graceful, though not very aggressive; in fact, I don't think Dale cared to sweat. Patty was more like my father, and would have been a terrific high school athlete. She was strong and athletic, and she liked to compete—but joined the cheerleading squads in high school and college instead of playing on any organized teams.

When Patty was teaching physical education at enormous Elizabeth High School, she challenged her students to beat her in a game of badminton. This was when she was in her forties and had put on some pounds. She offered a grade of "A" to anyone who could outscore her. She had plenty of takers, all boys, and many of them gifted athletes. And she never lost. Not once. She'd stand in the center of her side of the court and run those kids forward and back, and side to side. She didn't have to move much. One student, a Polish immigrant who was all-county in soccer and the county champ in the 800-meter run, came close. But she held him off. She retired undefeated.

I had trouble believing her claims. Elizabeth High had so many great athletes, and none could beat my middle aged sister in badminton?! I was skeptical. So on one of her visits to Portland, we went to the athletic club and competed head to head. I had played plenty of racquet sports (tennis, squash, racquetball) and I had played some badminton with my kids, so I was anticipating putting Patty in her place. I did. First place. As advertised, she simply stood in the middle of the court and ran me forward and back and side to side.

Dale, a Special Education teacher for twenty years, was more of a third parent than a sibling. She was the oldest, and she doted on her younger siblings, especially Doug, who was almost eleven years her junior. In fact, we all doted on Doug: he was the youngest by far, he was the cutest of kids, and he had his ongoing leg problems, which garnered him extra sympathy. We all loved being the doters, and my brother had no problem being the dotee.

For Doug, the whole family was there to applaud his first steps, his potty training, his learning to read and write, ride a bike, tie his shoe laces (in high school), hit a baseball, and change the grades on his report card.

But what Doug was able to achieve, athletically, was remarkable considering his physical disadvantages. He was born with an abnormality of his feet and legs. His feet were balled up like fists, and his legs were curled up with his feet turning inward. He came home from the hospital, age one week, with full casts on both legs, which remained on for a year. His first steps were with casts on his legs. He had surgery on both legs at age two and again at age five, followed each time with months of full-length casts. This resulted in him being very adept at getting around on casts as well as getting a huge amount of love and attention from his family.

When Doug didn't have the casts, he always had to wear corrective shoes. The shoes pointed out, so it appeared he had his shoes on the wrong feet. And at night he wore corrective shoes that were attached by a metal bar. I can't even imagine how uncomfortable that was. At other times he was in a wheelchair. Through it all, the rest of the family showered my brother with endless affection. Incredibly, he never complained about his legs and he was the happiest of kids.

Our back yard was adjacent to our grammar school. When I was twelve and Doug was three, I was leaving school to head home for lunch one day when I heard loud cheers from dozens of kids looking into our yard. My mother was pitching a ball to my brother, and pitch after pitch he was smashing high and far, some clear over our house. And with each hit the crowd cheered louder. It was as if they were watching Mickey Mantle. I got such a charge out of all these school kids cheering my little brother on. And it was pretty incredible that this three-year-old had such good hand-eye coordination and power.

My brother was never big in stature, his legs were/are chronically weak and they get very fatigued. Naturally, he had difficulty generating running speed. Having a lack of size, speed, and leg strength is not a formula for success in sports. But that never stopped Doug. He became an all-around athlete, participating in football, baseball, tennis, recreational basketball, and skiing.

Doug was on Columbia High School's Freshman Football team even though he weighed less than one hundred pounds at the time! So here was this tiny, slow kid, with little strength in his legs, but one who was totally fearless. He was also very smart and had great anticipation, so he was always at the right place at the right time. My brother's effort was hard to match. I've seen him make diving catches in baseball and softball which would make any Top Ten list on ESPN. And in football he would come up from his secondary position and totally give up his body to make a tackle. The thing I admire most is that he *never* complained about his disadvantage. And that remains the case today.

Every now and then I read stories of people with physical handicaps excelling in sports. Not many of the anecdotes are more impressive than what my brother was able to overcome and accomplish. He's remarkable.

You would think that the family's empathy for Doug would have prevented us from exposing him to any unnecessary angst. But my father once put Doug through the longest two minutes of his life. It was while singing about *The Land of the Freeeeee*.

AND THE HOME OF THE LOUD

Swede loved America. He always felt that in spite of its imperfections it was a great country that had saved many people in many places from many tyrants. Much of this attitude probably stemmed from his parents' appreciation for what this country had to offer. They felt so fortunate to have escaped from the widespread anti-Semitism of early twentieth-century Russia. Through hard work they were rewarded with a great life in America, in a terrific community where they were free from persecution.

It was in this context that my father changed Doug's life forever. At the age of eight, Doug attended his first basketball game, which (as is the custom) was preceded by singing the Star-Spangled Banner. Swede, former president (very briefly) of the Weequahic High School Glee Club, sang along—very loudly. He was bellowing our national anthem with pride.

Shy Doug had never before been exposed to this. He was panic-stricken and mortified. Convinced that everyone in the arena was staring at him and his crazy father, he wanted to leave immediately and even tried climbing under the seat, but there wasn't enough room. Tears welled up in his eyes, as he realized the only thing he could do was wait it out. By Doug's recollection, the anthem lasted three hours. His panic attack went totally unnoticed by Swede Pavarotti. Someday, if you happen to be in my brother's presence when the national anthem is being played, you will notice he's crying. It is not for love of country. It's because of his life-altering memory.

* * * *

As kids, we had different interests. Dale was a voracious reader, a real bookworm. Doug and I, besides liking sports, were both avid television watchers, albeit in different eras. One of my earliest memories was when I was five. I loved Farmer Gray cartoons, and these silent black-and-white animated shorts predated even Mickey Mouse. Once, I urged my father to watch with me. I *knew* he'd love it too. After a few minutes, Swede slinked out of the room, and I remember thinking "Doesn't he know what he's missing?!"

Later, while Patty was probably practicing doing homework, which she wouldn't be getting for another five years, and while Dale was reading every Bobbsey Twins book ever written, I became hooked on TV Westerns, such as *Cheyenne, Maverick, Have Gun Will Travel,* and *The Rifleman.* I got a little carried away. After seeing one too many Western saloon scenes, I'd pour milk into a shot glass and wolf it down like the cowboys did with their whiskey. I drank many shots of milk that way. And after watching one too many campfire scenes, I started drinking my milk out of a ladle, like the cowboys did. You'll be relieved to know I stopped the practice months ago. I think it's safe to say that as a child I was somewhat, well, how should I put it … odd. But I am here to say that I'm much better now.

When Sherry Curtin, one of my friends and colleagues at Columbia Sportswear, first met Patty, she asked for some "dirt" she could use to embarrass me. Naturally, Patty was eager to help, and told the story about me drinking out of a ladle. The next morning, straight-faced Sherry came into my office to talk business, nonchalantly drinking her cup of coffee … with a small ladle. I didn't notice at first, but when I did I exploded in laughter. Patty had struck. It might have been even funnier if Sherry had walked in drinking her coffee out of a shot glass.

Meanwhile, Dale was reading.

"Clever" is not a word often used to describe me. Once, my mother bought me a new coat, which was heavily insulated. I immediately went to the playground and challenged any of the kids to punch me in the stomach as hard as they could. With all that insulation, I was sure I wouldn't feel a thing. Someone took me up on the offer and punched me in the solar plexus. Barely able to speak, I gasped "See, told you it wouldn't hurt," as I staggered home, breathless and doubled over. Cheap coat.

Meanwhile, Patty was busy practicing being perfect.

And Dale read on.

So for many years, the Masin kids were busy being a "goody two shoes" (Patty); eating Devil Dogs and Yodels, watching Yogi Bear, The Flintstones, and Mr. Ed, and being spoiled rotten (Doug); and reading (you guessed it … Dale). In the meantime, when not watching the Westerns, I was busy being unusual.

Back in those days, none of us had a political bone in our bodies. But as grown-ups, we all took sides. My father and Patty were the family liberals, my mother and Dale were the conservatives, I of course was the voice of supreme logic and reason, and Doug was neutral so long as he had his Devil Dogs and Yodels. Dale's husband, Val, a Marine veteran, was always a willing (right-leaning) participant, and of course so was (left-leaning) Susie. It made for lively dinner table conversations.

Sometimes, as we were arguing at the table, it seemed as if virtually everyone was yapping at the same time, all in raised voices. I was always amazed that Dale was still able to read at the table with all that noise.

Okay, so I'm teasing Dale about how much she reads. But she *does* love to do so, from novels to biographies to history to gossip and more. So she certainly better read this book! But more importantly, Dale was always the most considerate of people. She was a terrific Special Education teacher for twenty years. And, as our third parent, she looked after the rest of us. I honestly don't remember Dale or Patty ever getting into trouble. Fortunately, Doug and I took up the slack.

It's impressive that the four of us got along so well, considering that we lived in very tight quarters. Our house on Mountain House Road was small. Dale and Patty shared a small room, and so did Doug and I. The four of us shared one small bathroom. There was really no place to hide.

A thin wall divided the two kids' bedrooms. On Christmas morning—remember that we celebrated both Hanukah and Christmas—I would tap on the wall to the tune of "Shave and a Haircut" … and Patty would tap back twice … "Two Bits." This would typically occur about 5 a.m. We'd then rouse our parents, who would usually tell us to come back in a couple of hours.

The four of us stuck together when the chips were down—for instance, when Doug got in trouble. Once, my mother bought an over-priced, fancy centerpiece for the dining room table, with many artificial flowers, berries, and such. Doug decided to pull some of the "grapes" out of the centerpiece and throw them at his buddy. When the damage was done, the centerpiece had lost maybe ten percent of its "fruit."

When my parents discovered the carnage, there was hell to pay. Estelle, in particular, was furious and lit into poor little, sweet Doug. Dale, Patty, and I mobilized and came to Doug's aid, knowing that the best defense is a good offense. Dale led the charge, challenging my mother, saying she was over-reacting, that the centerpiece still looked the same, and that it really didn't matter because it was ugly in the first place. Patty and I played the ugly centerpiece card as well (as we hid behind Dale), forcing my mother into a position of defending her investment. All of this shifted the attention away from Doug. Mission accomplished.

On the other hand, the tale of the missing bottle of whiskey doesn't have quite as happy an ending. Swede had brought home a case of whiskey, which he needed to deliver to a customer. A few days later he discovered one bottle was missing. Doug was in high school at the time, which meant that he had to fend for himself, since the rest of us were already out of the house. Swede confronted Doug about the missing bottle, and like any other red-blooded, all-American young lad, he denied knowing anything about it. My mother joined the conversation.

Estelle: "Swede, are you sure the bottle wasn't missing when you brought it home?"

Swede (disgusted): "Of course I'm sure. The case was full."

Estelle (at this point trying to save Doug's life): "Maybe a thief came in and stole it."

Swede (totally disgusted, using his Ralph Kramden voice): "A thief didn't bust in and steal *one* bottle out of the case!!!"

Estelle: "Don't yell at me, I didn't steal it."

Swede (yelling): "*I'm not yelling*!!"

Once again, Doug benefited from the conversation taking a different direction, at least for a while. But Swede kept after Doug, because he had little doubt on this one. He kept emphasizing that he just wanted the truth. Doug was too far committed to his "position" on the subject, and stuck to his story. Estelle helped him somewhat, but my father was not happy that day.

* * * *

To summarize, my siblings share certain characteristics: they are down-to-earth, modest, non-materialistic, and perhaps too passive for their own good. Individually, Dale was our leader and protector; Doug spent most of his time on other planets where he bonded with others just like him; and one-of-a-kind Patty, whose personality most matched my father, served as the glue for the family. And then there was …

PROBLEMATIC BOBBY

Yes, that would be me. The family oddity. There were times I couldn't quite get out of my own way. In retrospect, I suspect my parents often wondered what wavelength I was on, since it sure was a different one from the rest of the family. The following random anecdotes from my youth describe some of my unusual behavior. Naturally, in one way or another, they involved Swede ...

THE HOT SEAT

And I mean that literally.

When I was young my mother smoked cigarettes, so there were always books of matches in the house. I must have had aspirations of becoming a firebug, because I got into the habit of lighting a matchbook or two and watching them burn after throwing them into the toilet. (I know, I know, I had issues). One morning there was a mishap. I dropped the lighted matchbook, and somehow it ignited the bottom of the toilet seat. I was amazed at how fast the entire bottom of the seat got charred before I could put out the fire.

There was no way out for me on this one. I told my mother what happened, and showed her the damage. She must have been thinking her son was a perfect lunatic. But as angry as she was, I could sense that she felt very sorry for me for the same reason I felt sorry for me: Swede's eventual return from work. That entire day I moped around as if I were to be executed at sundown. My life, as I knew it, was over. I watched the clock all day, like Gary Cooper in *High Noon*, except he had to deal with the arrival of only four armed killers. I had to deal with the arrival of *The Mighty Swede*.

I wrote out my Last Will and Testament, leaving my twelve cents to my siblings. All South Orange residents left town; birds stopped chirping; crickets stopped cricketing. Finally, I heard Swede's VW pull into the driveway.

Motionless, I sat on my bed, panic-stricken, waiting for my date with the executioner. Out of earshot my mother told my father of the day's event. Soon, the biggest human on planet Earth, the mountain of a man, could be heard making his way toward my room.

A miracle happened. My father never, not once, raised his voice. He calmly asked me if I'd learned my lesson. He wanted to make sure that I understood what terrible consequences might have occurred because of my actions, and that I'd never do such a thing again. I clearly got the message. His lecture lasted a while, and when my father left the room my sigh of relief could be heard for miles around. I'll never forget that day. It may have been my longest.

Swede was like that. At times the little things would ignite his loudest reactions. But on major issues—unless a loved one was hurt—he was at his calmest. In this particular case, I think he wanted to make sure his son wasn't going to grow up to be an arsonist. His lecture worked. I haven't been to the bathroom since. Nor do I play with matches.

TALKIN TRASH

Dale and I both had the habit of climbing into bed with our parents almost every night. Dale stopped when she was four or five, while I broke myself of the habit when I left for college. Okay, maybe a little before that.

One hot, humid night I climbed in with my parents. Swede began a stern lecture, saying it was time for me to be a big boy and stay in my own bed, no more being a baby, etc.

His lecture in the dark of night lasted a couple of minutes. When he finished, the room became quiet. My parents were waiting for some kind of response, and they got one. I gave my father a solid backhand to the face—not a light tap, but a hard smack. Evidently I did not care for the content of my father's lecture. Swede's reaction was to explode in laughter, which got my mother laughing. What a break! My father's reaction could easily have gone in a different direction. Swede and Estelle told that story often. The moral: If I'm in bed with you, don't criticize me.

THE RECORD BREAKER

When I was a young lad I happened upon a brief conversation in which Swede was telling Estelle that one of his records had been broken. This got my attention.

Brilliant Little Bobby: "Daddy, weren't you mad?"

Swede: "No, not at all, Bobby."

Brilliant Little Bobby: "Why not?!"

Swede: "I expected it. I broke someone else's record, and I knew someday someone would break mine. And someday someone will break *his* record."

Brilliant Little Bobby (incredulously): But why does everyone do that, and why doesn't anyone get mad?!"

Obviously, I thought my parents were talking about the plastic disks that played music, not some track-and-field record. Are you beginning to conclude that it was quite clear, at an early age, that I was not destined to become a person of intellect? I'm just glad I didn't walk over to our record player and break a few records to test my father's claims.

PIP PIP, AND ALL THAT SORT OF ROT

Once, as a little boy, I approached the bathroom. My father was in there.

Me: "Daddy?"

Swede: "Yes, Bobby?"

Me: "What're ya doin?" (Yet another in a long line of brilliant questions on my part).

Swede, in a deep British accent: "I'm making a wee spot of doe doe." (Rhymes with yo-yo).

And from that day forward, "wee spot" (spoken like an English gentleman) became a permanent expression in the Masin household. It sure beats kah kah.

INDUSTRIOUS LITTLE BOBBY

When I was a young guy, maybe six or seven, I befriended a boy who lived with his mother around the block from us. They shared a small, basement apartment in a nice home, and if memory serves she was the housekeeper for the elderly woman who lived in the house. I believe they were German immigrants. The boy, Hans Hampf, and I hung out together. We lived very close to Mountain (train) Station, and unbeknownst to our parents we spent plenty of time there, watching the commuter trains stop and go, waving to the conductors, and unfortunately, putting bottle caps on the tracks and collecting the flattened remnants after the train ran over them.

Growing up where we did, I spent many a day observing the businessmen (then it was almost always men), dressed in their suits, walking to the station in the morning and walking from the station in the evening. Hans and I came up with the idea to sell the evening papers to the commuters as they left the station. We were ready for them, setting up in a strategic spot where the foot traffic was high. We had a nice stack of papers, ready to be sold for ten cents each, which was three cents more than the current going price for our product, *The Newark Evening News*.

The only catch, which Hans and I had overlooked, was that the newspapers we were selling were not current. They had been collected in neat piles by Mrs. Hampf, who must have been one of the earliest recyclers.

Industrious Hans and Bobby did this for a day or two or three, selling perhaps a half-dozen papers in all. It ended abruptly one evening when a man visited the Masin house, asking for Swede. He wanted his dime back. Seems he'd arrived home, sat down to catch up on the news with the paper we sold him, but found himself uninterested in re-reading the news from three weeks earlier. Picky. My father gave the ingrate his dime back, and asked me about my newspaper initiative. I proudly admitted my role, which made Swede laugh—at least outwardly. In his mind he was probably thinking about which asylum would accept me when I got old enough. By the way, do you believe that guy came back for his dime?! What a curmudgeon.

Years later I tried a similar venture. I offered Patty two lottery tickets for half-price. She was *very* appreciative: "Oh, that is so nice," she said as she gave me the money. She was somewhat less thankful when I pointed out they were the previous day's losing tickets. But what the heck! They were half-price!

PHOOEY!

When we were kids, we used to play a game in the car with Swede. If anyone spotted a station wagon, they'd yell "Beaver!" Whoever called it first got a point. The winner was the person with the most points at the end of the drive. Admittedly, there was a bit of a disadvantage to the driver, who had to glance occasionally at where s/he was going.

One day, when I was five or six, my father was driving, and we were playing the game. A station wagon came into view, and we both yelled "Beaver!" Swede just barely beat me to the punch. Frustrated, I shouted "Aaaah phooey!" Only I didn't say phooey. You got it … I dropped the f-bomb. Well, Swede, whom I never heard use that word in his life, exploded: "What did you say?! That's the worst word in the world!!" (I never knew they ranked the world's worst words). "Don't *ever* use that word again!!"

I burst out crying. I probably had heard this word from the older kids in the playground, but had no idea what it meant. I tearfully plead my case to my father, who quickly calmed down. But I'll always remember his "worst word in the world" speech. And I'm still furious he called "Beaver!" before I did.

THE BULLY

When I was five, my best friend and next-door neighbor was Peter Tzeses. One day, a local trouble-making bully (maybe fifteen or so), who was literally off his rocker, lured Peter and me behind the garage of the O'Brian's (our neighbor on the other side). He told us he had a secret for us, so we followed him. As I leaned in to hear his secret, he took Peter's head and smashed it into my face. Presumably, this guy "had issues," as they say now. Blood gushed from my nose. One of the few recollections I have is that the front of my shirt was completely red from blood. Peter and I ran toward my house, just a few yards away. The assailant was probably scared as well; there was a lot of blood. He bolted.

My father heard my screams, and he came charging outside. When Swede saw me, he exploded. Through my sobs I told him what happened. Peter and I both remember my father going into a rage. He spotted the bully fleeing through the adjacent grammar school playground. My other recollection is how fast he ran this guy down. Boom! He was on him.

If it were me, I don't think I could restrain myself from pummeling this guy after seeing the face of my five-year-old child covered in blood. I recall my father lifting him up by his shirt, so that their faces were an inch or so apart, and then putting the fear of God into this teenaged bully. Remember, my father was not only the world's largest man, he also had the most booming voice on the planet. In this case it was like a lion's roar.

It's hard to recall *anything* from such an early age. But this episode certainly made an impression on Peter and me (and my nose). And I'll never forget the way Swede got after this guy. He was faster than a speeding bullet, more powerful than a locomotive, and he caught this guy in a single bound. But he didn't use violence. He was like that his whole life. Very non-violent. It's a good thing.

DINING WITH THE MASINS

We all remember our "wonder" years, the period of time between Doug getting past his first year or two and before Dale left for college—roughly the years from 1959 to 1965. We were all home, it was the heart of our Shadybrook years (our family summer playground), our little house was the most crowded, and the kitchen table was the focal point of the house. Dinners brought all of us together, formally. It was a chance to bond as a family, talk about the day's events, and pour soda on Patty's head. More on that later.

Conversation always centered around the kids: stuff happening at school, doings at Shadybrook, Little League baseball, and so on. My sisters were perfect ladies at the table, always using good manners. Doug and me? Not so much.

My brother and I had poor eating habits. I'd wolf down the stuff I liked, and I'd labor over the stuff (vegetables) I didn't. If we were having beef as the main course, I'd spend five minutes trying to trim every last speck of fat off before I'd eat it. Invariably, Swede would offer to get me a magnifying glass so I wouldn't miss anything. Although Doug had allergies to certain nutritional foods, he certainly was *not* allergic to Devil Dogs, Scooter Pies, and Yodels. As a result, he was usually itching to escape the dinner table, grab some of the aforementioned junk food, and escape to the adjoining den to watch cartoons. Swede took it upon himself to delay Doug's escape as long as possible.

Dale was perfect. Just ask her. She always ate every item, and she liked having everything on her plate at the same time because she thought the various colors were pretty. She'd take a small, dainty bite of her chicken (or whatever), then some salad, then her vegetable, then her baked potato, blah blah blah. What a cornball.

Patty, like Dale, was also very mannerly at the table. But Patty did not like her various food items touching, and she prefers eating one item entirely before going on to the next. In other words, Patty was a kook.

The large fellow to my right would quietly, politely, and deliberately clean his plate—and I mean *clean* his plate—after which he'd clean Doug's plate, then my plate, then Dale's plate, etc. First, he'd ask "You gonna finish that?" Typical response, "no, dad, I don't want anymore," after which he'd dump it on his plate. Then on to the next kid. He was not happy that we were not finishing our meals, but deep down he was probably happy to be getting more food for himself.

We rarely had leftovers, and we *very* rarely wasted food. Swede made sure of that. In fact, my mother was very good at planning and preparing the right-sized portions.

In contrast to my three siblings who were well-behaved at the table, I was the family clown. I told bad jokes, I acted somewhat obnoxiously, and I ate like a hippo. (But I'm much better now). I *was* smart enough not to cross the bad behavior line, because I was within arm's reach of the world's biggest man.

However, one day at dinner my mother was making fun of me about something and Patty made the mistake of laughing at me. Unfortunately for my sister, I had a half-full can of soda, and I proceeded to pour it on her head. Yes, I rolled the dice on this one. The Giant Swede might have squashed me like a bug. But while Patty, in a pathetic display of over-reaction, was screaming in horror at my action, and Dale was semi-amused, probably relieved *she* hadn't laughed at me, Doug was laughing hysterically, and Estelle was using my actions to reinforce why she was making fun of me in the first place … Swede just sat there, shaking his head in disgust, with an expression that asked "Where did I go wrong with this numbskull?"

One thing we all loved was watching my mother eat. She made everything look *delicious*, just by the way she consumed it. She had excellent manners, but she ate with fervor and had a habit of getting food on her face. Surprisingly, she never seemed to notice, so it was up to us to inform her.

Swede was subtle about it, getting Estelle's attention and discreetly pointing to the spot on *his* face that corresponded to where the pesky food particle was on *her* face. (Sometimes it was remarkable how far the food was from her mouth).

Dale, Doug, and I were less subtle than my father. "Hey, ma, you got a corn niblet on your ear lobe!" Then there's Patty. For some reason, when she'd point out my mother's facial food, Estelle didn't care to hear about it …

Patty: "Ma, you've got food on your face."

Estelle (not overly appreciative): "Oh, shut up, Patty! Stop looking at me!"

More Estelle: "I can't help it if my mouth is too small!"

The apple doesn't fall too far from the tree. Patty reminded me that sometimes, dainty, mannerly Dale, while she's preparing food, gets food in her *hair*!

Patty: "Uh, Dale, you've got a cucumber in your hair."

Dale: "Oh, shut up, Patty!"

Such was life around our quaint dinner table in South Orange. It was intimate, delicious, and, if Patty laughed at me, unpredictable.

SHADYBROOK

Most summers from 1954 (when Dale was eight, I was six, Patty was three, and Doug was minus three) until the early 1970s, we had a family membership at Shadybrook Swim Club in Livingston, only ten minutes or so from home.

As the migration of families from Newark to the suburbs continued to build, many family-oriented private swim clubs sprouted up. Besides Shadybrook, there was Sun Valley, Spring Gardens, The Colony, Mountain Crest, Cabana Club, and others. At the same time, because some of the existing golf and/or tennis clubs in the area did not welcome Jewish members, the swim clubs became a good option for significant numbers of Jewish families. However, by the early 1970s, more community pools had opened, which were closer for most folks and less expensive—though there tended to be fewer features and facilities. Moreover, the golf and tennis clubs began opening their memberships to Jews. The decline of the private swim clubs soon followed.

For the Masins, Shadybrook Swim Club was perfect. There was a great day camp for kids of all ages, the membership fees were reasonable, activities were plentiful, and instead of hanging around our non-air-conditioned house, we could hang around with lots of friends in a huge pool, play softball or paddleball or basketball or tennis, or make arts and crafts (where my lack of ability provided some nice comic relief).

Some Saturday evenings, there was entertainment for the parents. There might be dinner and/or dancing, occasional live entertainment, and even a show produced by members of the club. There were also masquerade functions, and the photos of my parents in their costumes are some of our favorites—especially the one of Swede in a girl's cheerleading uniform.

Many of my friends from school went to various sleep-away camps in the Northeast. Most went for the entire eight-week summer, and I remember feeling so sorry for them, thinking they must have been so sad to be leaving their families for so long! How could they stand it? Of course, they absolutely loved it. But at the time, being the mama's boy that I was, I wouldn't have traded places with anyone. Summers at Shadybrook couldn't be beat.

A couple of times each summer, the family would go to "the club" bright and early. Basically we'd have this huge facility to ourselves. Swede, with his trusty eight-millimeter camera, would take lots of footage … swimming, diving, strutting around the pool, joking around, etc. These home movies covered many years of the Masin family growing up, summer to summer, and are now prized possessions. My kids love watching them: fascinated to see

Swede and Estelle, poolside at Shadybrook Swim Club, 1956.

Dressed as Burt Lancaster and Gina Lollobrigida, Masquerade Night at Shadybrook Swim Club, 1956.

their father, aunts, uncles, grandparents, great grandparents, etc. as young(er) people. They get a kick out of watching the 1951 Newark Thanksgiving Day Parade, with its antiquated "floats." They enjoy watching their father making a fool of himself as a young kid; they are so impressed with my mother's beauty and her athletic grace. And although he is less present in the movies because he was often behind the camera, my father makes Julie and Max (and Susie) laugh every time he hams it up.

Swede was very diligent about recording the growing up of the Masin family. There were birthday parties, snow storms, ice skating, frolicking at the beach, Passover Seders, a cruise my parents took, an occasional Little League baseball game, a high school or college football game, and holidays. But Shadybrook was the venue for a large percentage of the movies, and the movies taken there provide wonderful evidence of my parents' athletic ability. My mother was extremely well-coordinated, talented, and graceful. Swede was too, but he was more than that. His dives off the diving board were not only flawless, but the amount of spring he got off the board was awe-inspiring, even funny. His swim stroke was strong and graceful (naturally he won the men's race), he dominated the net in the volleyball games, and in the paddleball games he looks like an NFL linebacker playing among high school boys. He was quite something to watch.

There were lots of movies of swim races, which were held at Shadybrook throughout the summer. All the Masin kids fared well in the races, especially Patty, who dominated every race. Dale might also have dominated, but it was difficult for her to swim while she was reading.

Whether we were five years old or fifteen, the Shadybrook Swim Club was the perfect summer venue for all four of us. I wish all kids everywhere could have it so good, even those who might not be as perfect as Dale, Bobby, Patty, and Doug Masin.

CHAPTER TEN:
PAPA SWEDE

My wife Susie often remarked about how the four grown Masin children behaved in the presence of my father: like ten-year-olds. Total reverence. Totally respectful. We were hesitant to challenge him, to disagree with him, to make any decision that would not please him. We all soooo wanted to make him proud. Our behavior drove Susie a little crazy. Her family is also very close, but never hesitant to challenge each other directly.

Susie is right. We all craved Swede's approval, both as kids and as grown-ups. As much as he loved kibitzing his whole life, he was very serious about the health and welfare of his family. The four of us would worry about him worrying about us. Pathetic.

Not surprisingly, when I interviewed my siblings on this subject, their responses were virtually identical. Swede was *always* involved and engaged. Whether it was a school project, a sporting event, help with homework, or simply responding to childhood inquisitiveness, he was always there, willing to help whenever necessary. He had a great feel for right and wrong, for determining what was important in life and what was not. He was always the very best of company.

One of my strongest recollections is something that occurred one thousand times. My father would be reading a book or newspaper after dinner, and I'd approach him for any one of innumerable reasons. It may have been to talk about the New York Giants, or our favorite, Willie Mays, or sports in general, or homework help, or to ask him a question, or to request a raise in my allowance (against the longest of odds). It could have been anything, and he was always ready to engage, never showing a hint of impatience, and never rushing me. (Well, maybe he rushed me a bit on the allowance subject). Dale, Patty, and Doug have the same recollection, and it made a big impression on them as well. He was a terrific listener, and he was always so interested in us and our issues.

The bottom line is that I always felt Swede was a great father. I have tried to emulate him, but he is a tough act to follow. For a guy who never really showed much career ambition, he was tireless as a mentor. His patience with his kids, which was world class, is the hardest part to duplicate.

We all remember well how he got us up for school every morning, and prepared our breakfast. Although this was not a typical role for a father in 1950s America, Swede wanted to make sure we got off to a good start each day. Because he had such low tolerance for our missing a school day, Dale and I never missed one for a frivolous reason; Swede would have been on to us. Of course, Patty—the "Little Miss Goody Two Shoes" of the family—never *wanted* to miss a day of school. Doug always got up and left the house, but who knows where he went. I suppose he usually went to school.

Swede was always engaged in our schoolwork, and helped with our homework whenever we asked. He also used to encourage us to visit our teachers after school and ask for extra help if we needed it. Translation: he wanted us to take the extra step in our educations.

As kids, if we asked our father to play catch, or listen to a poem we had written for school, or to arm wrestle, or play hide and seek, he was always there. In fact, he may have been one of the greatest hide-and-seek players of all time, especially when he delicately sat on one of us. There he would be, nonchalantly reading the newspaper in the living room, while the "seekers" looked in vain for the small child who had become invisible, lying underneath the big Swede. Many years later, when he played hide and seek with my own children, he could stand so still that the kids would run right past him, never noticing that he was there.

We all remember Swede's tendency to over-react to trivial things and to react calmly and reasonably with major stuff. When Doug and I would rough house, it clearly made my father nervous. He did *not* want his kids to get hurt. Perhaps the fact that I was fourteen and Doug was five, with casts on both legs, suggested to Swede that my brother was at a disadvantage. Well, at least the little squirt wasn't blindfolded!

Swede took parenting very seriously. He made sure, at the appropriate time, to teach us how to skip, tie our shoe laces, brush our teeth properly, swim and dive, tie a tie, ride our bikes, drive a car, and, embarrassingly, the proper use of toilet paper. (I wish I were joking). He even took Dale and Patty clothes shopping—once; apparently, his taste in clothes was not very well aligned with Dale's and Patty's taste. He wanted to be the best, and if he wasn't it wouldn't be because of lack of effort.

There were things that were extremely important to Swede as a father and mentor. Some were vital (such as our health), and some were trivial (especially some of his idiosyncratic notions, ideas, and rules). But it was precisely these idiosyncrasies that help to define Swede ...

THE GREAT OJ BATTLE

No, not Simpson. I refer to orange juice.

While in the Navy, my father learned about the importance of consuming citrus fruit to help prevent scurvy. He took this advice seriously, drinking orange juice religiously. Naturally, as a father he wanted us to be as healthy as possible. Hence, he always made sure we had plenty of OJ on hand. He'd mix up a pitcher full every morning.

My sisters were no problem ... they liked it and drank it. I was a problem. I just didn't like it. So what did devious, five- year-old Bobby do? After my father filled my glass with the dreaded, scurvy-fighting, pulp-filled juice, I'd wait my father out. The moment he stepped out of the kitchen, the juice was down the kitchen sink drain. It worked for a while, but eventually my father began noticing drops of orange juice in the sink. He caught on, reprimanded me, and began staying in the kitchen.

But God forbid I should just drink the stuff. In my desperation I had to become more creative, so I started wandering into the adjoining den. The den was a dead-end; there was no way out. But there *was* a large, cushy chair. So, trapped like a rat, I poured the OJ under the cushion. Then I'd saunter back into the kitchen with my empty glass. Mission accomplished. In fact, this worked like a charm for a few days, until my mother noticed a nasty smell emanating from the den. It didn't take long before the smell was traced back to my actions. Fortunately my mother blamed the whole episode on my father for going over the top with his citrus campaign.

The good news postscript of the story is that I never got scurvy (whatever the heck it is), and I rarely pour my breakfast drink under chair cushions any more.

Ironically, after drinking healthy doses of orange juice every day, Dale, Patty, and Doug came down with scurvy. Just kidding. Luckily, all four Masin kids have dodged the scurvy menace to this day.

ALLOWANCE

In my father's lifetime, if the U.S. economy depended on his spending habits, the country would have been doomed. He needed and wanted nothing.

So when Dale, Patty, Doug, and I would initiate allowance discussions, he'd challenge us. "What do you need it for?" Then he'd tell us his college allowance story.

Swede: "When I was in college, I got five dollars per month allowance from Pop Pop Max. I used it for bus fare, haircuts, etc., and at the end of the month I'd have plenty of change left over." That's right, he actually said he had *plenty* left over! Go argue with that!

This is slightly off the subject, but as you can see, Swede was prone to exaggerate to make a point. When I was a young teenager, some of my buddies started lifting weights. I wanted to as well, but my father was dead set against it. He never used them, and he didn't want me to. He felt lifting weights made you too tight. I kept nagging, and he resorted to one of his gross exaggerations (really gross).

Swede: "I know a guy who lifted weights for a long time, and he got so tight and muscle-bound that when he went to the bathroom (number two) he had to call his wife to wipe him."

Yes, he actually said that, and kept a straight face. Let's face it, I couldn't make this stuff up. But we both knew he was kidding. Let's hope so, for the wife's sake.

But with the allowance, he'd finally give in. All four kids have the same recollection of the torture of asking for our weekly pittance. Invariably, Swede would be reading. One of us would gingerly approach and meekly remind my father that it was Thursday, allowance day. He'd always react the same way: He'd put down his book or newspaper, frowning all the way. He'd inhale deeply, exhale deeply, and shake his head as he reached deeply into his pocket. Finally, he'd hand over a few coins like they were the family jewels.

This is the same man who was incapable of passing a homeless person on the street without giving him or her something. In his later years my father would walk for exercise inside the Short Hills Mall, and would always stop at a small shop that not only sold cookies, but also offered free samples of broken cookie pieces. Swede always remembered to bring quarters with him so he could give them to the teenagers working behind the counter. He was an incredibly soft touch. But our allowance? What did we need it for? In retrospect, when we asked him for our allowance we should have brought pieces of broken cookies to soften him up.

In most cases, Swede was frugal to a fault, especially where it concerned spending on himself. He wanted his family to be the same way—though this did not resonate well with my mother; she liked nice things. Swede was the most non-materialistic person I've ever known.

However …

CHEERIOS

There are times when I think it would be a lot easier to just pull out your wallet and buy something. When I was nine I tried out for the South Orange Little League. I was drafted by the B'nai B'rith team, and if memory serves I was the last kid "drafted" into the majors. The coach of our team was Mr.

O'Brian, our next door neighbor and family friend, which is why I made the majors.

I hadn't played much baseball prior, and the only glove I had was an ancient hand-me-down from my father. It was old, had four fingers (not uncommon in the old days), and had no lacing. I could practically fold it up and put it in my pocket.

Now that I was going to be in the *majors* (!) I asked Swede about buying me a better glove. Typical Swede answer: "What's wrong with the one you have? A new one won't make you a better player."

But he did compromise. My father had noticed on the back of our Cheerios cereal box that you could buy a mitt from them for only one dollar and ten Cheerios box tops. Which is how I got my first, very own baseball glove. A Cheerios mitt! I also got very tired of Cheerios after eating what seemed like five bowls a day for two weeks.

But what I do remember most is that I absolutely *loved* the mitt! What did I care that it was purple?. I thought the pocket was great, it had five fingers, and it was laced. The best part? It was mine! I never let it out of my sight and I used it all four years in Little League.

I had so much appreciation for my first baseball glove, and so much *depreciation* for the taste of Cheerios. But looking back I wouldn't have wanted it any other way. In this instance perhaps Swede did the right thing in not getting me a "store-bought" glove. And in case you're wondering, Swede not only helped me down the Cheerios, he had more bowls than I did.

* * * *

My father's fretting about money, unbeknownst to him, used to concern me. We were about as middle-class as a family could be. Of course, South Orange was the home for many upper-middle-class and wealthy families. Compared to them it was easy to conclude we were poor. Our cars were inexpensive; for years Swede drove a VW, because it was affordable and barely depreciated, and to save a few bucks he bought it without a radio. Big, thick Swede wore that car like a suit. Our house was quite small; three small bedrooms for the six of us, and two small bathrooms. One of the bathrooms was so small you couldn't open the door all the way unless the toilet seat was raised. Many of our childhood friends went to sleep-away camp for the entire summer. We couldn't afford to. To be sure, we were far from poor, but it was easy for me to think so in our environment.

So naturally, Swede's reaction to allowance reminders reinforced the feeling. Especially when I was younger, I would literally feel bad for my father and his financial fretting. One time, I had a five-dollar bill—probably a gift from Pop Pop Max. I decided Swede needed it more than I did, so anonymously I put it in his top bureau drawer, where he kept all his miscellaneous stuff. At dinner that night Swede asked the family about the five.

Swede: "Did somebody put this five-dollar bill in my bureau?" Silence from the kids. Then my mother spoke up.

Estelle: "I must have put it there by mistake."

So Swede handed it to her. I was not happy, since my goal was to ease my *father's* financial burden. That evening, I took it from my mother's pocket book and returned it to the drawer. And that was the last I heard of the mysterious five.

The anecdotes about OJ, allowances, and Cheerios are memorable, but one remembrance was practically life-or-death-like in seriousness. It was, simply ...

REPORT CARD DAY

It was hell. And in retrospect, if I spent as much time studying as I did strategizing how I was going to present my report cards with the least possible damage, I would have ended up a Rhodes Scholar.

My father was fanatical about our grades, especially with Doug and me. Dale, and especially Patty the Miss Goody Two Shoes, did very well. On more than one occasion I was pulled from a sports league by Swede due to poor grades. There were endless lectures about how unimportant sports were to our futures, and how important scholastic success was. Unfortunately, Doug and I were not wired to be driven, studious types. We did well in subjects to our liking, but in the others (at least speaking for myself) my mind would be miles away.

I may not have been a great student, but I was smart enough to know never to be disruptive or disrespectful in school. Swede had a no-tolerance policy for bad behavior in school.

Every marking period was the same drill. Dale's grades were very good, Patty's were exceptional, and mine consisted of a few Cs, a few Bs, and an A in gym, which Swede didn't count. We were never sure about Doug's grades, because if he didn't approve of them he simply took the liberty of changing them.

The dreaded report card day? The tension would build for a week or more before the actual cards were issued. I wanted to do well—especially because many of my friends were excellent students—and I really didn't want to disappoint my father, particularly on something that was clearly important to him. (Estelle pushed us to get good grades as well, but on this issue, it was all about dealing with Swede). I still remember the conversations as my father slowly waded through my report card. He'd have this grim look on his face, he'd shake his head in disappointment, and he'd say something like, "I hope you understand that you are not hurting me. You are hurting yourself." Oy.

One of the rare light moments would be on the infrequent occasion when I'd get an A in a non-gym subject. For a brief moment Swede would let up a bit and ask "Don't they give plusses in that school?" Strict.

After each of the dreaded report card encounters, I'd make up my mind that I was going to get very serious about my schoolwork. By the next day those feelings had passed.

Once in a while my grades were even worse than my mediocre standards. Swede would get downright angry. He was always convinced that I was capable of doing much better if only I would apply myself. He had a booming, intimidating voice, and these were the times he used it.

You might be asking yourself why, if I didn't want to disappoint my father, I didn't work harder in school. I have psychoanalyzed myself on this subject for decades and I can only conclude that I was just a lazy jackass.

When Doug got older it was his turn, and his siblings were not around to take some of the pressure off. His strategy of changing his grades hit a slight snag once when he neglected to change them back when he brought the signed cards back to school.

Funny, but as genteel as Swede was, his voice at times was loud and scary … it had a bit of a growl to it. He never threatened to send us to the moon, but sometimes he reminded me of Ralph Kramden: big, loud, and physically intimidating. In fact, when I was a little kid, I remember being sure that my father was the biggest man in the world. Literally, a giant and always a gentle giant, unless we brought home a bad report card. Then we would need earplugs. But possibly his loudest reaction was one night when Doug and I were horsing around, resulting in …

SEEING RED: DOUG'S CUT ARM

Doug and I shared a small bedroom. One summer evening, when I was twenty and he was eleven, we were horsing around, playing an improvised game of "basketball," using a tennis ball. (We'd make a contest out of anything).

During the action, I blocked one of Doug's shots, and the ball was deflected backwards and up, and it hit the light fixture hanging from the middle of the ceiling. The fixture broke and fell. Doug instinctively put his arm out to break the fall of the fixture to prevent it from shattering. As a result, he got a nasty slice on the inside of his forearm, which spurted blood badly. I grabbed my brother and we hustled down the hallway to the bathroom. We knew the cut was serious and we needed to stop the bleeding, but we "scampered" as quietly as possible. We both knew how Swede would react to this.

My father did not handle a loved one's misfortune well at all. And an unnecessary injury like this one? He was going to be *very* upset. So Doug and I were trying to solve this without alerting him.

I held my hand tightly over the wound to try to slow the bleeding. We kept the cold water running, and occasionally I'd loosen the pressure to let cold water onto the cut. Each time I did so the blood gushed aggressively. We repeated the process a couple of times: pressure, cold water, gush of blood. This entire sequence took perhaps sixty to ninety seconds.

At this point an alarm must have gone off in Swede's head. He'd been down the hall in my parents' bedroom, doing business-related work. Something about our scurrying around and loud whispers must have aroused his senses. So Doug and I are in the bathroom, trying to make some progress (we weren't) and we heard (and felt) what sounded like a herd of hippos stampeding down the hallway towards us. I reached over and opened the door as my father arrived.

Swede: "What happened?!" (loudly and excitedly)

Me: "It's gonna be okay, dad," I calmly lied.

Swede, pointing to Doug's arm: "Let's see! (Very impatiently, with a real sense of urgency).

As the doorway filled with my mother and Dale, I slowly removed my hand from Doug's injury. Naturally, the blood gushed just as before.

Swede: "*Gragharghaaararraagraaa!!!*"

That unintelligible growl was Swede's way of announcing to us and the rest of the world that he was livid (at me), upset, worried, scared, livid (at me), frustrated, infuriated, and livid (at me). He followed that with what today we laugh at, but we were not in a jovial mood at the time:

Swede: "*All right!!! Calm down!!! Don't panic!!! Relax!!! Calm down!!! Take it easy!!!*

Obviously we were all worried; this was a deep gash. But my father was extremely upset. Seeing a loved one injured like that was his worst nightmare. Fortunately, his entire initial reaction and explosion lasted only a few seconds. We calmed down and agreed to get some professionals to help us with Doug's wound. We called for an ambulance, and they took Doug to Saint Barnabas Medical Center, where he was treated. The tally: fifteen stitches.

We all lived happily ever after. But none of us will forget my father's torment upon seeing his young son bleeding like that. And because of the distraction my selfish brother caused with his injury, no one remembers my beautiful blocked shot that started the fiasco.

* * * *

In some ways, my father was ahead of his time. He often did the family food shopping. The supermarket would be filled with housewives and Swede. It was hilarious listening to his stories of food-shopping frustrations at the local Shop-Rite. "Boy, I can't believe how inconsiderate some of these women are with the way they shop! They block the aisles with their carts, they ram my cart, and one woman even took one of my items out of *my* cart!" I know the way my father was, and I can just picture him focusing in the Shop-Rite, making sure he was in no one's way, always being considerate, turning the whole shopping experience into a science. To do it any other way would be illogical, and Swede wouldn't have that. But to hear him come home and talk about his weekly shopping "adventure," trying to survive among the other aggressive shoppers, was priceless.

The Masin kids much preferred that my mother did the food shopping. Unlike my father she would occasionally bring home some kind of "junk" food (or in Swede's vernacular, "garbage" or "poison"). If he found us eating candy, he'd come up behind us and whisper in our ear "*Bzzzzzzzz*". He was emulating a dentist's drill, knowing how much we dreaded getting cavities filled.

My father was tireless with Doug, whose first few years, with his foot and leg problems, were brutal. There were many nights (and I know because I shared a room with Doug) when my brother would awaken, crying from discomfort, ten times or more. Each time Swede would get up and try to comfort him. My father never fully recovered from years of constant listening for the cries of my brother. He never slept well thereafter.

So based on his early physical problems, the fact that he was the youngest Masin child by six, nine, and eleven years, Doug was, frankly, spoiled. All of us loved him to death, coddled him, played with him, entertained him, smothered him with affection, etc. Soon, Swede was the first to recognize that the family had created a monster, and Doug would have to be de-spoiled.

One evening, as little Doug was leaving the dinner table en route to the adjoining den he stated that he wanted some cookies (with the implication that he wanted them *now*). Swede immediately replied "Okay, Nikita," suggesting Doug's attitude likened him to the intimidating Russian Premier, Nikita Khrushchev. Obviously, it was not a compliment, and Doug knew it by my father's tone as well as the fact the rest of the family was laughing so hard. His response? Without stopping and without even glancing toward my father, he dismissed Swede with a wave of his arm and shot back "No, you!" Translation: I don't know who this Nikita guy is, but I ain't him. *You* are!

My father's love was unconditional, even if he had reason to be quite furious. Once, Doug got into a beef with some guy in a bar, and he ended up at a police station in Orange. Swede had to retrieve my brother, and on the drive home, gave Doug one of his world-class lectures: the ones about being a good person, taking the right road, doing the right thing, right and wrong, keeping out of bars, etc., etc. This was a very unusual incident for our family, and Swede was not happy, even though while at the station he befriended one of the cops who had been at the scene of Doug's altercation.

A court appearance ensued. Prior to it, my buddy Dave Fargnoli, who was a probation officer in Essex County for many years, made a few phone calls on Doug's behalf. And just in case, my buddy Eric Perlmutter, who had recently passed the bar exam, represented Doug. The police dropped the charges and we all lived happily ever after. Soon after, Eric began a highly successful career in the wholesale liquor industry, so he is one of the few trial lawyers who can boast of retiring undefeated (1-0).

* * * *

My father sometimes seemed just like a big kid. His whole life, he loved to play. Even in his seventies, playing hide and seek with the grandkids, he enjoyed the "competition." He loved to tease and kibitz, though never in a mean-spirited way. This was his playful side.

But I also remember his serious side. He fretted about money, to the point where it concerned me. He complained about politicians he viewed as villains. He openly criticized prejudiced people, and often fretted about anti-Semitism. None of the above was meant for us kids to hear, but it was hard to miss.

For instance, my father was very uncomfortable with ethnic jokes. He found them mean-spirited, and he felt if it was okay to poke fun of Italians, Polish, Blacks, and others, then it would be equally acceptable to poke fun of Jews, which tended to strike a nerve with him. I was less sensitive, and I would occasionally try the latest joke I'd heard on Swede. He usually cringed (perhaps my delivery was poor). But once he couldn't hold back ... he got quite the chuckle at this beauty:

Bobby: "What is the Jewish football teams' favorite cheer?"

Swede, reluctant to even ask: "I give up. What is it?"

Bobby: "Let's get that *quarter* back!!

Swede was quite the social liberal, often fretting about class and ethnic divisions, the plight of the needy, and "greedy pigs." At the same time he could be *very* traditional in his views. He was extremely impatient with us if we misbehaved; after all, isn't misbehaving inconsiderate and illogical?

* * * *

We *loved* our visits to Olympic Park, a huge amusement park on the Newark-Irvington border. For us kids it was the best, even though I was always afraid of rides that went high, fast, in a circle, or up and down. That left only the motor boats, which I loved. If it snowed or if it was cold enough, my father would gather up the family and take us sledding on Flood's Hill or skating on the frozen duck pond in South Orange.

We all remember how much my father loved little kids and animals. He connected so well with them, and they did the same. For instance, a neighbor's daughter, Susan Capiello, loved my father so much that one day, when she was eight or nine, she came to our house and asked if Swede could come out and play.

He was soooo gentle with cats and dogs. And rats. One day a bunch of kids caught a rat in a heavy paper bag. They were going to burn it! Swede intervened and said he'd get rid of the rat. He ended up letting it go in the brook that runs through South Orange. Right or wrong, he couldn't kill it. He certainly wasn't going to let those kids burn it.

Swede led by example. He was always very aware of others and he went overboard being considerate to them. And he treated *everyone* so respectfully. I remember my father going to great pains to limit how much trash he left for the garbage men. He tried to make sure it was neat and easy to collect.

And punctual? To not be would be inconsiderate, so naturally Swede was as punctual a person as I've ever met. If he was to be at a function at 7:01 p.m., he would arrive by 7:01 p.m.

TEACHING MOMENTS: SWEDE TO BOBBY

I still remember my first Little League home run. I was ten, and I was incredibly elated when the ball cleared the fence. Try as I might, I couldn't wipe this huge grin from my face as I rounded the bases. My next at bat, the umpire suggested that my father should give me a dollar for my "heroics." At home that evening, I passed along what I considered the umpire's excellent suggestion to Swede, but he pooh-poohed the idea. Instead, he used it as a teaching moment, explaining why I should play sports for fun, not for any material rewards, blah blah blah. I think he should have given me the buck and *then* start his teaching moment. But truth be known, I did not care one bit about the dollar. I didn't even want to ask for it. I was so pumped about hitting my first homer, I would not have traded my experience for anything … not even a dollar.

Swede's attempts to display a good perspective about sports were occasionally tested. For instance, our Junior Varsity basketball team was outstanding during my first year at Columbia High School. We would have been a viable contender in the Essex County Tournament (JV division), and with our impressive record we wanted to go. But the South Orange/ Maplewood Board of Education had a strict policy regarding games *not* being played on school nights. The administrators did not want to over-emphasize sports, and always maintained an "academics first" approach. The tournament in question did have games scheduled on weeknights, so it looked like the administrators would not permit us to participate.

Nevertheless, some folks decided to appeal the policy. A special meeting was called, and the issue of our JV team going to the tournament was the subject. Many concerned folks, including my parents, attended. One of the Board of Education officials stood up to start the meeting and announced something like: "Regardless of the arguments made tonight, our JV basketball team will *not* be playing in the tournament." This opening salvo created a mild explosion of protest. But bottom line, we didn't go.

My parents came home and broke the news, which of course was disappointing. My mother was quite angry, both with the decision as well as the approach taken by the Board. My father was not happy about it either, especially for my buddies and me. But he didn't dwell on it and encouraged me not to either. I think he was sending a message with his apparent indifference. In the long run, it really didn't matter. We'd had a great season, and nothing was going to change that. But I still wish we had gone to the tournament!

My father worked hard not to impose himself in my sports life. It was obvious that he wanted me to have my own identity, to benefit from the positive aspects of sports, and, most importantly, to never try to be him. But there was one time when he couldn't resist trying to help.

It was when I was a sophomore at Columbia, weighing maybe 160 pounds, and going to be starting both offensively and defensively in a football game that day against the New Jersey state champs that year, East Orange High School. They had numerous stars on their team, including two of New Jersey's best-rated players ever, Jim Oliver and Quincy Yarborough. As my father drove to drop me off, I had my game face on the whole way, not saying one word. Actually, I was feeling quite intimidated with visions of carrying the ball into the line and being annihilated by Jim and Quincy. I'm sure my father sensed this, because it was one of the few times he ever gave me some pre-game advice and encouragement. That alone got my attention. As we arrived at Underhill Field, he looked me in the eye and reminded me that football was a rough, nasty sport, and if I was going to play I had to play it the right way: fearlessly and savagely. I'll never forget his use of the word "savage", as it was *very* un-Swede like. His simple but serious words both inspired and relaxed me. It may be a coincidence, but that was perhaps the best game I ever played at any level in any sport. I *know* my father's brief pep talk made a difference.

* * * *

Swede had a few idiosyncratic views on clothes. He virtually never wore long-sleeved shirts because they made him uncomfortable. And once, when I was with Columbia Sportswear, I sent him a plaid shirt (short-sleeved, naturally), which I thought he would like. A few days later, while talking to my father by phone, I asked about the shirt:

Bob: "Dad, did you get the shirt I sent you?"

Swede: "Yeah, thank you, but I won't wear it."

Bob: "Why not?"

Swede: "It's got buttons on the collar. I don't wear shirts with button-down collars."

Bob (incredulously): "Why not?!"

Swede: "Eh ... you gotta button 'em, then unbutton 'em ..." He explained this as though it was as tedious as building the Great Pyramids of Egypt.

Bob (more incredulously): "*What*? Why don't you just leave the collar buttoned all the time? Then you won't have to bother with it."

Swede: "Yeah, but then the buttons break."

Remember, this is the same guy who bragged that he still had (and wore) ties from his college years, and who wore pants two inches too short and with zippers that appeared to be broken. ("My fly is not broken ... it just *looks* like it's broken").

Doug points out how fortunate he was to be able to spend significant time with my father as an adult. Doug's one-hour photo store in Central Jersey was not far from Trenton, where Swede had business meetings every Friday morning. He spent most of those Friday afternoons helping Doug at his store. After Swede retired, he worked as a volunteer two days a week, helping in any way he could. Doug did most of the interacting with customers, but remarked that those customers who got to know Swede "just loved him."

Every December, on two consecutive Saturdays, Doug brought Santa Claus to his store. Actually, it was right outside the store, and I doubt it was the real Santa ... just someone dressed up like him. There, he'd pose with families and their children. The photos were taken by Patty, a spectacular photographer, with an incredible knack for getting everyone, including little kids, smiling and looking at the camera. Swede managed (and entertained) the long lines of parents and kids, and Doug processed and printed the photos. It was always a very successful promotion for Doug. As busy as they were, Doug and Patty were entertained by Swede's "management" skills, as he prepped the families for their turn with Santa, and coached Patty on her picture-taking techniques. "Patty, when you count to three, don't snap the picture as you say three; snap the picture just *before* saying three. Snapping while talking might cause the camera to move and blur the picture." He then carefully explained to the folks the post-photo instructions. He kept things efficient, he kept things moving, and naturally he did plenty of kibitzing with each family. He was in his element. It was always comical to watch Swede try to convince little toddlers why they shouldn't be crying. He kept a straight face as he explained (remember, these are toddlers) how illogical it was to cry just for the sake of crying. The little ones would typically look at my father like he had several heads, but they often were distracted into stopping their crying.

Another example of Swede being in his element took place over several days when he held a garage sale at his Mountain House Road home. In his late seventies at the time, my father wore an apron with multiple pockets and served as the cash register. My siblings were entertained by Swede's sharpness and engagement with the customers at the garage sale. He was negotiating, joking, collecting money, making change, challenging, entertaining, teasing, and selling. And he was having a blast.

Swede's influence as a father clearly had the most impact on Patty. In so many ways, Patty *is* Swede. And like her father, virtually everyone who meets Patty loves her. It was remarkable the way Patty and my father clicked. Their interests, their humor, their disposition, their gentle nature, their generosity, and more were so much in synch. And there was something else that I can't put my finger on. The best way for me to describe it is that there are not many people who clearly make the world better. They do.

Just as Swede was the ever-present silent warrior when his parents needed him the most, Patty assumed that role when her parents needed her the most. Not only did she not complain; she was energized to take on the challenge. There are few people like my sister Patty.

However, ... Patty wasn't always the perfect angel. Little Miss Goody Two Shoes had her moments, as evidenced by her behavior in the following anecdote.

KIND, CONSIDERATE, GENTLE PATTY

One afternoon in the mid-1950s, Swede and Estelle took all the kids to a Saturday matinee movie. Earlier that day, my parents had taken us to a shoe store; Dale and I needed new shoes. Evidently Patty didn't, so she didn't get any.

The theater was crowded, and Swede had his hands full trying to use logic with five-year-old Patty, who felt left out due to the shoe snub. She was quietly explaining to my father about the unfairness of it all. Apparently, she didn't feel as though she was getting her point across.

Suddenly, she climbed over my father and leaped into the aisle, and in her loudest possible voice screamed: "*Hey Daddy, I'm gonna kick you in the eye!*"

Ah yes, my kind, rational sister Patty.

As for Swede, he was always remarkably fast for a big guy. But I believe that day he set a world record for jumping out of his seat, scooping up a five-year-old and sprinting out of a theater.

And ever since this episode, if any of us is out shopping with Patty, we make sure to buy her something.

* * * *

Swede had great parenting skills, but that's not all. According to my Aunt Shirley Swede was not only "the greatest father," he was also "the greatest son." She added that he was an adoring brother to Leo as well. "Leo and Swede never had a harsh word. But as a youngster Swede nagged Leo all the time; he always wanted to hang out with Leo and his buddies. And in some ways they were very different. Leo spent too much, and Swede was very tight; he spent nothing."

Always a devoted son, Swede worked tirelessly for his parents as they neared the end of their lives. Max had increasing dementia during his last five years, and my grandmother had similar symptoms—though not as serious—which caused her to deteriorate after Max's death. They required constant attention. My father and Uncle Leo hired a young Haitian immigrant named Pat (who was an absolute princess of a person) to assist my grandparents. During this time my father visited his parents at least once every day and arranged *everything* for them. Pat and my father worked so hard to get my grandparents through every day. They had a difficult job ... one that never lets up. But Swede never complained about this task; he would never let himself do so. He loved his parents the way he loved his kids, unconditionally. He was an incredible role model.

Aunt Shirley remarked that when my Uncle Leo, Swede's beloved older brother, started to fail, my father was there for him every day. Swede was in a bit of a decline himself; it wouldn't be too long before he moved into the assisted living facility. That was Swede, he was always there. One of the all-time great foul-weather friends, Swede Masin.

On a very sad note, my grandparents' aide, Pat, suddenly passed away not long after my grandmother died at the *very* young age of twenty-nine. If anyone deserved a long, healthy, happy life, it was her. All of us were heartbroken, especially my father, who attended Pat's funeral in Newark. She and my father had worked so hard together to take care of Max and Sonia.

Greatness in people can be measured in many ways, and the greatness label can be a very subjective thing. But this young woman, whose last name none of the Masin siblings ever knew, left a lasting impression on me. The world needs more great people like her. I regret not being able to publicize her full name. She deserves the recognition.

Clearly my father worked hard at setting a good example. He had so much honesty and integrity, and he was remarkably fair. It's no wonder my siblings and I craved his approval and his happiness, both when we were kids and as adults. We idolized Swede.

CHAPTER ELEVEN:
IDYLLIC SOUTH ORANGE

I have been very fortunate to have lived in some wonderful places. The beautiful West Hills of Portland, Oregon; the tranquil, rolling hills and open country of Landenburg, Pennsylvania; spectacular Laguna Beach, California; and historic Queen Anne Hill in Seattle, Washington. All are great places to live, but paled in comparison to growing up in idyllic South Orange, New Jersey. It's been decades since I've lived there, but I always love going back.

On my visits, I stayed at my father's house, and I'd always go for long runs, just so I could take in as much of the town as possible. I'd start from our quiet street, Mountain House Road, and run to the park. Then I'd run up and down Flood's Hill ten times, just to prove to myself that I still had it. (I didn't). Then I'd run from the top of the hill along Ridgewood Road to Forest Road, where I'd turn left. Running up Forest was tough. It's quite steep, but my close friend in high school, Jim Deutsch, used to live near the top of Forest, so I took that street for old times' sake. Then left onto Wyoming Avenue. Occasionally I'd stay on Wyoming for a long stretch, across South Orange Avenue, working my way to Maplewood (South Orange's beautiful sister community). For a time Uncle Leo, Aunt Shirley, and family lived on Lewis Drive, off Wyoming (Dionne Warwick also lived on that street for a while), and I'd turn right onto it. That street is *very* steep, and I'd have to be feeling very energetic to not stop and walk. My other route was to snake my way up through the South Orange hills, across Mayhew Drive and Harding Drive, to Newstead. All along the way, the streets get prettier the higher you climb. The homes, the yards, the trees are world class. There are few places I can imagine being nicer than a cool, sunny, fall day in the hills of South Orange.

I remember my father telling me that as a boy he liked to go outside and run long distances, invariably winding his way to and throughout Weequahic Park. He had also related how many endless hours he spent in nearby playgrounds (I assume either Maple Avenue School or Chancellor

Avenue School), playing sandlot sports. It got me thinking about the many parallels between my parents growing up in Newark's Weequahic section and my siblings and I growing up in South Orange. The similarities are striking.

The Cameron Field Park in the middle of South Orange, where I spent much of my youth, could not be better. It had the best sledding hill (Flood's Hill) in the area, a duck pond that offered good ice skating when conditions permitted, a Little League diamond with a fence, four softball fields, open fields for soccer and touch football (not to mention Ultimate Frisbee, which was invented by Columbia High School students several years after I graduated), a spacious community pool and playground, tennis courts, bocce courts, a major league baseball diamond, platform tennis courts, basketball courts, and a great Community Center building.

Back in the 1960s, even on cold winter afternoons and Saturdays, Mike Abramson, Marty Brafman, Bruce Chait, Roy Greenman, Bobby Katz, Neil Kramer, Steve Kruvant, Steve Pasko, Eric Perlmutter, Peter Tzeses, and other kids and I would be there *all* day. We'd shovel away the snow and ice so we could play hoops. Once we couldn't stand the cold any longer, we'd go inside and play ping pong or bumper pool. There was a TV room for those who wanted to watch a ball game. Once we warmed up enough, we'd be back outside on the courts. It was heaven. I've always thought how wonderful it would be if all kids were lucky enough to have the same facilities and opportunities that we had in South Orange. It was a very healthy atmosphere. To top it all off for me, it was a five-minute walk from our house.

A long, long time ago—October 29, 1929, to be exact—probably unbeknownst to most current South Orange residents, there was an exhibition baseball game played on the baseball diamond in the park. One team happened to have Babe Ruth and Lou Gehrig playing for them. Legend has it that Gehrig hit an absolutely monstrous home run, one that seemed to have traveled further each year after it was hit. By the time I was in high school, considering where the ball reportedly landed, it traveled about four miles.

Near my parents' home in Newark was huge, beautiful Weequahic Park with its rolling hills, an eighteen-hole golf course (which opened in 1904, making it one of the oldest public courses in the United States), the largest lake in Essex County (eighty acres), and countless other facilities. It's certainly more massive than our Cameron Field/Meadowland Park in South Orange, but both were great venues for kids and families.

The Village of South Orange itself is quite special. The Fire House has been featured for its distinctive Norman style. The train station, in the middle of the Village, is right out of a 1940s Cary Grant movie. And of course everyone had their favorite eating spot: the great delicatessens (The Famous,

Village Pantry), a favorite bakery (Romoser's), a good burger joint (Bun and Burger), and the popular Chinese Restaurant, Alex Eng. But today they are all gone. Other popular spots (Bunny's and The Reservoir) have passed the test of time and remain Village landmarks. And lest I forget Sonny's, a small, nondescript little joint that has my favorite bagels.

But there were eating establishments in the Village whose renown went beyond the local residents. One of those places was Gruning's, where most teenagers hung out. There were actually two Gruning's restaurants: one was in the middle of the Village on South Orange Avenue; the other was half a mile up the road (I think it's officially in Maplewood), which was known as "Gruning's at the Top." On a clear day it had a great view of the Manhattan skyline. Both establishments were classic malt shops/burger joints. Gruning's made its own ice cream, which was hard to beat.

In the late 1970s, my buddy Mike Purzycki and I went on a two-week backpacking trip through the Cascade Mountains in Washington. We were in some very remote spots and went days without seeing any other humans. However, when we did encounter some folks from Chicago, we learned that one of them had gone to college with someone from South Orange. To our great surprise, he went on and on about Gruning's ice cream—not something I expected to hear in the wilderness of the Northwest.

Then there is Town Hall Deli, home of the "Original Sloppy Joe," which is not to be confused with the Sloppy Joe that consists of chopped meat on a bun. The Town Hall Sloppy Joe is a large, layered sandwich, cut up into eight individual sandwiches, made on great rye bread, with many different combinations of meats and dressings. My personal favorite is roast beef, turkey and Swiss cheese with Russian dressing and Cole slaw. It is not uncommon for college students and people who have moved away from South Orange to have Town Hall Sloppy Joe's packed in dry ice and shipped overnight to them. In fact, we've done this a few times ourselves.

My parents' eateries were equally significant. Take, for instance, the Weequahic Diner (established 1938). It certainly was as important to the Weequahic crowd as Gruning's was to us Columbia kids. It was *the* place to go. And who can forget Syd's (established 1941), located across the street from the high school? Great hot dogs. Once in a while, after we'd visit my grandparents on Grumman Avenue, we'd hit Syd's for a mustard/kraut dog. Or two. Hit the spot.

South Orange schools were terrific—and in the 1960s were consistently ranked among the top school systems in the country. The teachers were dedicated, caring, and highly respected. Even the school buildings themselves were impressive. When the current Columbia High was completed in 1927, it was pictured in the *Encyclopedia Britannica* as a state-of-the-art educational institution. And when South Orange Junior High (now South Orange Middle School) was completed in 1956, it was described, with a little bit of envy, by educators in surrounding towns as the "pink palace."

My very first day at the beautiful junior high had some controversy. It seems someone had blown up a toilet in one of the boys' bathrooms with a cherry bomb. The principal, Ray Sterling, called a special assembly after classes for every boy in the school. And did he put the fear of God in every one! He stood on the stage with a microphone, and growled warnings. And I mean growled! He scared the living daylights out of me, and I hadn't even done anything. Old School (no pun intended) Ray Sterling got our attention that day. There would be no more incidents during my three years at South Orange Junior High School.

The Board of Education took academics *very* seriously. Besides the high caliber of teachers throughout the school system, the students were brilliant, at least from my perspective. There were so many smart kids I sometimes found it a little intimidating. So many went to great colleges (such as Williams, Colgate, Amherst, all the Ivy League colleges, Haverford, NYU, Hamilton), and my closest friends (including Marty Brafman, Jim Deutsch, Roy Greenman, Bob Katz, Neil Kramer, and Eric Perlmutter) went on to become very successful in their fields ... doctors, lawyers, professors, authors, business leaders, etc.

Every Weequahic alumni with whom I've spoken has raved the same way about their public schools as I do about mine: So many smart kids! Teachers who were demanding but great. I've seen it written more than once—and I'm sure most of the alumni would concur—that the Weequahic High School of the 1930s, 1940s, and 1950s was the most accomplished school, academically, in the country. I doubt there is a way to validate that, but it's fun to think it's so. And just as Weequahic produced many highly successful people, so too did Columbia.

To name just a few ... the entertainment industry success stories include Zach Braff, Lauryn Hill, Frank Langella, Roy Scheider, Andrew and Elizabeth Shue, Joel Silver (who also was a key figure in the invention of Ultimate Frisbee!), Max Weinberg, and Teresa Wright. The great athletes include Mark Bryant, who played fifteen years in the NBA; Joetta Clark, a world-class track star for twenty years; and her sister Hazel who was an Olympian as well. Peter Connor was posthumously awarded the Congressional Medal of Honor for his bravery in the Vietnam War. Paul Auster is an acclaimed writer, screenwriter, and director—and perhaps more importantly, he was the star player on our B'nai B'rith Little League team. And let's not forget my cousin Artie Bartner, now well into his fourth decade as the director of the University of Southern California's famed marching band.

All of us—my parents and their contemporaries, my siblings and my friends—had it pretty darn good growing up in the1930s-1940s South Ward section of Newark and 1950s-1960s South Orange, respectively. They were wonderful times and places, many of our peers were good role models, there were strong families, and plenty of good, strong mentors/teachers. One other thing in our favor, particularly for my siblings and me, was that even though South Orange was a very affluent town, our family was about as middle-class as we could be. Because we were surrounded by many wealthy people, I used to think we were poor. In fact, we weren't, but that was my perspective. If nothing else, it made my siblings and me appreciative of what we had. Another similarity between the two communities was that both had large Jewish communities. Of course, many of the parents of my Columbia high School classmates, like my own parents, had graduated from Weequahic High School in the 1930s and 1940s.

Clearly, I lived a sheltered life, growing up in South Orange, with everything it had: the affluence, the schools, the beauty, the lack of crime, etc. Not many kids have it so good. Just one more similarity to my parents' generation growing up in the Weequahic section. To a person, they all said their time and place was incomparable.

What made me realize even more how sheltered my upbringing was in South Orange was going away to college at the University of Delaware. Newark, Delaware, is only 125 miles away from Newark, New Jersey, but in the mid-1960s it sometimes felt as if it were in the Deep South. My University classmates, who came primarily from South Jersey, Philadelphia, and Delaware talked differently than my North Jersey friends. My roommate from southern Delaware may as well have been from Mars, and he probably thought I was from Uranus.

Moreover, whereas most of my peers in South Orange were social liberals, that was certainly not the case at the University of Delaware. Growing up in South Orange, the "N" word was *never* used—not at home, not in school, not in the park. Admittedly, there were not many black families in South Orange, and frankly (and unfortunately) there was not much socializing between the black and white families. But in sports and in school, there was good interaction; and from this white person's (perhaps naïve) perspective, I never sensed animosity between the two groups. At the University of Delaware, however, I heard the "N" word used routinely and I remember arguing with guys about it. I recall thinking at the time how lucky I was to have grown up in a more progressive town like South Orange, and how lucky I was to have been raised by such enlightened parents.

THE SUBURBAN GUYS

I stay in touch with my boyhood friends, even though we live on opposite coasts. These are the kids who came to my house often, played with or against me in Little League, played with me in high school sports, and went with me to Hebrew School. We had similar interests, our parents knew each other (in fact, Bobby Katz's father took my mother to the high school prom), we slept at each other's houses, and more. My parents loved my friends for being such good influences on me. (I needed it).

All of us spent endless hours and days in the South Orange parks, where much of the sports action was: Little League baseball, hoops, sledding, tennis, touch football, softball, and even occasional ice skating. The Baird Community Center was our focal point. We all followed pro sports, and we loved to get into spirited arguments over who was better: Mantle, Mays, or Snider, the Giants or the Yankees, the Giants or the Dodgers. Naturally, since my father was a big Willie Mays fan, I was too. That's pretty much always the way it worked in my family ... I followed Swede's lead.

Below are some anecdotes of my lifelong friends from South Orange and Columbia High School, all of whom in some way have made me what I am today. (Yeah, it's *their* fault).

Bobby Katz was our take-charge guy. If we wanted to arrange a sandlot football game against the grade above ours or below ours, he was the one to make it happen. Planning to take in a Knicks game? He handled it. Going to the movies? He took care of it. He always had the nicest car once we reached driving age, so he always drove. He wouldn't have it any other way. "Coach Katz" loved having the responsibility to manage our affairs, and he did it well—though it didn't occur to me at the time that he just liked being bossy.

He was the coach of every one of our teams in every sport in every league, well into our adult years. He did all the thinking and all the planning. If there was a schedule change or we needed more players, etc., he was all over it. He was always planning ahead. Fortunately, the rest of us had confidence in Coach Katz ... we felt quite comfortable being his pawns in the game of life. Often, after he'd declare what our next action was to be, we'd look at him and then remind ourselves that "It's good to be the king."

Jim Deutsch and I were inseparable during our junior high and high school years. We had similar senses of humor, such as when we made phony phone calls together, we played sports on the same teams, and we were world-class experts on *The Twilight Zone* television series—and in fact still think we are.

Like many of my childhood friends, Jim was a brilliant student and graduated from Williams College, but the more interesting part comes next. From then until now (almost four decades), Jim set out on a routine where he'd move from place to place, generally at one-year intervals, trying new experiences each time. He was a reporter for the *Indianapolis Star* newspaper, a forest ranger in Alaska, a librarian in Montana, a monorail driver at Walt Disney World, and the sole reporter for a very small newspaper in Yazoo City, Mississippi. While there, one of his fellow employees, learning of Jim's background, admitted "I ain't never met a Jew before." I once had some business in nearby Jackson, Mississippi, and met Jim for dinner, which he was nice enough to mention in the paper's next edition. I guess it was a slow news day.

Jim speaks six languages, and has taught at the college level in many countries. In recent years he seems to have finally settled somewhat, living in Washington, D.C., where he works for the Smithsonian Institution, and continues to teach. A fascinating life, but not something many of us could or would endure.

My buddy Marty Brafman lives in Cincinnati but we speak on the phone monthly, as we have done since our college days. In fact, we've been close since we were teammates in Little League baseball. In the seventh grade, Marty and I became avid fans of Pro Wrestling, and went to several wrestling events in the old Newark Armory (coincidentally, the same arena where Weequahic and South Side had their epic basketball battles). Marty even got into an altercation with one of the wrestlers when he had the nerve to ask Red Gruppe (the designated bad guy) for his autograph just as he was approaching the ring. The Evil Mr. Gruppe responded by sending Marty flying to the floor with a stiff arm. Marty was so excited he came sprinting back to where we were sitting and slipped on a bunch of peanut shells. It looked like a perfect slide into a base, and it sure entertained those sitting around us.

Roy Greenman and I played sports together from the time we were ten, and in the fifty years since I've *never* seen him lose his temper. He became an outstanding athlete, and always seemed to have a smile on his face while competing. A highly successful attorney, he looks the same as he did in high school. (Don't you just hate guys like that)?

Neil Kramer was our Renaissance Man: an all-around athlete, brilliant student, (he went to Williams College too), sophisticated, and with a good sense of humor, etc. He was also respectful, responsible, honest, and courteous; in short, he was a distinguished guy before his time. Naturally, my parents really liked it when I would hang out with Neil. Swede regarded Neil as a perfect model and hoped he would rub off on me. To a degree, he did; we're both right-handed.

But unbeknownst to my parents, Neil was in fact fallible. One day he, Eric Perlmutter, and I took a bus to Asbury Park on the Jersey Shore. We had a great day at the beach, then spent a little time on the boardwalk, where we bought some saltwater taffy. It was one of those deals where they give you a box which you can fill on your own with the various flavors of taffy. Well, the three stooges figured we'd be charged by the box, so we tried to jam as much taffy as physically possible into the box. That's right. That's the strategy the brilliant Eric Einstein and Sir Neil Newton came up with. Me, the sap, went along with their clever idea. At one point, if memory serves, Eric even stood on the taffy so we could jam more into the box. (Okay, I made that up). To our dismay, the taffy establishment charged by the ounce, so our taffy would have cost one thousand dollars, or perhaps a little less. We quickly emptied about three-fourths of our box into the bins so we could afford the stuff.

Then we get on the bus home. There was a young lady sitting across from us, eating a candy apple, *painfully* slowly. We watched as the inside of the apple started to turn an increasingly darker shade of brown. Don't ask me why, but this little incident entertained us the whole ride. We were already somewhat giddy as we mocked ourselves over the idiotic taffy scheme, and for some reason the candy apple girl got us laughing uncontrollably. And the brilliant, sophisticated, erudite, genteel, man about town, the accomplished Mr. Kramer … was drooling. He was laughing so hard he was drooling—this, the same guy my father wanted me to emulate! Finally, the three geniuses reached our destination. The whole day, which we still enjoy revisiting, was like a Seinfeld episode … about nothing.

Eric Perlmutter could be president. Yes, of the United States. He's that impressive and a true leader. He and his wife, Judy, have been close to me since junior high school. Even further back in time, my father dated Judy's mother, Vita, when both resided in the Weequahic section. Naturally, my parents adored Eric and Judy, as they did my other friends.

In the late 1990s, my mother was eating dinner with friends at Solano's Restaurant in Orange, and was opining about how today's movie stars don't come close to equaling the stars of her day: Cary Grant, Gary Cooper, Clark Gable, and others. Across the room she spots this tall, well-built, handsome man, dressed in a suit. She tells her friends, "Now that's what I call a handsome man." Suddenly the handsome man approaches their table. "Hi, Mrs. Masin!" It was Eric. My mother hadn't seen him in years and didn't realize it was him. She was so excited to see him. Then Judy, who was at their table on the other side of the room, stomps across the restaurant towards my mother. "So, what am I, chopped liver!?" It was a terrific mini-reunion for my mother, as she proudly introduced Eric and Judy to her friends.

I've had one fight in my life, and Eric played an integral role. He started it. At the beginning of my junior year at Columbia, Eric, along with football teammate Steve Price and me, decided to check out a back-to-school dance at West Orange Mountain High School. Foolishly, we were wearing our

Columbia letter jackets and encountered a large group of thugs standing between us and the gym entrance. They started baiting and taunting us, not liking interlopers coming to "their" school. There were at least fifteen of them, and they were clearly drunk. As they became louder and more aggressive, we kept walking, silently, hoping they'd lose interest. No chance: they wanted a fight, and they weren't going away. Suddenly, one of the more aggressive taunters, a big lug, jumped in front of Eric, blocking his path. With his index finger pointed in Eric's face, he screamed, "I'm talking to you!! What the &@%# are you doin' here!?" In an instant, convinced there was no way out of this mess, Eric decided he might as well get the first shot. He briefly looked away and then *crack*! He sucker-punched this thug with a mighty right. I still remember the sound. After a split second, in which everyone froze from the shock of the punch, all parties engaged in what must have looked like a rugby scrum. Miraculously, as the "scrum" detached, three separate one-against-one fights ensued. Driven by about ten percent rage and ninety percent fear, I zeroed in on the face of the moose I was fighting and threw as many punches as I could. Everything seemed to be happening so quickly, like a speeded-up movie. Fortunately for us, one of the many student spectators ran into the gym and summoned a security officer, who quickly called in the police. They pulled all the participants inside, questioned us, yelled at us, and then let us go.

When I got home after midnight, I woke up my parents to tell them all about it. I stood at the foot of their bed, re-enacting the scene, blow by blow. They acted just as I expected. First, they were both relieved that I wasn't hurt—though I found out the next day that I had broken my left hand, which I didn't notice that night because I was so worked up. Swede was not happy that we had put ourselves in this position, but I detected a slight smile when he learned my fight was one-sided. Eventually he got around to one of his mini-lectures about avoiding risky situations and using better judgment. Typical Swede. Estelle? She got charged up. She was practically shadow boxing as I related the story. I think if my mother was at Mountain High School that night she would have tried to get a few shots in.

Eric wasn't rattled that night, but I *have* seen him flustered—just once. It was when he shook hands with legendary football coach Vince Lombardi ... who was naked. (Yep, that's what I said). I'll explain. Eric's father-in-law Larry Orenstein was good friends with Frank Scott, a sports promoter who put deals together—a precursor to today's sports agents. That's how Frank invited Eric and me to Dickinson College in Pennsylvania, where the Washington Redskins were conducting their pre-season work-outs. Coach Lombardi and a couple of Redskins players were working on promotional opportunities with Frank. As we're driving to Dickinson, Frank asked several times about our correct names, since he wanted to introduce us properly. We responded each time he asked, but for some reason it didn't seem to take. So he kept asking.

When we arrived, Frank brazenly barged into the office of Lombardi, who had just finished toweling off after a shower. Frank seemed like a fearless guy, but now he was in the company of royalty. Buck naked royalty. He excitedly introduced us, Bob Masin and Eric Perlmutter, as "Bobby uh, Bobby uh, Mollins and Errol, uh Putzmutter." No one cared much, certainly not Mollins and Putzmutter. After all, how many people can say they've shaken hands with Vince Lombardi while he was putting on his skivvies?

Then Lombardi invited us to join the team for lunch. Eric and I got our food and went into the hallway, looking for the team. Coach Vince, by now sitting at one of the tables, spotted us in the hallway and said, loud and forcibly, "Come on in, boys." When he spoke, half the Redskins players glanced our way, curious as to who we were. So here are these two dopes, now feeling extremely self-conscious, trying to walk through the doorway with our lunch trays … at the same time. It was like a Laurel and Hardy routine. First we both try to walk through, then we both back up and insist the other go first. Then we both try to go through again, doing all of this as the players snickered. What a couple of winners.

To this day I am so impressed with my boyhood friends. They were good influences, they were good citizens, and they were relatively trouble-free. My parents loved all of them, because they knew I could use all of the help I could get.

WISE GUYS

We all are molded, to a certain degree, by our life experiences. Growing up in tranquil South Orange was going to offer different experiences than growing up in a city like Newark, New Jersey. Whereas South Orange was true suburbia, and my high school classmates were just the kind of friends and mentors my parents wanted in my life, some of the friends I met in college were pure city.

Take, for instance, Joe Purzycki, youngest son of Swede's South Side High rival, Iron Mike Purzycki. We hit it off right away. And over time I became very close to his family and his friends, such as Joe Abruzzese, Dave Fargnoli, Al Avignone, Frank La Bruto, Terry Cunningham, Barry Prezioso, Steve Samich. They grew up in Orange, East Orange, and Newark, minutes away from my home, but light years away in their environment. In their blue-collar neighborhoods, there were plenty of street thugs (wise guys, and they were everywhere), low levels of organized crime, and genuine and growing racial tension. And while we were enjoying multiple activities at the South Orange

Community Center, Joe and his crowd hung out on some street corner in Newark's Vailsburg section, outside a candy store, taunting each other.

So the difference in these two distinct groups of my friends was (and still is, but to a lesser degree) palpable. The South Orange crowd was serious about schoolwork, genteel in nature, generally affluent, protected from the seedier side of life, and non-violent.

Primarily Italian, the Purzycki crowd were not from affluent families, were much more aggressive in nature (engaging in brawls was not uncommon), were not overly dedicated to hitting the books, and were far more exposed to a tougher side of life. And, as mentioned, they had a smart remark for everyone.

But there were also some striking similarities: Both groups are extremely sharp, creative, entertaining, quick-witted people, and are successful in their chosen fields. The South Orange guys have excelled in medicine, law, teaching, and business, etc., and the city guys have excelled in law enforcement, coaching, and the entertainment industry.

One of my father's Swede-isms—"You hang around bars, you're looking for trouble. Bad things happen"—was often proven to be accurate by the city guys. The closer I got to them, the nearer I came to harm's way. In the center of it all was always the outgoing, personable Joe Abruzzese, the same guy who has become one of the most successful people in his industry. A lasting image I have is of Joe being escorted/shoved/carried out of bars by large bouncers—as a direct result of his smart-alecky trouble-instigating behavior.

* * * *

Joe Purzycki and Joe Abruzzese grew up near each other in the Vailsburg section of Newark. They were like brothers then and remain just as close today. Growing up, they were, well, usually up to no good. But today these men are distinguished, highly responsible industry leaders, and I feel there is no need to air the dirty laundry of their *most* unfortunate youthful behavior. Besides, if I did, they would beat me up.

But they sure are entertaining. Two years ago I received an email from them, which went something like this:

Joe and Joe: "Mase, we want to come to the Northwest this summer and climb Mt. Rainier with you."

My response: "Guys, it's great you want to come out, but I *strongly* recommend we lower our sights and climb something easier than Mt. Rainier."

Joe and Joe: "Fat Boy, you're still a pampered little punk from South Orange. We're tough guys from Newark. Stop being a girl and get ready for

Rainier. Besides, if something bad happens, and you die up there, we can live off your carcass for eighteen months."

Me (now a little more motivated): "Okay, dummies, I'll set it up. I'll arrange for the guide, the equipment, etc. I'll get crampons, tents, etc. We'll be on snow most of the time."

Abruzzese: "There's *snow*?!"

Funny stuff, and for some reason the two macho guys from Newark (who probably never climbed anything higher than their Little League pitcher's mound) haven't brought up mountaineering since.

* * * *

One day in 1988, four of us (Joe Purzycki, Joe Abruzzese, Dave Fargnoli, and I) decided to get together for a friendly round of golf in what must have been the motliest foursome ever seen on a golf course. Abruzzese played occasionally and was good. Fargnoli, a lifelong golfer, was excellent, and still maintains a handicap of four. He (always at arm's length) referred to Purzycki as the worst male, adult golfer in the history of the planet, but I knew that was a stretch, seeing as how Joe played better than me.

Joe Purzycki and I had no clubs; luckily Fargnoli had multiple sets, which he graciously loaned to us. The teams were Abruzzese and Masin vs. Fargnoli and Purzycki, but three of us teamed up to root against, distract, and taunt Dave on virtually every shot.

On one hole, as Dave was driving his cart toward his ball in the fairway, Abruzzese hit an iron shot that appeared to be headed on a collision course with Dave. Spontaneously and simultaneously, the three of us yelled … not "*Fore*," but "*Hit him*!!" Regrettably, the ball missed; but we succeeded in getting a few interesting glances from the golfers on the parallel fairway.

On the eighteenth green, Dave was set up for an important putt to win for his team. It was about a seven-footer, not an easy putt, but very doable for Dave. As he completed his backswing and was about to hit the ball, we all screamed at him. It worked like a charm. Dave missed, and his disgusted, curse-riddled, f-bomb-laden diatribe towards us was one for the ages.

And to rub salt in the wound, Dave's "partner," Tiger Purzycki, lost not only a dozen or so of Dave's golf balls during the round, but three of his clubs, to boot! Shockingly, that was the last time the four of us got together for a friendly round of golf.

* * * *

So there you have it: the beauty and the security of growing up in bucolic South Orange, which was made that much clearer once I left for college and was exposed to the real world. I look forward to my next visit: to my long run to the park, up Flood's Hill, up Forest Road, along Wyoming Avenue, up into Newstead, then back down to the Village, where I will reward myself with a bagel from Sonny's bagel joint, a Sloppy Joe from Town Hall Deli, and a pizza from The Reservoir. The perfect day.

CHAPTER TWELVE:
UNIQUELY SWEDE

The following stories help define who my father was. These anecdotes made an impression on me, since I remember them many years later. They touch upon Swede's athleticism, his sense of humor, his personality, and his quirkiness.

SWEDE IN ACTION

In the early 1960s, the Village of South Orange held a fundraising basketball game, pitting some of the town's basketball stars of the past against a team consisting of the South Orange Police Department and ... Nick Werkman. Werkman, a recent Seton Hall University graduate, had led the nation in scoring, and averaged nearly thirty points per game during his career. Most of his scoring was the result of his strength, his great moves, his aggressiveness near the basket, and his quickness—hence his nickname, "Nick the Quick."

And who was given the assignment of guarding Nick the Quick? None other than my father—even though he was approaching his mid-forties and nearing his heaviest weight—almost 250 lbs. As a husband and father of four, he didn't have much time nor the opportunity to exercise often. This did not bode well for Swede and his team.

The South Orange fathers, besides Swede, featured Dick Duckett and Richie Regan, great players who had excelled professionally. All the players were past their prime, (especially my father, who was the oldest player), and most were overweight, but it was a fascinating game to watch. The "fathers" were incredible. I was so impressed with their court savvy, their shooting skills, their passing, and their ball handling. They were like the Harlem Globetrotters! Magical.

In fact, this was one of the only times I saw my father actually play in an organized basketball game. My family and I were thrilled to see how impressive he was, despite his age, his weight, and his lack of practice. Although the police were younger, and very game, they were not in the same talent league.

Having Nick Werkman on their team kept the score respectable, but the "fathers" still won handily.

Later that night my father chuckled as he told us that while he and Werkman were on the free throw lane, awaiting a foul shot, the 6' 3" Werkman put his hand on the 6' Swede's shoulder and said respectfully "you're a big one!" My interpretation of the gesture was that "Nick the Quick" had to work *much* harder than he had ever expected. I saw my father play basketball only a couple of times, and each time he was well into his forties or older. Each time I was astounded with his knowledge of the game, his court sense, his defense, ballhandling, passing, and more. Above all else, he was remarkable near the basket. He was seemingly immoveable and dominated the action around the hoop both offensively and defensively. Besides his incomparable all-around strength, he had the quickest of feet and was an extraordinary jumper. On top of all that were his freakishly strong hands. Once he got his hands on the ball it was over. All in all, a tough combination to compete against near the basket. That is what I suspect Nick Werkman was expressing with his comment.

Swede later joked that "if Werkman had me guarding him [during his college career] he'd have been the *world's* leading scorer." Self-deprecating Swede, at it again. Swede did allow that considering his responsibility of guarding Nick, he held his own, but he did not let us forget that Werkman certainly scored his share of points.

In his article about the game for the local newspaper, Len Morris noted the impressive roster of the "fathers," but raved about Swede. He observed how Swede had dominated near the basket, always at the right place at the right time, and making everything look easy.

One other impression has lasted until this day. I was stunned to see how great some of these "over-the-hill" ex-stars were. They played as though they had been teammates for years. They were all top athletes, but more impressive, they were *brilliant* basketball players. Any true fan would have been totally entertained by this brand of ball. Richie Regan and Dick Duckett, in particular, were soooo good in every aspect of the game. Magicians. And Swede? I kind of feel like Jim Delany did. Swede was …

FABULOUS!

Jim Delany, currently the commissioner of the Big Ten Conference, lived across the street from us in South Orange, and was one of the toughest competitors I have ever seen. Utterly fearless, he captained the basketball team at the University of North Carolina in 1969-70. Once, I watched him and Swede guard each other in a pick-up game at the South Orange Community Center. In spite of their age differences—Jim is my age, and was nineteen or twenty at the time, while Swede was in his late forties—it was inspiring to see two very competitive athletes going at it in a very physical way. What Jim later remembered most about my father's "game" was his "incredible bounce." In addition to all of his other skills, what differentiated Swede from other players was his amazing spring. That's how Jim remembers it.

A buddy of mine ran into Jim at Madison Square Garden, introduced himself, and dropped my name. They got around to talking about Swede. At one point in the conversation, Jim said "Yeah, Bob was a good athlete, but Swede was *fabulous.*"

FIBER A DAY …

My father's approach to eating and diet, especially in his later years, was interesting—or a better word might be eccentric. He had become quite the health nut, which meant there were certain foods he advocated and other foods that he condemned. One of the latter was mayonnaise, which Swede referred to as poison. He could not even bring himself to utter the word mayonnaise. It was always, "You're not going to put that poison on your sandwich, are you?"

On the other hand, the food he praised most was Fiber One cereal. He would extol the virtue of this dish every chance he could. He knew all the stats about Fiber One: how much sodium, fiber content, calories per serving, etc.

One year, Doug's wife Sue spotted a great deal on Fiber One, so with Swede's birthday approaching, Sue gave him twenty boxes. *Twenty!* Can you imagine getting twenty boxes of cereal for your birthday?? Well, my father was thrilled! He generously tried to give each of his kids a few boxes. I don't think he had any takers. He couldn't believe we were turning down such an offer!

In fact, I had tried eating Fiber One occasionally myself because of the health benefits, but found it rather tasteless. Patty also tried it and didn't care for the taste either. The difference between us is that Patty dared to tell my father it tasted like sawdust. Naturally, he leapt to the defense of his pet cereal, and seemed insulted by Patty's poor taste. Swede said he loved it so much that he was saddened when finishing his bowl in the morning because that meant his eating pleasure was nearing the end. *Saddened!* We all howled at that one. We used to have so much fun with Swede when he'd make over-the-top comments like that, especially when said in a very dramatic, passionate way. But if he was indeed so sad, he should have tapped into his twenty-box stash and had another bowl.

Around this same time, *Consumer Reports* magazine conducted research on health cereals in the marketplace and rated them in various categories.

When it came to Swede's favorite, the magazine reported that Fiber One had many virtues ... "despite its sawdust-like taste." Patty and I loved that, and of course immediately shared it with Swede, who totally rejected such a subjective critique—as if his own opinion was objective!

Once in a while I'll have a bowl of Fiber One. But Patty? Never. However, unlike my father, I don't feel sad as I near the bottom of the bowl. In fact, I'm quite happy.

Fiber One wasn't the only life-saving food on my father's must-eat list. He also swore by Smart Beat Cheese: no calories, no fat, no sugar, no sodium, no carbs, no nothing—and in my opinion, no taste. I take that back ... it tasted like wax. Naturally, Swede objected to my review and set up a scientific taste test. On a subsequent visit, he blindfolded me, fed me samples of Smart Beat along with a more conventional brand of American cheese, and then challenged me to distinguish one from the other. Honestly, I was surprised that I couldn't tell the difference. So I took a stab and guessed ... wrong. If I didn't know better I would have sworn my father cheated.

Patty and my father both loved track and field, and attended many major high school meets together. There was just one thing about these outings Patty didn't like: the fact that Swede would bring lunch for both of them, consisting of ... Smart Beat Cheese sandwiches with Gulden's mustard on whole wheat bread. *Every* single track meet. Is it possible to make a sandwich more bland? Only if you sprinkled some Fiber One on it. Of course, good-natured Patty always acted appreciatively as she ate her sawdust-like sandwich, even though she had to wash it down with a gallon of water. And Swede? He loved every bite. Perhaps he even got a little sad as he was nearing the end of his sandwich.

THE GIFT OF GIBBERISH

My father had a huge vocabulary. Unfortunately, a fairly large percentage of his vocabulary was not of the English language, nor for that matter of any other recognized language. Swede had his own language—a combination of Hebrew, Italian, Martian, Yiddish, Toddler, North Jersey, and inebriated—which he spoke fluently. Unfortunately, no one else spoke this particular language of gibberish, but that never stopped Swede from using it. It seemed to work best when he conversed with babies and toddlers. For instance, when my son Max was fifteen months old, he and Swede engaged in a wonderful, heartfelt, serious discussion, totally in gibberish. It's hilarious to watch the video we have—the two of them with their faces only two inches apart. No one else had any idea what the subject matter was, but the dialogue sounded quite serious, and it looked as if they both knew exactly what the other was saying. Finally, Max, with cat-like quickness, reached across, grabbed my father's eyeglasses and threw them to the floor. One lens popped out. Swede cursed, but in gibberish.

Judy (Wilner) Stein, a fellow Weequahic graduate who had dated Swede a few times when he was on leave from the Navy, graciously told me how thoughtful and gentlemanly my father was, and what a great dancer he was. Then she asked, "Do you know how your father swore?"

Me: (somewhat confused by the question): "No."

Judy: "He'd say, *Flotula Mingala Jingala.*" She actually tried to spell it for me.

I don't know the meaning of Flotula Mingala Jingala—nor did Judy—but I might start using it.

Not many people knew that Swede, the former glee club president, had a strong, beautiful singing voice. And whenever he prepared our breakfast as we were getting ready for school in the morning, he would sing ... in gibberish. Perhaps he didn't know the words to many songs, but with his own personal language, he would simply match his nonsensical words to the music.

When my father entered the last stages of his life, his vocabulary diminished dramatically. He was in an assisted-living facility, and even though his use of English was deteriorating, his gibberish stayed pretty much intact. He began using it more and more, with family, other visitors, and staff. Some of the staff even gibberated with him on occasion.

I've tried over the years to emulate Swede's gift of gibberish. I suppose I'm okay, but definitely not in my father's league. He was the Socrates of gibberish.

TIED AGAIN!

I used to race my father all the time. It started when I was seven or eight, and continued right through high school. Normally we would be in the Montrose Grammar School playground, adjacent to our back yard, having a catch, when I'd challenge Swede to a running race. He always obliged, and the result was always the same. He'd let me stay close the entire sprint, and then he'd just barely nip me at the finish line. I'd always yell "*Tie!*" (even though it wasn't) and my father would burst out laughing. By my junior year I was as fast as anyone on the high school team, but even then I could not beat my father in a sprint. The best I could do was stay even with him.

Fast forward a few decades to 1991. Swede was visiting the family in Oregon. He, Julie (about seven at the time), and I went to a beautiful park near a lake for a picnic. I had my camera and decided it was time to get my father racing again. He was game (even though he was north of seventy) and still competitive. Julie was likewise always ready for competition. They raced toward me and my camera. It is still one of my favorite all-time family pictures. Swede and Julie have the same expressions: broad and determined smiles. Their strides looked identical too. And guess what? They were tied!

The great race: Julie, age seven, versus her grandfather, age seventy-one.

The next race took place in 1997 on the Oregon Coast. This time the contestants were Max (age 7), Julie (13), Swede (77), and me (49). Susie, the smart one, was behind the camera. I orchestrated a staggered start. Max started closest to the finish line, then Julie a couple of yards behind, then Swede, then me. Unfortunately, I was too generous with the stagger. The race finished as it started: Max, Julie, Swede, me. But more importantly we have another great race picture. Everyone smiling, especially Max.

HENNY MASIN

Susie, the kids, and I often climb Beacon Rock, a distinctive 900-foot-high monolith on the Washington side of the Columbia River, which was named by Lewis and Clark on their famous expedition. The views from the "rock" are spectacular, and thanks to a series of carefully constructed switchbacks, it is neither a long nor particularly strenuous ascent.

In the summer of 1999, during Swede and Patty's annual visit to Oregon, the three of us climbed Beacon Rock. It was a wonderful day for being outdoors, so there were many other folks hiking as well. At nearly every switchback we would cross paths with other hikers of all ages. And for every one, without fail, my father had an original one-liner ready. Whether it was an elderly woman, a toddler being carried, teenagers, an athlete, a father with his kids, it didn't matter. Swede was ready for each one, and his quip was perfectly tailored to his audience. Patty and I were cracking up, and wondering with excited anticipation (and a little embarrassment) what his next line would be. All were funny, all were teasing and/or self-deprecating, and all were original. None were mean-spirited. That was Swede. He loved to make people laugh and smile, especially the elderly and little kids. And his originality was amazing. He certainly entertained Patty and me that day.

Unfortunately, every once in a while one of my father's one-liners might fall flat. For instance, when we were traveling Oregon's spectacular coastline that same summer of 1999, we found ourselves high on a cliff, enjoying the view of the Pacific. Some distance away a large ship sounded its foghorn, very loudly and very long. At the same time, a middle-aged woman was strolling past. As the deep toot of the foghorn ended, Swede politely and gently asked the woman, "Was that you?" For implying that the noise was caused by the woman passing wind, Swede received only a stern scowl in return. On the other hand, Patty, Susie and I, all very much appreciated his juvenile humor. You might have also if you had heard the sound of the foghorn.

MY FATHER, THE SECURITY BLANKET

In November 2003 Steve Kelley, veteran sportswriter for the *Seattle Times*, wrote a tribute to his father, who had recently passed away. He talked about how supportive his father had always been, how secure he felt when his father arrived at his sporting events, their mutual enthusiasm for the University of Delaware football team, and more. As I recall, one of the last things his father said before passing was, "How did Delaware do against Navy?"

Besides the Delaware coincidence, the column really hit home with me. I vividly remember looking for my father before all my sporting events. The moment I spotted him I felt a blanket of security fall over me. It was like "well, dad's here … nothing bad is going to happen." The feeling was palpable, and I can remember it no matter if it was a Little League baseball game or a college football contest. Once I spotted Swede (and I made sure to find him before *all* my games), I could concentrate on the business at hand. After all, my father, the world's biggest man, had arrived. All would be okay.

I wrote to Steve Kelley, sending condolences for his father and complimented him on his wonderful article, describing how his column had sparked strong memories for me of spotting Swede as he arrived at Delaware Stadium. Steve thanked me, and said he remembered me when I played at Delaware. He and his father had been in the stands, rooting. Small world.

FIRST AND LAST

Even into his seventies, my father was quite the physical specimen. So when my close friend Tim Boyle, the president and CEO of Columbia Sportswear, heard about the growing popularity of senior track and field competitions, he thought Swede might be interested. When I mentioned this to me father, he initially said no; but with just a little bit of encouragement he reconsidered. Patty was able to borrow a shot put from her school so Swede could practice. Unfortunately, he had suffered a serious injury while in the Navy to three fingers on his right hand, which kept the top half of his middle finger frozen in a bent position. This did not lend itself to shooting a basketball or putting a shot, but Swede gave it a try anyway. He signed up for a meet in Long Island, where he competed in the 75-to-80-year-old shot-put competition. I was back in Portland, anxious to hear how he did, so I called that evening.

Bob: "Hey dad, how'd it go today?"

Swede: "Okay"

Bob: "Did you win?!"

Swede: "Yeah, I won" he answered sheepishly.

Bob: "Good for you!!"

Swede: "I guess," he said, unimpressed with himself.

Bob: "So, tell me about it"

Swede: "I wasn't that impressive. There were only two other guys in my division, and frankly they were kind of scrawny."

Bob, laughing: "Dad, at seventy-five to eighty you're not gonna see too many musclemen."

The shot putting did bother his fingers, and it hindered his performance, so he decided to try entering the discus competition (which was easier on his fingers) the next meet. Again, I called that evening.

Bob: "Hey dad, how'd it go?"

Swede: "Okay"

Bob: "Did you win?!"

Swede: "I came in first, and I came in last. There were no others in my age group."

Swede lost interest after that. He preferred the shot, but it was going to be a problem due to his hand. And there weren't many competitors around. I should have suggested he look into the sprints or hurdles competition. In any case, he retired undefeated in two events in senior track and field.

DOLLAR BILL

Basketball star and Senator Bill Bradley happened to be at a high school football game my father was attending in the early 1990s, when Swede was in his early seventies. I recall the senator was there campaigning. My father was always a big fan and supporter of Bill Bradley, so he veered over to shake his hand. He did, and Swede's grip and overall appearance prompted Bradley to exclaim, "Wow, you're in shape!" To which my father lamented, "Yeah, for the shape I'm in." I'm not sure what that witticism means, but the senator got a kick out of it.

SWEDE'S TREKS

My father was one of the first joggers. He told us that as a young guy he enjoyed going out for long runs, often throughout Weequahic Park. Later in life he resumed his distance running, followed by bicycling. Later still, he became a walker.

Once retired, Swede took weekly trips by train into Manhattan, a place he rarely ventured during his working life, and he'd walk. And walk. You name it, but if it's in New York City, my father walked there. He always loved being outside—even though the streets of Manhattan are not my idea of the great outdoors—and he thoroughly enjoyed exploring all the things there are to see in the city. Mind you, these were not thirty-minute strolls my father was taking. These were hours of steady walking, with a break for a light lunch on a park bench somewhere. Often my father covered ten miles or so ... not bad for a guy in his mid-to-late seventies.

Manhattan was not the only venue for my father's treks. He occasionally drove down to the Jersey Shore for long walks on various boardwalks. He frequented Seaside Heights because it has one of the longer stretches of boardwalk in the state. He used to lament that he'd stop frequently along the way to eat "garbage." A hot dog here, a slice of pizza there, sometimes followed by an ice cream cone. He'd vent about his lack of willpower, but it never stopped him from going back for more. Sometimes he'd walk along Ocean Avenue in Deal, New Jersey, with its magnificent homes.

He also frequently walked in and around South Orange as well as South Mountain Reservation, a wooded area of some 2,000-plus acres, just a few minutes from the house. Having the Reservation so close was great; it's big, beautiful, and not what most people expect to find in Northeast "Joisey." During one of his walks there, a young girl, high school age or so, came up to my father and asked for help. She was being followed, perhaps even stalked, by some nut in his car, and she was terrified. Swede scared the guy off with some intimidating words along with his Ralph Kramden (booming) voice. The young girl was thankful and relieved. She got my father's name, and must have told her parents about the episode, for her father called Swede that night. He was extremely appreciative, gushing with thanks. And he told my father about all the great things he had heard about him over the years. The Swede legend strikes again.

One late winter day, while in junior high school, I hiked with a buddy into the Reservation. We went quite deeply into the woods and discovered what we later learned was Hemlock Falls. This twenty-five-foot waterfall was beautiful, and the volume of water, which was very large and impressive, was encased in ice. We had a blast frolicking around the falls, which were a very pleasant surprise.

I got home and raved about the sight to Swede. He was quite interested, as he was not aware of a falls in the Reservation. He made a mental note to check it out sometime, and months later my father got around to hiking the Reservation, carrying Doug, age four, on his shoulders. I was excited for them, anxious to hear the report of their journey. Finally, they returned home.

Bob (excitedly): "How was it, dad?"

Swede: "How was what? Oh, you mean Hemlock Trickle?"

Apparently, the water volume shrinks just a tad from late winter to late summer. I suppose my build-up may have been a bit inflated. In any event, at least in the Masin family, the name Hemlock Trickle stuck.

One of the problems my father had when he walked in South Orange was that he knew everybody. So what should have been an hour-long walk would turn into a two- or three-hour journey of short walks and then chit-chat. Swede was always so friendly, that not to stop and visit would have been rude. He always blamed the people he was talking to: "They wouldn't let me leave!" But we knew better.

When the weather turned foul, my father drove to the Short Hills Mall for his daily walks. Sometimes, when I was visiting, I'd join him—and hear him point out a little lady who also was a regular walker at the Mall. He always expressed his frustration that he could not keep up with her. "I don't get it. My strides are longer than hers, I'm taking as many strides as she is, and she's still pulling away! How does she do it?" The big guy did not like that he was being out-walked by this woman. Always the competitor.

From his teenage years running in Weequahic Park, to his walks almost seventy years later at his assisted living home, Swede was always on the move. He was running and walking before it became popular. And none of us were able to keep up with him.

Other than the little lady at the Mall.

THE STRONG MAN

My father rarely demonstrated his natural strength. He never lifted weights, he didn't do push-ups, pull-ups, or anything else like that. As a kid, when I asked him to flex his bicep, he always claimed he didn't have one. But based on the few times I watched him on the basketball court, his core body strength must have been phenomenal, and his hand strength was legend.

151

Documentary proof that Swede did indeed have a bicep—a massive one at that.

One evening in 1995, when Swede and I attended a high school basketball game together, we walked into the gym lobby and I noticed where the ticket window was situated. I scooted over to purchase the tickets, figuring I would treat. But heaven forbid I should pay for the tickets! When my father realized what I was doing, he came up behind me, grabbed my arms, pinned them against my body, lifted me up, and removed me away from the window. He then proceeded to buy the tickets himself.

I remember this story very, very well, for two reasons: 1) Swede's typical reaction to me wanting to buy the tickets (remember his yearbook inscription, "God-like in giving, but the devil to pay"), and 2) the ease with which my seventy-five-year old father man-handled my 200-plus-pound body. I felt like a helpless rag doll in his hands, and I cracked up laughing at the time. In fact, I still laugh about it. His physical power was simply amazing.

SWEDE HAS AN ANNOUNCEMENT

Swede "Rudyard" Masin had a creative streak that occasionally blossomed. He wrote the music and the lyrics of a love song while at war in the Navy that was very sentimental. He'd often write humorous poems to my mother on Mother's Day and her birthday. And he started a small tradition when Dale was born; he wrote a short poem to announce her birth:

"A TAX EXEMPTION IS BORN"
(1946)

Dale Iris to Estelle and Swede
was born
A new little doll their home
to adorn
7 lbs. 6 ozs. was the weight
you know
In the Beth Israel Hotel she did
start to grow
27 December was the day
so grand
And that's the story of the pride
of the land.

The Happy Masins
194 Davis Ave.
Kearney, N.J.

"Edgar Allan" Masin followed up with more of the same when I was born ...

"ANOTHER TAX EXEMPTION IS BORN"
(1948)

Robert Gregory was the name we gave
To that little fellow of whom we rave

7 lbs. 12 ozs. was the weight of the lad
In the Beth Israel Hotel he arrived unclad

The 24th of August he let out a wail
And joined the family of Estelle, Swede and Dale

Still The Happy Masins
765 Valley Street
Orange, N.J.

And then Swede, "Lord Tennyson," announced Patty:

"AND STILL ANOTHER TAX EXEMPTION IS BORN"
(1951)

Patricia Carol is the name of the lass,
And she entered this world to show her class

7 lbs. 14 ozs. in her birthday suit
In the Beth Israel Hotel she did take root.

T'was the 1st of July that our Pat came to be
And that's the story of Exemption number three.

And Still The Happy Masins
765 Valley Street
Orange, N.J.

And finally, "Edna St. Vincent" Masin announced Doug:

"AND STILL ANOTHER TAX EXEMPTION IS BORN"
(1957)

Douglas Scott is the newest one
And he joined this world to have some fun

8 lbs. 4ozs. for our biggest yet
In the Beth Israel Hotel his folks he met.

T'was the 12th day of August that he let out a roar
And that's the story of Exemption number Four.

Still The Happy Masins
60 Mountainhouse Rd.
South Orange, N.J.

So naturally, since I never had an original idea of my own, I tried the same thing when Julie and Max were born. To say the least, I used some poetic license. My announcements were not as good (nor as original) as Swede's, but hey, they were longer:

"BABY MASIN"
(1984)

It happened not quite midnight
On August 23rd
A little person joined us
Without uttering a word
Susie worked so hard that day—
You should have seen her toil
But it was worth the effort
She produced a baby goil
Her length was 19 inches,
Her weight 5 lbs. 1 oz.
Mom and daughter are just fine
I'm happy to announce
Her name is Julie Anna
And just before I close,
Let's all hope she has Bob's brains

But please God, not his nose.

Bob and Susie

Okay, okay, so I was being a little presumptuous with the part about wanting *my* brains. Luckily for Julie, she didn't get them.

And of course, Max:

MAX
(1990)

Susie, Bob & Julie are happy to announce
That Max Stuart has arrived, weighing 7 pounts.

T'was late July he was born (the 22nd I think)
His hair was blond, his nose not small, his skin was very pink

3 times 7 inches was his newborn height
He finally showed at 9 AM (he made us wait all night).

But now he's here and you should see Susie's weight reduction,
Since giving birth to little Max, our newest tax deduction.

Susie, Bob & Julie

How unfortunate that I took the low road and teased my one-day-old about his nose. And how pathetic that I plagiarized the "tax deduction" angle. Hopefully, when Max and Julie have children, they'll return the birth announcement creativity back to its lofty beginnings. In any case, it's clear to me that my own goofy birth announcements were a perfect example of how much I wanted to be like my father. I tried to emulate him in various ways my whole life. But he was an impossible act to follow … even when it came to our frivolous birth announcements.

LET'S STRETCH THAT LEG

Like many high school athletes, I was anxious for my senior year to begin. Heck, it was my last year, and I did love competing. I was ready to go. But early in the football season, in a game against Orange High, I suffered a bad knee injury. I was taken directly to Beth Israel Hospital in Newark, where I was thoroughly examined. Afterwards, as I was alone in the examination room, waiting for a verdict on the seriousness of the injury, I had time to ponder stuff.

I recalled what I thought had been a similar injury during my sophomore year, when I was back playing the following Saturday. In fact, a feeling of embarrassment started creeping over me, suspecting that this episode would be very much the same ... that I'd be playing in a week or two. How was I going to explain the big fuss (i.e., being rushed to the hospital via ambulance) for what I suspected was a not-too-serious injury?

After what I remember to be a long wait, my father came into the room alone. He was very matter-of-fact as he told me I would be operated on the next morning, that I should forget about playing football and basketball this year, and that I would have to be very diligent about rehabilitating my knee once the cast was removed. My anterior cruciate ligament, ACL, and my medial collateral ligament had been "shredded."

I was in a state of disbelief after hearing the news. I would miss the rest of football season *and* all of basketball season?! In my mind I was already determined to prove that wrong! But my father's demeanor clearly got my attention. I still remember it to this day, four decades later. He was working hard to act calmly, attempting to convey that it was *not* the end of the world, and convincing me to forget about the trivial stuff (sports), so that we would work hard to rehabilitate the knee once the cast came off. He wanted me to handle this setback like a man, and to look forward, not backward. But I also knew my father. He felt *terrible* for me. He did *not* handle misfortune for his loved ones well at all. The next morning, after the surgery, Dr. Saul Firtel, to whom I owe a great deal, reassured my parents that the operation had gone well. My mother later told me that Swede was so relieved to hear the news that he broke down in tears. What a softy.

People today are amazed to hear I was in the hospital for fourteen days, had a full leg cast, and used crutches for three and a half months. When the cast was finally removed, I can't tell you how shocked I was at the sight of my leg. I could barely bend my very swollen knee, all the muscles were gone, the leg was very discolored, and there was dead skin everywhere. This was a major psychological setback. As anxious as I was to start rehabilitation, that first day I was wondering if I'd ever be able to play anything again.

As usual, my father took the leadership role in helping me try to get the leg back to normal. Numerous times a day I'd lie on my stomach on the floor as my father (gently but firmly) would bend my leg back as far as it would go. He had a great feel for how hard to push to improve flexibility but not injure me. We did this many times every day for months. I hated it, but Swede made sure I never missed a session. Then he got ankle weights for me so that I could sit on the edge of the kitchen table and do trillions of repetitions of lifting and lowering my foot, rebuilding the quad muscles. And once able to do so, I ran up and down our one flight of stairs (to the basement), enough to make me dizzy. All the while my father was there, encouraging me, making sure I didn't overdo it and making constructive suggestions. Most importantly, he would never let me skip the leg-bending exercises. Those were my least favorite (and Swede knew it) but the most important. There was no way he was going to let me slide on them.

I had imagined that my senior year would be something special, since I was looking forward to playing three sports; football, basketball, and baseball. Accordingly, after the injury, I was hugely disappointed. And adding insult to injury, I contracted mononucleosis just several games into the baseball season, which effectively ended my high school sports career. So, for all my anticipation, my senior year at Columbia High, sports-wise, consisted of a couple of football games and a few baseball games. But I actually got over it surprisingly quickly and surprisingly well. It taught me some good life lessons. And thanks to Swede's prodding and hands-on support, my leg recovered well, to the point where I was able to play sports in college. He wouldn't let me dog it, and he was there with me every step of the way. That was my father.

One unintended benefit of the injury may have had huge implications. It eliminated me from military duty, which in those days meant the probability of going to Vietnam. My lottery number of 36 was very low, which meant I would have been drafted into the Army. Who knows, the bad luck injury may have saved me from a far worse fate.

SWEDE-ISMS
My father had pet phrases, which he used his whole life. Many are self-explanatory, some need explaining. Here's a small sampling, all of which are fondly remembered (and still used!) by the Masin kids:

1) "SOMEBODY'S GOTTA GET HURT!"
This was directed primarily towards Doug and me. Even though I was nine years his senior, I had no qualms about wrestling with Doug. Or boxing. Or playing one-on-one tackle football in our small living room. Sure it was lopsided in my favor, but winning is everything, I always say. My advantage was further enhanced because Doug spent a lot of his early years with casts on both legs. We never let that stop us.

Well, big, strong Swede didn't care for rough-housing, especially among his own loved ones. It made him nervous. When he came upon us roughing it up, he'd shout out his warning: *"Somebody's **gotta** get hurt!!"* For him there was no question about it; if we didn't stop, an injury was inevitable. Typically we'd reluctantly stop and then wait until my father was out of earshot. Then

Doug would attack, casts and all, and I'd have to teach him another lesson. And sure enough, Swede was right: one of us usually got hurt.

2) "LATE TO BED ..."

My father drilled us on fundamentals. Most of his major directives were related to our health, our happiness, and of doing the right thing. One fundamental he always stressed was getting enough sleep. Most of the Masins were early risers, which would logically suggest we were early to bed. Not always. And Swede would be on the lookout for (self-imposed) sleep deprivation. His warning? *"Late to bed, early to rise, you're lookin' for trouble."* Of course, in our more mature years we get smarter and realize how important good sleep habits are. So I've plagiarized Swede on this one ... I use the same expression with my kids.

3) MISTER CONSIDERATE

Swede Masin, Mister Considerate, would never stand up while cheering at a sports event if there was someone sitting behind him. He wouldn't want to block someone else's view. So what was my father's Swede-ism for the less considerate person he always managed to sit behind at every sporting event he ever attended?? *"The world's fastest riser."*

4) "100 PERCENT?"

My father enjoyed a healthy debate as much as the next guy. And his guard was up for over-the-top exaggeration, for which my mother was well known. When making a point, Estelle was prone to using words like "never," "always," "all," "none," and "totally." Some examples: *"All* left-handed people have low IQ's," or "Bobby *always* gets a good report card" (wait, bad example).

Swede would respond to my mother's bold statements with *"Estelle, you're 100-percenting again"* (in a very condescending tone). This never deterred Estelle. She was quite comfortable with her definitiveness.

Of course, my father used the expression with anyone against whom he'd be debating or arguing, though my mother was by far the most frequent target. But if he had trouble making an impression with his mild reminder, he used another Swede-ism that was more attention-getting. To make a rebuttal point, my father, with his booming, foghorn voice, would bellow ...

5) "FAAAAALSE!!"

It wasn't very cerebral, but it was loud. And funny. And it spread. One year my parents drove Patty back to Springfield College in Massachusetts. As Swede was carrying bags through the dorm, an occasional student would see him down the hall. They'd simply shout "*Faaaaalse!*" to him. Yes, Patty had spread this Swede-ism to New England.

6) "BAD THINGS HAPPEN"

My father was a liquor salesman for fifty years, but he wasn't a drinker. Perhaps he'd have one drink at a social function, but he was not one to alter his mind. He had a point of view about bars, too. Namely, he didn't want us in them. This was reflected in his Swede-ism: "***Ya hang around in bars, you're lookin' for trouble. Bad things happen.***" And once again some of my experiences proved him right.

7) HELPING SWEDE

We had small yards in the front and back of our house. Swede did the yard work, and I think he enjoyed it. When I was a kid I would occasionally go outside and offer to help—usually when my father was watering the lawn, since that looked like an easy job. The conversation:

Me: "Hey, dad, can I help?"

Swede's Swede-ism response: "Sure, ya wanna help?," said appreciatively and cheerfully. "***Then keep outta my way!***"

He was having fun with me. But I did notice that after I'd watered the lawn for about three seconds he'd thank me and ask for the hose back.

* * * *

SWEDE'S MALAPROPISMS

This is simply another category of Swede-isms, the ones where he used the vicinity rule: if the word or phrase he used was wrong but close enough, he was okay with it. Here are just a few examples:

WHAT SWEDE MEANT TO SAY	WHAT SWEDE SAID
"Piscataway" (a New Jersey town)	"Piccadilly"
"Meat Loaf" (the singer)	"Moss Beat"
"Robert Redford"	"Robert Redwood"
"Alfalfa" (of *Little Rascals* fame)	"Sassafras"
"State Farm" (insurance)	"State Fair"

These were fun to remind Swede about, and in fact he was entertained by them more than any of us. But years later his malapropisms couldn't compare with those of one of my closest buddies at Columbia Sportswear Company, Jim

Lukich, the national sales manager. Jim, a *very* bright guy, took the vicinity rule to the extreme:

WHAT JIM MEANT TO SAY	WHAT JIM SAID
"San Luis Obispo"	"St. Louis Nabisco"
"A shindig" (a big party)	"A shing ding"
"Long pants"	"Long-sleeved pants"
"Shiitake Mushrooms"	"Shitcake mushrooms"

Not surprisingly, many of my Columbia colleagues and I adopted Jim's versions rather than the correct versions. After all, who doesn't like going to a great shing ding, wearing long-sleeved pants, in St. Louis Nabisco … especially if they're serving shitcakes?

CHAPTER THIRTEEN:
SWEDE AND SUSIE

My parents went out of their way to foster good relationships with the extended family, including the in-laws. They would overlook idiosyncratic personalities, cultural differences, and/or downright goofy points of view.

The first time I brought Susie, my wife-to-be, to meet Estelle and Swede was for Thanksgiving dinner in the late 1970s. As we drove north from Delaware to South Orange, Susie was clearly nervous. She wanted to make a good impression, but did not know what to expect. In retrospect, she had nothing to worry about. I knew that my father was going to be easy for her. And because I hadn't had a date for several dozen years prior to meeting Susie, I knew that my mother was going to be thrilled with whomever I showed up with—female, male, animal, vegetable.

The day went smooth and easy, and as we started our drive back to Delaware, Susie was happy and relieved. She had connected with both of my parents, and observed, "I think your mother really liked me." My response might have been just a little deflating: "Susie, I could have arrived with a real live elephant and my mother would have complimented it on its trunk."

In any event, Susie always hit it off well with both Swede and Estelle. Like my parents, she has a terrific personality and has always had a great deal of interest in people. Susie has never been shy about offering her point of view, but she does it in such a way that her suggestions and ideas are always well received.

Susie and Swede very much enjoyed sparring over stuff—be it politics, people in the news, improvements that my father's house needed, my father's choice of clothes, the timing of the next vacation, and so on. Not much was off limits—especially from Susie's perspective.

One time Susie, my sister Patty, Swede, and I all went to a large wholesale clothing warehouse to buy a suit for me. Susie happens to be a world-class shopper: she likes to shop, she likes to find bargains, and she is battle-tested from years of experience. In other words, she's a shoppin' fool. Swede was the opposite: he shopped for clothes as a very last resort, he did not pride himself on his fashion sense, and he really didn't care. The two of them were on a collision course that day.

When I first tried on the suit, and emerged from the dressing room, there was something about the fit Susie didn't like. She asked if I knew the name of the salesman who was helping us—but who had momentarily stepped away. Although I had no clue of his actual name, I told her it was Sid. I shared the joke with my father and sister as Susie boldly called out "*Sid*," in an attention-getting manner. Needless to say, the object of Susie's call did not respond. But, coincidentally, another salesman *was* named Sid, and he *did* respond from a different side of the warehouse. To which Susie replied, "No, no, I meant the *other* Sid." Even though I had made them uneasy with my little prank, Swede and Patty were laughing—a little nervously, but mostly hysterically. They even started to drift away from the scene because they didn't want to be associated with Susie or me. At this point I started howling. Finally, Susie caught on, and while she saw the humor in the whole thing, I don't remember her laughing as hard as the rest of us. In retrospect, the funniest part for me was watching Patty and Swede, who were so embarrassed for Susie. And their nervous giggling, as they distanced themselves from the scene, is etched in my memory.

Once we settled on the suit, Susie's next goal was to find a dress shirt and tie. She picked out a striped shirt, which she took to the tie section. She held a tie she liked against the shirt, and appeared satisfied. The tie's pattern seemed to me rather "busy," but far be it from me to offer a better solution. However, my father, "Oleg Cassini" Masin, looked both confused and concerned, and asked incredulously, "Wait a second. You want him to wear *that* tie with *that* shirt?!" Susie responded patiently (or perhaps semi-patiently), "Yes, dad. *That* tie with *that* shirt. It looks very nice." "I can see that" replied Swede. And then pausing a few seconds for effect, he repeated "But *that* tie with *that* shirt?!" Susie again (even less patiently), "Yes, dad. Believe me, it looks very nice. I know what I'm doing." (Translation: "*Butt out!*").

After a few dozen more barbs about the tie and shirt combination, we headed towards the slacks. Susie wanted me to get a new pair of dress slacks, picked out a pair, liked the way they looked and fit, and added them to the purchase. My father took the liberty of checking the price tag.

Swede: "*Fifty dollars,* for *pants*!!?"

Susie: "Dad, that is not too much for nice dress slacks."

Swede: "Fine. But *fifty dollars,* for *pants*!!? I recently paid fifty dollars for pants, but I got *five pair!*"

Susie: "They look like it, dad."

On and on they went. What a joy it was to shop with Susie and Swede. Just ask Sid. No, the *other* Sid.

Susie's decisiveness and willingness to take the proverbial bull by the horns always impressed my parents and siblings. No matter how small or how large the issue, Susie would take charge. And in the case of our family—where deciding whether to take food out from an Italian restaurant or a Chinese restaurant could become a *major* issue—Susie's no-nonsense decisiveness was very much appreciated. Admittedly, when you have people of Jewish and Italian heritage together, trying to decide about food is never simple. So, while the Masins would be going back and forth, everyone saying, "I don't care if it's Italian or Chinese, whatever the rest of you want is okay with me," Susie would make the decision for us.

Needless to say, there were other things besides food that the Masins were very hesitant to deal with. For our annual visits to the East Coast, Susie made *all* the plans. Arranging for a Broadway show? Susie did it. Which train to take? Susie. Restaurants? Susie. Home repairs? Susie. When to visit Aunt Shirley? Susie. When to inhale and exhale? Susie. And don't think for a minute we Masins didn't appreciate Susie for taking charge. She was a lot better at it than we were. Plus, if something went wrong with the plans, whom did we blame? Susie.

Moreover, Susie's fearlessness has been beneficial for my sister Patty, who has a timid side to her. As they have become very close over the years, they find that they truly complement each other: daring, adventurous Susie, who is not afraid to mix it up if she feels wronged; and shy, non-confrontational Patty, who appreciates the little things in life. Patty loves Susie for getting her to experience things that she otherwise never would have. And Susie loves and appreciates Patty for her genuineness, her sense of humor, and, most importantly, the fact that she can boss Patty around.

In the summer of 2002, Patty brought my father to Portland for about ten days (for what would be his last trip to the West Coast). Susie, Patty, and Susie's close friend Cheryl Tonge took a cruise to Alaska—a perfect example of something Patty *never* would have experienced without Susie's prodding and pushing. They had a blast; and at the end of the voyage, the passengers filled out a "what did you think of your experience" questionnaire for the cruise ship. The responses demonstrate some of Susie's and Patty's differences:

Some of Susie's remarks:
—"You really needed to have more melted butter on Lobster Dinner Night."
—"The pillows need to be a little more fluffy."
—"The microphone at Bingo Night wasn't quite loud enough."

—"The shrimp fork was rather small."

—"Can't you do something about the ship rocking back and forth?"

—"Can't you do something about the constant smell of salt water in the air?"

—"Did I mention you need more melted butter on Lobster Dinner Night?"

And some of Patty's remarks:

—"This has been one of the greatest experiences of my life!"

—"I felt like royalty!"

—"Everything was so luxurious!"

—"The staff was wonderful!"

—"The food was superb. Delicious and plentiful."

—"Thank you for all the melted butter on Lobster Dinner Night!"

In other words, Patty's approach was "I loved every minute of the trip and I wanted the staff to know it." Susie's approach was "I loved every minute of the trip, but the staff will want to know how to make the experience even better." It's hard to argue with either of them.

All kidding aside, Susie is her own person. Her verbal exchanges with Swede were often entertaining to observe, and always a change of pace from what we were accustomed to. Dale, Patty, Doug and I rarely challenged my father. Susie was quite comfortable doing so, and I think the big guy truly enjoyed the back-and-forth repartee during their debates. They were great sparring partners, and they never hit below the belt.

Well, maybe Susie did.

CHAPTER FOURTEEN:
THE DIVORCE

So many family memories are wonderful for my siblings and me. I thought we were a loving family, with caring parents, making for a great extended family. We were generally very healthy. We were active, we laughed a lot, and did many things together as a family. My father's job didn't require overnight travel, so he was always at the dinner table. We were pretty darn secure.

I have traveled extensively on business for decades, and I always hated the part about being away from my family. It made me feel very guilty. It's hard to beat the security of having two loving parents who are always there for you and engaged in your activities.

Growing up we felt (as I am sure many kids do) that our parents were special in many ways. They looked great together, they did many things together, they had many wonderful friends. I always had the distinct impression that my parents' friends viewed Swede and Estelle as being a very fun, happy, special couple. For example, my Aunt Shirley absolutely adored my mother and my father. "They made a wonderful, beautiful couple," she told me on many occasions.

So, other than their deaths, nothing is more difficult for me to talk about than my parents' divorce. In fact, I have dreaded writing this chapter of the book, because it was such a negative experience for everyone.

The divorce did not become final until 1984, but the preceding three years were a depressing, downward spiral. The divorce was precipitated by my mother, and my father never really "got it." And in fact he would never fully get over it.

For several years after the divorce there was a noticeable pall over the family. My siblings and I were almost as disappointed and bewildered by my mother's actions as my father was. Even though Estelle could be bright, loving, and personable, she *did* have a tendency to do and say things that defied logic.

No one (other than my father) took it worse than I did. I was furious with my mother. I was convinced her actions were foolish, mean, illogical, and selfish. But over time, even with me, relations normalized.

Doug's and Dale's marriages and subsequent births of grandchildren helped to thaw things out. My parents lived apart, but both were still in South Orange, perhaps a mile away from each other. Eventually, the whole family got over the shock and we started doing many things together again as a family. But clearly, especially at first, it was more than a little awkward.

Years later we even had a joint, surprise birthday party at the Crestmont Country Club for my parents. Swede was turning eighty, Estelle seventy-five. Aunt Shirley got my parents there together. Needless to say they were shocked. Many great friends and relatives were there, and everyone had a terrific time. Patty had prepared some wonderful picture collages of both my parents, and placed them on large easels. Prior to the party, as club members walked through the party room, they noticed the pictures. Several stopped and remarked that the pictures were of Swede Masin, as if he were a celebrity.

Surprise birthday party in 2000 for Swede (center) and Estelle (far left), with the Manoffs, Feins, Dorfmans, and Wrights.

This party was undoubtedly the first time in years some of my parents' mutual friends—couples who were close to both Estelle and Swede—were back enjoying each other's company. It was a terrific, memorable evening.

Afterwards there were many family dinners where we either squeezed into Swede's house, Estelle's apartment, or occasionally in a room we'd reserve at Pal's Cabin restaurant. These dinners were characterized by lots of great food, lots of laughter, and plenty of arguing, usually over politics.

Even though the whole family would occasionally get together, it obviously wasn't the same. My father always prided himself on succeeding at whatever he tried: as a parent, as a son and brother, as an athlete, and as a husband. The failure of his marriage (which lasted thirty-eight years, most of which were exceptionally good) was a shock to him and a blow to his ego; it had a profound impact on his personality for quite a long time. He really had the wind knocked out of him. Time healed him, but never one hundred percent.

Why the divorce? There's not one, simple answer, but divorces are not a one-way street. My mother and father had much in common, but they had plenty of differences. My mother was very demonstrative; my father was not. My mother was very opinionated and shot from the hip; Swede would usually listen first, then opine. Estelle was right-wing; Swede was not. My father prided himself on being logical; my mother could say the darndest things. My father clearly loved my mother, but he was never an outwardly affectionate guy. Many people, including my mother, need reinforcement and encouragement, and affection is a good way to show it. Swede was very frugal. My mother liked to spend money on nice things. They had their share of arguments over money. As the four kids grew up and left the house, I'm sure some of my parents' differences started becoming more exposed.

I have discussed my father's frugality elsewhere in the book, mostly in humorous ways. He surely was a contradiction in terms. Swede was a very giving person his entire life. But he clearly went out of his way to do more with less, and he tried to influence his family to be the same way. Remember his high school yearbook, which called him "Godlike in giving, but the devil to pay"? I think he was very admirable in that regard, but he should have been more flexible. I have never known anyone quite so un-materialistic. Estelle, on the other hand, had a more "normal" approach to spending money, and she clearly got tired of listening to Swede's "jabs" about her spending habits.

It is possible that my father took after his father, Max, in this regard. After all, my grandfather came to the U.S. alone, as a teenager, with only two Russian Rubles in his pocket. It must have been very frightening in those days, not knowing from one day to the next if he would have food to eat. With his background, it is easy to understand why he was always so intent on not "needing" anything. In that regard, my father was a chip off the old block. But Swede's brother Leo had no such inclinations. He and my father, with all their similarities, were miles apart in terms of spending money.

One telling example of how my parents were not always on the same page occurred when I was in my late teens. Swede had a bunch of medals from high school and college track and field meets. They were for various events (shot put, discus, hurdles, etc.), they were from a variety of city and state and regional meets, and they were actually very cool looking. My father kept them in a shoe box in the basement, buried with a lot of other stuff. My mother decided to surprise Swede one holiday season by mounting the medals and framing them so they could be displayed on the wall. The final product actually looked great. There were a couple of dozen different medals, placed on a navy blue felt material, behind glass and beautifully framed. Patty still remembers that "I couldn't wait to see daddy's reaction!" And I remember my mother being quite excited as well. She had put a lot of thought into this gift.

Well, Swede unwrapped his gift, and exploded. He was furious that my mother would think he'd want to have something like this hanging on the wall. I'm sure he felt it was very tacky to display his medals for people to marvel over. He preferred they remain stuffed in a shoe box with other junk. My mother attempted making her case, but it didn't matter. She had been so excited to have done this for Swede, and she was so deflated and disappointed by his reaction, just as the rest of the family was. We were all mad with my father. Now I understand that he didn't believe in displaying this stuff; it just was not his style. But he could have and should have handled this better. He calmed down, and realized he'd over-reacted, and actually thanked my mother for the thought. But it was too late. What was supposed to be a special present turned into a negative event. Swede should have sidelined his humility at the time, pretended that he loved it (it was actually a wonderful piece), and moved on. Should my mother have foreseen that this gift was not the perfect idea? Maybe, but this one was badly mishandled by Swede.

When my mother joined the South Orange Rescue Squad, she tried to convince Swede to join. He didn't want to. And my mother's commitment to the squad, while admirable and good for the town, was divisive for the marriage. Estelle developed new friends, her schedule was pervasive and (based on the nature of the job) could be spontaneous and inconvenient.

I can still remember my father's frustration when the relationship was unraveling. He would express it to me, and I felt very helpless. I was *really* hoping my mother was going through a stage, but I suspected the worst. I also knew that my mother, who was very bright, could at times be totally unreasonable and impossible to get through to. She probably felt the same about me. And during this time she did not want to hear anything. It was a lousy time for the family.

My initial reaction, unfortunately, was very lopsided. I felt terrible for my father, and I was angry with Estelle. Once, when Susie and I were living in Seattle, Swede came to visit. One day he and I took a ferry ride to Bremerton, the naval base where my parents lived right after they got married. Obviously, it was a very nostalgic day for my father. I could see the sadness, and it just made me angrier with my mother. Today I regret being as one-sided as I was at the time. But to this day I can't quite understand Estelle's thought process. I think it (the divorce) ended up a lose/lose scenario for all.

As tough as this episode was, things did improve for my father over time. Actually, there were times when I sensed Swede was pretty comfortable with his independence. He had his own schedule, he did what he wanted, he traveled—whereas my mother was not a traveler. I'm sure he was lonely at times, but the kids and grandkids stayed close to him. And he had many great buddies. He definitely missed my mother's cooking, but within a few years after the divorce, we were all re-uniting for holidays and such, and quite often Swede had his share of spaghetti, meatballs, ziti, etc.

There was one unintended positive consequence of my frequent business travel combined with my parents' divorce: the opportunity for my father to travel and see much of the country. With my mother's aversion to flying, my parents hardly ever took long trips. But with quite a few frequent flyer miles I was able to make it affordable for Swede to join us on yearly adventures in and around the Western U.S. In his later years, my father was able to visit Hawaii (twice), Sun Valley, Idaho (twice), Alaska, Yellowstone National Park, Vancouver and Victoria, Banff, Vail, numerous locations in California, Mt. Rainier, Mt. St. Helens, the San Juan Islands, the Olympic Peninsula, Seattle, and of course many visits with us in Portland, where we would often indulge ourselves in the incredible beauty of Oregon. We did plenty of hiking in and around the Columbia River Gorge, Beacon Rock, Mt. Hood, Crater Lake, and the Oregon Coast. Swede was great company on all these vacations. He appreciated the scenic beauty like few people would. And having his personality along with us was a great bonus.

Getting back to the dreaded subject, my Aunt Shirley does not mince words. She knew my father from when he was a young boy. She and Leo went to see my father's games all through high school and college. She calls Swede the greatest father and the greatest son and the greatest brother anyone could ever have. She still talks about it to this day. But she also adored my mother; her incomparable looks ("Wow was she gorgeous!"), her magnetic personality, her laughter, her outspokenness, etc. Aunt Shirley took my mother under her wing during the tumultuous times following my parents' bi-religious marriage. She and Uncle Leo were the saviors for Swede and Estelle. Leo was the voice of reason who was able to re-assure Grandpa Max after his Seymour married out of the faith. Shirley was

"Mount Swede" at Mount Rainier, Washington, ca. 1992.

my mother's protector and advisor on everything. She remembers that my parents were the perfect couple: looks, personality (although she says Swede was somewhat of a square!), they even were the greatest of dance teams (something I did not inherit). When the divorce came Leo and especially Shirley, who is very family oriented, were devastated. My aunt still talks about it as if it were a terrible death. To this day, the pain in her voice as she talks about it is palpable. She was angry and frustrated with my mother, but she certainly knew my father's shortcomings as well.

Virtually every divorce is a lousy thing to witness, especially from the inside. My sisters, my brother, all of our aunts and uncles, all of our friends, etc. viewed the break-up of my parents as a shocker and a negative, and the end of a storybook union. Many probably concluded that if Swede and Estelle's marriage could fall apart, anyone's can. It certainly is unpleasant writing about it.

If my father were here today, and if he were to look back on his life, there is very little he would change. But he would try to change the divorce. Swede always played hard in order not to lose, and he took the divorce as a major failure. He would try to figure out how to reverse that.

CHAPTER FIFTEEN:
SWEDE AND THE NEWARK
GREATS

When discussing Weequahic High School's legendary alumni, the list of accomplished people is too long to mention. There are so many successful people in the fields of medicine, law, the arts, education, and more. But a couple of names rise to the top of the recognition meter. Most would start with Philip Roth, the globally acclaimed author. Right behind is Alvin Attles, a terrific athlete, mentor, world-championship winning coach, and business executive—someone who all Weequahic graduates are proud to call one of their own.

Weequahic's longtime rival is South Side High School, now the Malcolm X Shabazz High School, which has produced its own share of distinguished alumni. Among them are Edward Koch, the former New York City mayor, and Lonnie Wright, not only one of the most extraordinary all-around athletes of his era, but also one of the most versatile athletes *ever* … and I'm including the ones we've watched on television over the years.

Neither Attles nor Wright were Swede's contemporaries, teammates, or competitors. But in their own way, they are linked to each other through school affiliation, city affiliation, their athletic legends, and the hearts of Newark sports fans. Like many of my father's contemporaries, they are exceptional, original, and under-appreciated.

Four other Newark greats also deserve mention here: Richie Regan, Bert Manhoff, Les Fein, and Sid Dorfman. All four are in the Newark Sports Hall of Fame—along with Wright and Attles—and all four were close to Swede. Their lunch "meetings" were a terrific source of fun for my father, who truly admired these impressive men.

ALVIN ATTLES

Born in Newark the year my father was a junior at Weequahic High School, Alvin Attles would go on to become a legend of his own; in fact, among members of the NBA's Golden State Warriors organization, he is known as The Legend for his athleticism, toughness, and leadership. There aren't many better role models than Alvin (the so-called "Destroyer") Attles.

I had never met Al in person, but hoped to speak with him as I was writing this book in order to get his perspective not only on his Weequahic days, but also on my father. I called the Golden State Warriors front office and left a voice mail message for him. I identified myself as Swede Masin's son and explained why I was calling. But I didn't leave my number; I figured I'd try calling again the following week.

A few days later Patty telephoned from New Jersey. Al Attles had called her, looking for my number. I don't know how he got Patty's number, but I was very surprised and appreciative he had gone to the trouble of tracking me down. I sensed that he was anxious to talk to me about my father. He left his home number with Patty, and that is where I reached him.

The ex-Weequahic star and I had a great conversation. The only problem was that his extreme modesty kept him from talking much about himself. He was more eager to talk about the mentors he had as a teenager growing up in Newark's Weequahic section, graciously telling me how his coaches in Newark would use my father as a "template" for how the game of basketball should be played. But getting Al to talk about himself was almost impossible. He reminded me of my father that way. Both loved talking about their teammates, competitors, coaches, and mentors, and both were very hesitant to talk about their own exploits. You really had to coax it out of them.

Swede often spoke very admiringly of Art Lustig, his football and basketball coach at Weequahic—not so much about Lustig's expertise in the X's and O's, but more how the coach was a great leader and mentor. Art Lustig was also Al's coach and made the same impression. Al referred to his old coach as "very tough but very fair," someone who treated all his players equally—unlike many other coaches, who treat their star players more equally than others. Al always remembered Art Lustig's approach, even in the 1970s and 1980s when he was coaching the Golden State Warriors and leading them to the NBA championship. In fact, he stayed in touch with Lustig for tips on how best to handle personnel and player issues.

Al Attles was sixteen years younger than Swede, but knew a lot about him, in part because Coach Lustig brought up Swede's name frequently. For instance, many basketball coaches still use a fundamental drill, which helps big men develop the use of both hands as well as their footwork and agility around the basket. Today it is known as the Mikan Drill—named for the 6' 10" George Mikan, who was the game's first dominant big man. But, according to Al Attles, Coach Lustig referred to it as the "Swede Masin Drill," saying that nobody executed this drill, or benefited from it, as well as Swede.

In the category of "it's a small world," Al Attles remained close to his seventh-grade playground coach, who was none other than Les Fein, one of Swede's "lunch bunch" group. Les became one of the most successful New Jersey high school basketball coaches *ever*. He had many dominant teams at Weequahic, and two of his teams in the 1960s were considered the best in the country. .

I asked "The Destroyer" how he got the nickname. Al laughed off the moniker, suggesting it was an exaggeration. However, at one point in our conversation he did allow that he "asked no quarter, and gave none." If anything, that's an understatement. On one of the fishing trips in Montana that I took with Bob Knight and John Havlicek (see Chapter Four), we were debating who was the toughest NBA player ever. Several names were discussed, but there was no real consensus. Then I suggested Al Attles. Knight and Havlicek looked at each other and nodded. There was no one tougher than the ex-Weequahic star.

Al Attles' name also came up during the 2007 Super Bowl, when both football teams had African American head coaches—a first for the NFL, but a milestone that the NBA had reached thirty-two years earlier, when Al Attles and K.C. Jones coached the two teams in the finals. The best part of this history-making event, according to Al, is that there was little fuss made about it. He had it right.

It was also fun listening to Al talk about his close friend Wilt Chamberlain, who was always a favorite of mine. We compared notes on several Wilt legends, but I particularly enjoyed the story of Al and his family visiting the star's well-publicized bachelor mansion in Los Angeles, with its huge circular bed, covered in a wildly expensive wolfskin bedspread. Al had to keep his kids from jumping on Wilt's notorious bed.

In 2006, Alvin hosted a fundraiser at Newark's Robert Treat Hotel to establish the Alvin Attles Scholarship Endowment Fund. The host attracted many friends, classmates, and teammates, including Governor Jon Corzine, basketball great Earl Monroe, Newark Mayor Cory Booker, super coach Les Fein, and super-athlete Lonnie Wright. Over $120,000 in contributions made the evening a huge success. There were alumni from many generations present. And leading the way to help many of today's Weequahic students was Attles.

One year later, in April 2007, Susie and I had a wonderful dinner with Al and Wilhelmina Attles while we were visiting the Bay Area. Al asked if we'd like to attend a Warriors game. When I replied yes, but only if I could get

Wilt Chamberlain, close friend of Al Attles, poses with Swede, ca.1961. Swede is the one on the left.

some playing time, he chuckled nervously, and then checked the schedule and saw that the Warriors were not at home that weekend. Al is a very impressive person, and so is Wilhelmina. I brought a few pictures; one was of Swede posing with Al's old friend and teammate, Wilt Chamberlain.

In Al's words, "Swede sure impressed a lot of people." I've always believed that as well. And Alvin Attles, another true original, certainly impressed me—reminding me in many ways of my father. Their styles of play were very similar: both were defensive stoppers, very strong, very determined, fearless, and tireless competitors who never quit and refused to lose. They were the kind of players you hated to play against, because you *knew* nothing would come easily. Another obvious similarity is their humility. We need more role models like them.

When I asked Al about his Weequahic experience, he answered quickly: "I loved it!" And Wilhelmina, who grew up in Florida, is taken by the amount of school spirit among the Weequahic alumni. That helps explain why a former star player and championship-winning coach like Al Attles always stayed in touch with his two great Weequahic mentors, Art Lustig and Les Fein. The Weequahic bond is formidable.

LONNIE WRIGHT

Swede was always modest about his press clippings, but there were two instances that made him very proud. One was an article in which Matty Begovich, a highly successful coach and official who saw my father play many times, claimed that Swede was the equal of Bob Davies, Seton Hall's All-American and a future All-Pro and MVP.

And then there was Lonnie Wright.

There were very few athletes anywhere, from any era, comparable to Lonnie. Of all the top stars my father and I watched compete over the years, none impressed us the way he did. He had it all and could do it all: speed, smarts, strength, size, athleticism, versatility, and unquestionable leadership. Moreover, he always looked so poised and under control, playing as if he were a man among boys. One night after attending a high school basketball tournament game, Swede could not stop talking about this superstar's all-around ability, and particularly some effortless slam-dunks he executed during the game.

After leading South Side High to the state basketball championship, the Newark papers raved about his performance, and how (as a quarterback) he had also earned first team all-state in football. Highly respected Art Lustig, my father's high school football and basketball coach, attended South Side's championship victory, and was quoted as claiming that Lonnie and Swede were the greatest athletes ever to come out of Newark. This was the other newspaper article that made my father very proud. He was so impressed with how special an athlete Lonnie was, and to be compared to him was a great honor. He loved it!

Lonnie Wright went on to star at Colorado State University in basketball and track. In the shot put, which was practically an afterthought, he set a school record, which is an unusual feat for a basketball star, since the two sports are not very compatible—though Swede happened to be great in both sports as well. What's perhaps most remarkable about Lonnie is his versatility. There have been *very* few athletes who have played two professional sports; Dion Sanders, Bo Jackson, Dave DeBusschere, and Danny Ainge, and a few others; the list is understandably short. But Lonnie was the first and only athlete in the modern era *ever* to play both professional football (for the Denver Broncos) and professional basketball (for the Denver Nuggets).

When the Newark Sports Hall of Fame was established in 1988, Swede and Lonnie were in the first group of inductees. It was the first time I met Lonnie, and I went up to him and told him he was my idol when I was a teenager. He said Swede was *his* idol, which was wonderful to hear.

In 2000, the *Star-Ledger* of Newark published a thirty-two-page section in which they named the New Jersey high school athletes of the century. The rankings covered both boys' and girls' sports, selecting not only all-decade teams in all sports, but also their "Nifty Fifty" … the top all-around New Jersey high school athletes of the twentieth century, based on all-around versatility. Number one on the list was Milt Campbell, a pro football player, hall of fame swimmer, and track star who won the silver medal in the decathlon as a high school junior in the 1952 Olympics, and then won the gold medal four years later.

Swede and Lonnie both made the Nifty Fifty. Lonnie was ranked number five, and Swede was ranked further down, just one notch behind Carl Lewis, the track-and-field star. Pretty impressive, when you consider that the ranking covers hundreds of high schools and one hundred years.

More accolades and raves about Lonnie came from Al Attles, who played with, and against, the likes of Wilt Chamberlain, Oscar Robertson, Jerry West, John Havlicek, Bill Russell, and others. Al told me he was glad he wasn't playing basketball against Lonnie in the Newark City League. And Al observed that "when Lonnie gave you a stiff arm [in football], he knocked you out."

It's too bad Lonnie Wright's name isn't better known nationally. From the perspective of my teenage eyes, he was the most amazing, impressive athlete I've ever seen. He did things no one else has, and he made it look easy.

Lonnie isn't the only family member who has made his mark in the world of sports. For instance, his father was an undefeated heavyweight boxer, retiring with a 24-0 record. The Columbia High School Girls Basketball team was (and still is) one of the top programs in Jersey, thanks to the coach, Johanna Wright, who happens to be Lonnie's wife. And for several years the team's star player was none other than their own daughter, Jazmine Wright.

Johanna is one of the most acclaimed coaches in the country. Her career won-loss record is phenomenal, and in 2001 she was one of an elite group to receive the Frank Maguire Foundation Award. She has also coached in the McDonald's All-American all-star game.

Swede and a handful of other senior citizens missed very few of the games in which Jazmine Wright played. Sometimes, Lonnie would pick up Swede at home and take him to the games, where they would sit together, rooting for Johanna and Jazmine, and becoming good friends in the process. My father adored Jazmine, and she would sometimes refer to him as Pop Pop. Later, when Jazmine was at Syracuse University, where she excelled for the hoops team, she would keep in touch by mail; and when Syracuse came to town to play Seton Hall University, my father and Patty watched her play, and as always she was terrific.

Years later, when Swede's ability to recall the past was fading, he had no trouble remembering Lonnie:

Patty: "Dad, did you see Lonnie Wright play?"

Swede: "Yup," he answered quickly and confidently.

Patty: "How good was he?"

Swede: "He was great!"

Patty: "Is he a nice guy?"

Swede: "He's the greatest"

Patty and I visited the Wrights at their home in South Orange. Theirs is a great family, and as accomplished as Lonnie is, Johanna and Jazmine have "resumes" that are just as impressive. I hadn't realized that Jazmine topped 2,000 career points and 1,000 career rebounds while at Columbia High. Those are *huge* numbers at any level. Jazmine is tall (maybe 5' 10"), but not 1,000 rebounds tall. And she went on to excel at Syracuse, where often she played inside, even though she was very undersized for that position. She made up for it with her strength, know-how, and aggressiveness. Like father, like daughter.

I had forgotten that she was also a terrific shot putter and discus thrower in high school, among the best in the state in both events. I don't want to hurt Lonnie's feelings, but I wonder if he realizes he's no longer the best athlete in the family?

Patty and I are both sports junkies, so we had a great time visiting the Wrights, and could have talked with the family forever. Lonnie had great stories about his coaches, teammates, and competitors in high school, college, and professional sports. For instance, he told of his playing in a college basketball all-star game, and being approached afterwards by the Dallas Cowboys' Gil Brandt, who was ready to sign him to an NFL contract. Lonnie was also being sought by the AFL and by the great coach, Paul Brown. However, asking for a guaranteed contract, as Lonnie did with Paul Brown, was asking for the impossible; that is how he ended up playing instead for the Denver Broncos (AFL) and the Denver Nuggets (ABA).

There was some family taunting going on as well over the issue of sports memorabilia. Between the three family members, there were too many plaques, trophies, framed photos, and mementos to display on the main floor of their home, so it seems that Lonnie unilaterally decided that *his* memorabilia would remain there while the ladies' memorabilia would be moved to less traveled areas of the house. Jazmine and Johanna let Lonnie hear about that.

It was easy to see why Swede thought the world of the Wright family and was thrilled to have become close to them. They are not only special athletes; more importantly they are a wonderful family. And Lonnie? They don't make athletes like him anymore.

And keep away from that stiff arm.

THE "LUNCH BUNCH"

In his later years, my father was invited to join a group of his contemporaries for monthly lunch get-togethers. The group consisted of five Newarkers: Sid Dorfman, Les Fein, Bert Manhoff, Richie Regan, and Swede. All but Regan had Weequahic roots, and for their varied accomplishments, all were early inductees into the Newark Sports Hall of Fame. Based on the personalities of the group, all of them strong, larger-than-life characters, the lunchtime back-and-forth repartee must have been entertaining. Les Fein told me that whenever any one of the five could not join the lunch for some reason, the others were very disappointed. (Les also made sure to point out that forty years ago or so he had loaned five dollars to Sid Dorfman, and was wondering when he'd get his money back).

Swede *loved* those lunches. He was so impressed with his very sharp and accomplished (and funny) buddies. Knowing my father, and based on my impression of the others, I suspect Swede was the quietest of the bunch, but certainly the most entertained. I often asked about his latest lunch when I'd call from Oregon. He always claimed to have had a terrific time and was looking forward to the next one. Sid Dorfman said the same thing ... how much they all looked forward to the next meeting.

Richie Regan was a terrific basketball player and coach, and an institution at his alma mater, Seton Hall University. His sense of humor and quick wit made him a perfect fit for the "lunch bunch."

Bert Manhoff was extremely accomplished. Orphaned at age seven, he spent his life giving of himself, as a teacher, sports coach, and counselor. He was the ultimate volunteer, lending his time to endless causes throughout his life.

Legendary coach Les Fein was an extremely strong man, and I'm not talking about physical stature. Listening to him was an inspiration in itself. He was self-assured, positive, and undoubtedly was one of the "lunch bunch" leaders. (I suspect he and Regan were the wise guys of the group).

Les Fein passed away in 2007, but I will never forget the wonderful things he said about my father. For instance, in the preview article for the inaugural group of inductees into the Metro West Jewish Sports Hall of Fame, Les was quoted as saying, "Swede Masin is a very special person. It's an honor to go into the Jewish Sports Hall of Fame with Swede. He was a great athlete in his day and he's such a nice man." Wonderful words from a terrific man.

And then there's Sid Dorfman, the unofficial leader of the group. He is the only one of the five still with us. His newspaper column still appears regularly in the Newark *Star-Ledger*, and it's always written with pragmatism and insight, just as it has been for many years. He remains an institution in New Jersey sports reporting.

As a very interested bystander, I appreciated that my father had the opportunity to bond with Dorfman, Fein, Manhoff, and Regan. Their personalities, their accomplishments, and their active participation in *so* many good things are inspirational. I know my father felt fortunate to have their friendship.

CHAPTER SIXTEEN: THE REAL SWEDE (MASIN, NOT LEVOV)

One evening in 1997, my father received a phone call from an old friend who had attended Weequahic High School with him. She was calling Swede to tell him that she had seen a preview of the new Philip Roth novel that was about to hit the bookstores, and that a major character sounded eerily similar to my father. The award-winning author was a Weequahic grad as well, and often used Newark locales in his works. Moreover, some of his previous fictional characters had seemed very similar to real-life folks. So when he introduced a new novel with the Weequahic section of Newark as the backdrop, interested readers had their antennae up, looking for fictional characters "inspired" by someone they might have known. The Weequahic Alumni Association is not only large, but also very close-knit. As a result, they have become accustomed to looking for familiar characters in Roth's fiction.

My father did not quite know what to make of the phone call. He pretty much forgot about it. But as more previews of the book emerged, even Swede's interest must have been piqued. However, Swede being Swede, he still pooh-poohed it. Knowing his typical thought process, he figured it was a minor, insignificant character, and was a non-issue.

But when an author of Philip Roth's status is about to introduce a new novel, it gets a lot of attention. Many in the know refer to him as one of the greatest, if not *the* greatest, novelist of our time. So when his *American Pastoral* debuted, the reviews, virtually all of them glowing, were everywhere. I will never forget my reaction when I first read those reviews. My eyes would jump directly to words that seemed identical to something I had read one thousand times before, and had heard even more times before: Seymour "Swede" Levov, legendary all-around athlete from Weequahic High School in Newark, New Jersey. If you change the name Levov to Masin, it is practically word-for-word identical to the endless entries in my father's scrapbook, other newspaper clippings, and elsewhere.

Whether I was reading the review of Roth's book in the *Star-Ledger, New York Times, Time, Newsweek*, etc., the words and phrases were incredibly familiar. And yet, this was a work of fiction. It was a very strange feeling for me. And as my father's great friend, Sid Dorfman exclaimed, "Come on, how many big, blond, blue-eyed Jews lived in the all-Jewish Weequahic section, were legendary athletes, with the nickname of Swede?!" Another interesting coincidence was that the Levov character married a non-Jewish beauty queen, as did the real-life Swede.

So in a sense I felt I was reading about my father in all of these newspapers and magazines. Admittedly, it was not exactly the same. The plot of *American Pastoral* itself had few similarities to my father's family. But the Levov character? He was identical in so many ways it was funny, and to the Masin kids very exciting.

One review describes the Levov character: "As handsome, modest, generous and kind as he is gifted, Swede takes pains to acknowledge the blessings for which he is perceived as the most fortunate of men. He is patriotic and civically responsible, maritally faithful, morally upstanding, a mensch." Well, the Masin kids (as well as others) have used every one of those adjectives to describe my father. We could not have described the real Swede any better. At the time, and even to this day, reading that stuff is fascinating to me.

Still, the stoic Swede (Masin, not Levov) did not make much of it, even after he received dozens of letters and telephone calls from old friends as far away as California. About this time my father went on one of his journeys into Manhattan, prepared for a long walk. As usual, he visited Columbia Sportswear's New York showroom to say hello to my buddy Joe Mangan. Joe had been following the *American Pastoral*/Swede Levov issue and said to my father: "Hey, Swede, let's go over to Barnes and Noble and see if the book is out yet." My father was less than excited; he wanted to get going on his long Manhattan walk. But he went with Joe to the bookstore. The book was not on the shelves, so Joe asked a clerk who said, "Hold on, we may have just received it." The clerk went to a basement storage area and several minutes later returned with copies of the brand-new novel. My father casually opened it to page one; and, according to Joe, suddenly had an expression of shock on his face. Swede Masin certainly did not expect the first sentence to read simply, "The Swede." Nor did he expect Roth's second sentence to note that this was "a magical name in our Newark neighborhood, even to adults just a generation removed from the city's … ghetto and not yet so flawlessly Americanized as to be bowled over by the prowess of a high school athlete." As my father paged through the book for several minutes, he began to understand why he was suddenly hearing from so many old cronies and classmates. But did he buy the book that day? No, because he was going for a long walk and didn't want to lug it around all day.

One week later, my father was back in Manhattan, prepared for another trek and to buy books for his four kids. But talk about sticker shock! He couldn't believe how expensive it was, which led to this phone conversation:

Me: "Dad, did you get the book?"

Swede: "No, I couldn't believe how expensive it was!"

Me: "How much was it?"

Swede: "It was almost thirty dollars!"

Me: "How much do you think a book costs now-a-days?"

Swede: "I thought it'd be five dollars, seven dollars, something like that."

Me: "When was the last time you bought a book?"

Swede: "I don't know, maybe fifty, fifty-five years ago."

Naturally, I got a good laugh out of that. The funny thing is that my father was an avid reader. He read books constantly, but he got them all from the South Orange Public Library. He *really* liked their prices.

Once the book was on the shelves, a series of articles were written about my father and his similarities to the Levov character. Two articles, by columnists Sid Dorfman and John McLaughlin, were printed in the *Newark Star-Ledger;* there was a long article in the North Jersey edition of the *Jewish News,* and then a full-page article (with a sketch of my father) in *The New Yorker* magazine. The articles were very flattering and interesting. I particularly enjoyed some of Dorfman's comments: "But what about his athletic career? Was Swede Levov really an athletic Masin? Well Mr. Levov, not to be critical, but I know Swede Masin, and you're no Swede Masin. There could be only one." He ended his column with "If Roth's early Levov was almost too good to be true, it's not surprising. After all, Swede Masin was."

My father particularly enjoyed hearing from so many men and women from his past. That was the favorite part for him. He also got a real kick out of being invited to be a guest of book clubs featuring Roth's novel. He told me the club members were so gracious, and they treated him like a celebrity. A dose of his mostly self-deprecating humor put everyone at ease with the "celebrity."

Swede told me at one such gathering, he was reminding the club members that *American Pastoral*'s story had no similarities whatsoever with my father's life, other than the sex scenes. That comment got a great laugh.

Some people, including lawyers, suggested to my father that he sue Roth for invasion of privacy, or some such violation. The chance of that happening was nil. My father clearly had an absolute blast with the whole *American Pastoral* experience.

In the book, Levov's daughter, Merry, becomes an anti-war radical, blows up a post office, and kills an innocent person. If anyone should have considered suing it was my sister. But which sister? Dale and Patty always argue that the "Merry" character was inspired by the other.

The fact that both Swede Masin and Swede Levov had the same given name of Seymour was probably not coincidental. In the case of my father, he never really cared for his given name. He liked the nickname, which was bestowed upon him when he was seven years old, while at summer camp. The counselor was telling a story in which one of the characters was Swedish—tall, blond, and blue-eyed. One of the other kids, Tim Lesnick, a lifelong friend of my father, announced that Seymour was tall, blue-eyed, and blond-haired. Hence, he should be called Swede. The nickname stuck.

In some circles the nickname "Swede" was not uncommon. But in the mostly Jewish Weequahic section of Newark it was most distinctive, if not unique. My father's size, blond hair, and blue eyes were also most distinctive. To this day, if the name Swede is mentioned among a group of Weequahic High School alumni, it almost certainly refers to my father.

When *American Pastoral* was published in 1997 my father had still never fully recovered from the divorce from my mother. There was always still a sliver of sadness. The trauma (and the embarrassment) of living through the break-up of a marriage, which he had felt was ideal, had taken its toll. I'm not sure he *ever* understood how it could have happened. Fortunately, when the book was published, it truly diverted his attention to a much happier subject. For the first time in years, my father was back in the limelight, and in a very energizing way. The McLaughlin article in the *Star-Ledger* had a great paragraph at the end that hit the nail on the head: "Seymour Masin is pushing eighty. His fame has long faded. But he has experienced what amounts to a second coming. He runs for touchdowns and grabs rebounds and soars over hurdles, not in his memories like other old men. But on the pages of a book read by hundreds of thousands of people." At last he was once again fully engaged with endless friends (and strangers) about a fun subject. He should sue Philip Roth? Not a chance. On the contrary, the book experience was just what the doctor ordered.

* * * *

When Philip Roth was honored at the New Jersey Performing Arts Center in 1997, my father was invited to attend, and met his fellow Weequahic graduate for the first time. Upon being introduced, my father told the author: "You changed my life, Phil." Answered Roth: "No, you changed *my* life."

Swede later told me that Roth was very friendly and gracious that evening. Many people had their cameras, and asked the two Weequahic grads to pose together. Philip Roth is reputed to be a very private person. But, according to all accounts, he was wonderful and most gracious with my father on that occasion.

After my father died, his obituary appeared in papers all around the United States, as well as in Europe, Asia, and South America. His death was reported on the news ticker at the bottom of the screen during a broadcast of New Jersey news. In many announcements of Swede's passing, his being an "inspiration" for Roth's *American Pastoral* protagonist was mentioned.

Thinking that the author might be interested, I sent Roth a brief note with a copy of my father's obituary. I also added a few comments about the unique bond among the Weequahic community, as well as a reminder of the fun my father had with his connection to *American Pastoral.*

Roth wrote back, saying he had heard of my father's passing. He mentioned his meeting Swede at the Performing Arts function, and added, "I liked him enormously right off." He went on to point out that, in spite of what others had commented, he did not "base his character's life on your father's." Roth explained, "I just used his nickname and his legendary athleticism." He concluded by pointing out that Swede was revered by many people, and he was glad my father got a kick out of the book and the attention it had brought him.

I am hesitant to be too specific with the content of Roth's letter because it was intended to be private. But, for the record, I would like to say that this world-renowned and Pulitzer Prize-winning author treated my father with grace, kindness, and respect at a very emotional time for the Masin family. The Masin kids surely appreciate him and Seymour "Swede" Levov.

After the Newark function, my father and Roth corresponded a few additional times. One note from Roth, perhaps referring to the Pulitzer Prize he received for writing *American Pastoral* read simply:

"Dear Swede,

Couldn't have done it without you."

Short and sweet, and to the point. And my father couldn't have had such a fun experience without Philip Roth.

CHAPTER SEVENTEEN:
THE MAGIC OF WEEQUAHIC

Many people look back upon their high school years with nostalgia. Their recollections of friends, incidents, teachers, places, coaches, principals, etc., often remain with them forever.

But when it comes to displaying pride in one's geographical origins—as well as fond memories of friends and even one's school—the graduates of Weequahic High School are in a league of their own.

During the course of my research, I have spoken with many people who grew up in Newark's Weequahic section. The consistency of everyone's love of Weequahic is remarkable. Admittedly, this should not have been surprising to me, because I heard nothing but raves about it from my parents over the years. And despite all the changes seen over the years in the city, the South Ward, and the schools, the special pride in "things Weequahic" endures.

The consistent raves of so many alumni about the school, the incomparable teachers and administrators, and the multitude of brilliant, driven students are almost too glowing to be believed. Could the school have been *that* great?! Even my parents, neither of whom were extraordinary students in their high school days, always spoke in awe of their teachers and fellow students.

My siblings and I went to excellent schools (Columbia High, South Orange Junior High, and Montrose Elementary) in a terrific town. South Orange was as good as it gets, and we all still remain in touch with our school friends. Yet, curiously, there was neither a 35th nor a 40th reunion for my graduating class.

In contrast, I doubt that the Weequahic Class of 1966 (or any other class back in the day) would ever go ten or fifteen years without a reunion. I remember my parents *loving* theirs. Weequahic alumni even gather for reunions in distant states, such as California and Florida.

In addition, Weequahic athletes from every era plan joint reunions every two years, which are extremely popular among the old (and even not so old) jocks.

In 2003, Patty took my father to the 65th reunion of his Weequahic class. She was taking a chance because Swede had already been transferred to the Alzheimer's wing of his assisted living facility. But everything worked out positively, with both Swede and Patty having a great time.

They sat at a table with some of my father's oldest friends: Stan Gilbert, Elmer Konwiser, and Donny Kurtz. Hal Braff, the master of ceremonies, said some wonderful things about Swede. My father had to apologize to many of his classmates for not remembering their names; but knowing him and his lifelong habit of not remembering names, I suspect that he had to do the same at his fifth high school reunion! In any case, Swede was remarkably social that day and had a great time seeing so many of his old cronies.

Patty came away awed by this reunion. "There was a great turnout; I was shocked at the attendance. After all, virtually everyone in the room was eighty-three years old. And everyone knew each other." In contrast, Patty recalled that by her twentieth high school reunion, she was trying all night to read everyone's name tags. "For their ages, I was so impressed with how sharp everyone was. It was obvious that they were all great friends, the majority of whom hadn't lost touch."

So what accounts for this Magic of Weequahic? Exactly what is so special about the Weequahic section of Newark? One explanation may be that most of the inhabitants were "in the same boat." Virtually everyone was a Jewish immigrant (or off-spring thereof) from Europe. This "sameness" was bound to provide a comfort zone and feeling of security because you were among "your own." Moreover, the South Ward had some of the newer, nicer, one and two-family homes, which were attractive for upwardly mobile families. In addition, the beautiful new school, named Weequahic High School, opened in 1933. It was the perfect destination and magnet for members of the Jewish community and their traditional emphasis on arts, learning, and education in general.

As a result, many observers regarded Weequahic as one of the best high schools academically in the country during the 1930s, 1940s, and 1950s. Swede certainly thought so; and William Helmreich in his excellent book, *The Enduring Community: The Jews of Newark and Metrowest*, agrees: "In its halcyon days, Weequahic students were amongst the best in the land." Helmreich also notes the "esprit de corps that characterize their reunions" and the tradition of Weequahic's superb teachers. One of them, Hannah Ginsberg Litzky (whose nephew was famed poet Allen Ginsberg), "described her experience at Weequahic as 'a love affair' between her, the students, faculty, and the school as a whole" (pp. 112-13).

I also had the opportunity to speak to several former teachers, including Hilda Lutzke, who taught at Weequahic from 1938 until well into the 1970s.

Now in her nineties, she is still incredibly sharp! She informed me that Philip Roth was not in her class, but that she did hand him his diploma upon graduation. As for school pride, her position was consistent with everyone else's:

>Bob: "Was there a lot of pride in the school?"
>
>Hilda: "Pride? You have no idea how much pride there was in the school!"
>
>Bob: "Did you love it?"
>
>Hilda [once again with a tone suggesting a dumb question]: "Are you kidding?!"
>
>Bob: "As a teacher, what did you think of Principal Herzberg?"
>
>Hilda: "He was so nice, and he was brilliant!!"

From the other side of the classroom, former student Ruth Fien told Heimreich, "I loved my experience at Weequahic High. The teachers were fabulous, the breadth of courses was spectacular. I thought it was an extraordinary educational experience. My teachers had a profound influence on me."

As impressive as the above quotation is, it is far from unique. In fact, it is remarkably similar to those offered by almost everyone I talked to about the school. A very small sampling from some of Swede's contemporaries:

>Judy (Wilner) Stein: "I was in awe of them [Weequahic's teachers]."
>
>Marie Purzycki: "The teachers and principal were wonderful!"
>
>Dotty (Doyle) Blackstone: "The teachers were demanding and wonderful."
>
>Stan Gilbert: "We had super teachers. But I didn't realize how great they were until later."
>
>Milton Lurie: "The teachers pushed us and pushed us, and Max Herzberg was a terrific principal ... They were wonderful years. The best years of my life. My best friends in high school remained my best friends my whole life. There were no cliques; there were no divisions between rich kids and poor kids (we were all middle class), the top students and the top athletes were friendly. It was a great time."
>
>Saul Berkowitz: "The teachers were great and the principal, Max Herzberg, was great."
>
>Julie Kramer, a couple of years older than my father and an excellent basketball player himself: "Did I love Weequahic? I *loved* it! Best years of my life!"

On and on the accolades went—almost all of them the same, demonstrating without a doubt not only the enormous respect accorded the teachers and the administrators, but also the genuine seriousness almost everyone had about their own education.

Another example comes from the film, *American Gangster* (2007), in which Russell Crowe plays the part of Richie Roberts, a detective in Essex County who prosecutes a drug kingpin played by Denzel Washington. The real Richie Roberts happens to be a Weequahic graduate (Class of 1947), and must have worn his Weequahic pride on his sleeve because the Australian actor gave every member of the cast a sweatshirt with "Weequahic High School" printed on the sleeve.

And then there was the success of the sports teams. The stereotype of Jews in sports has never been flattering—including the old joke about *Famous Jewish Athletes* being the shortest book in the world. There are many individual examples and anecdotes that could debunk that stereotype, even though there is some truth to the notion that many Jewish immigrants from Europe and Russia (such as Swede's parents) did not consider sports a high priority, especially when compared with hard work, education, the arts, and other more intellectual pursuits.

Another stereotype was that Jews were smaller of stature, further inhibiting their ability to advance in sports. For instance, in *When Boxing Was a Jewish Sport*, Allen Bodner describes many accomplished boxers in the 1920s and 1930s of the Jewish faith, virtually all of them in the lighter weight divisions. Nevertheless, this particular stereotype, whether accurate or not, certainly did not apply to my father and his brother Leo. They were big bruisers, right from the start, and were part of a new generation of Jews in Newark who had a much greater interest in sports than their parents. In fact, I am often amazed that my non-sports-supporting grandparents could have raised two sons who both loved and excelled at sports.

As a school that was born in 1933, Weequahic was able to capitalize on this new generation of Jewish athletes, and has always maintained a high interest in sports. I mention elsewhere in the book the huge fan interest in the great basketball rivalry between South Side and Weequahic in the mid-to-late 1930s, when the Newark Armory would be packed with nearly 5,000 extremely avid fans. My "second mother," Marie Purzycki, who attended the games to watch her future husband, South Side star Mike Purzycki, recalled, "It was so loud in there you could barely hear yourself think!" Basketball, in fact has been a hugely successful sport at the school almost from the beginning (starting with All-Stater Irv Keller) to the present day. Over the years, other stars such as Chris Pervall, Herb Krauplatt, Gerry Greenspan, Mo Layton, Dana Lewis, and of course, Al Attles. Oh ... and Swede.

In football, the record is less distinguished; Weequahic rarely excelled on the gridiron. I was even reminded of this by an older gentleman, who happened to be my roommate in Newark's Beth Israel Hospital, where I was recovering from knee surgery in 1965. The man was a Weequahic graduate and remembered my father well, but went out of his way to tell me how bad the football team was. He said they referred to them as "Weequit." (Ouch).

Nevertheless, Weequahic fielded an outstanding football team in 1951 and won the city championship. That squad and its stars—such as Andy Zupko, Al Lubetkin, Marvin Feinblatt—have attained legendary status among the alumni, and are *still* talked about and greatly revered.

Indeed, over the years, there have been a number of legendary coaches at the school. One is Les Fein. This larger-than-life man started as a playground director in the Weequahic section shortly after World War II. He later became incredibly successful as the varsity basketball coach, leading the school to several state championships. But he was more than a great coach; he was a strong, bright, energizing leader, who invigorated all those who heard him. When he spoke, people listened.

Another is Art Lustig, whom my father adored. Swede never said so, but I suspect that Lustig, his high school basketball and football coach, was like a second father. From as early as I can remember, my father spoke of Lustig frequently and with total admiration and reverence. Swede idolized his coach, and with mutual admiration the coach forever sang the praises of his all-around athlete. For instance, when the great Lonnie Wright was featured in an article about the all-state basketball team in 1962, Lustig was quoted as saying, "You see such a schoolboy athlete only once or twice in a lifetime. I've seen two … Swede Masin and Lonnie Wright."

When this newspaper article appeared, a friend called Swede to tell him about it. It was one of the very few times I saw my father demonstrably proud. To be compared to the incomparable Lonnie Wright, and for it to come from his beloved Art Lustig? Well, for my father it could not get any better than this. I only wish my father could have heard what Al Attles vividly remembered during his playing days at Weequahic: that Coach Lustig always used Swede Masin as the "template" for how the game should be played.

Like Les Fein, Lustig was much more than a sports coach; he was a great teacher of life lessons. Camp Weequahic, the summer camp he founded in Pennsylvania, is still owned and operated by Lustig family members and still stresses the same core principles and positive message he preached as a coach decades ago: that the principles of teamwork, fairness, and including everyone are far more than how to win.

Al Attles spoke highly of both Fein and Lustig, and consulted with them all during his career as a player, coach, and executive for the Golden State

Warriors. Hal Braff opined that Art Lustig could have been very successful in almost any field. But Lustig's most appreciative supporter might be Arnold Keller, the nephew of Weequahic's first great hoopster, Irv Keller. Arnold's father left home before he was born, and his mother had two "devastating" marriages afterwards. With little or no money, the family was constantly moving around; for instance, Arnold attended four different elementary schools. He also remembers living at his grandparents' house, where he would sleep in his Uncle Irv's room (who by this time was away at college or in the service). Arnold loved reading Irv's scrapbooks, and everything else "Weequahic." So when he entered the high school, he made the basketball team. He was never a star, but he cannot describe how much it enriched his life. "Art took me under his wing," he explains—and credits Lustig with filling a huge void in his life as basketball coach, mentor, and surrogate father. It would be hard to find a stronger advocate of the Weequahic experience than Arnold Keller.

The enormous pride in Weequahic High School that everyone felt reminds me of a comic routine with Carl Reiner interviewing a psychiatrist played by Mel Brooks:

Reiner: "Doctor, tell me about some of your patients."

Dr. Brooks: "Well, I had a man who loved his dog."

Reiner: "That's not so unusual. A lot of people love their dogs."

Dr. Brooks: "No, no, never mind ... this guy *loved* his dog."

That's like asking Weequahic alumni about their school. They didn't love their school. They *loved* their school!

The anecdotes go on and on about Weequahic—which brings us back to the question of what accounts for "the magic of Weequahic." Another factor was that the neighborhoods were extremely safe, which perhaps heightened the optimism. I asked my Aunt Shirley about the time and place.

Shirley: "It was beautiful. We loved the neighborhood."

Nephew Bob: "Was it safe?"

Shirley: "Safe?!" [Said as if it was the dumbest question of all time]. "Of course it was safe! It was all Jewish!!"

Similar sentiments came from Vita Orenstein (the mother of Judy Orenstein Perlmutter, one of my high school classmates): "The Weequahic Section was terrific. It was very safe, the school was excellent, and the social life was very good. We all went out in groups."

And likewise from Dotty Doyle Blackstone, my mother's life-long friend:

"The Newark we grew up in was the greatest place in the country. Estelle and I would go to the movies and walk home at midnight, totally safe ... It was *never* an issue not being Jewish ... we had many great friends."

And Stan Gilbert, Swede's buddy: "It was just a super place. Very safe. We had a brand new school, and many of the families were upper middle-class. I'm not sure we appreciated how great it was."

My own conclusion about Weequahic is that there was a "perfect storm" going on at that time and place, what with a plethora of great teachers and coaches, hard-working, ambitious families who were striving to improve themselves, people whose past lives were quite probably difficult at best, and more. There were many appreciative folks that were coming together, many in the same boat.

That was Weequahic then. But what of Weequahic today? If Max Herzberg, Art Lustig, Les Fein and all the other great teachers of my parents' generation were to be transported into today's high school, what would they find?

According to Ronald Smothers' report in the *New York Times* (December 4, 2006), Weequahic's test scores in recent years had "plummeted to the lowest of any school in Newark, and its classrooms were plagued by violence, drugs, and gangs. Students cutting class brazenly shot craps in the hallways, sometimes holding the dice up so they could be seen on security cameras."

Why such a reversal of fortune? The reasons are numerous, and it would take an urban historian and sociologist to explain what happened. Certainly, one factor was the migration of families moving from the city to western suburbs such as South Orange and Livingston, where new, larger homes were being built with larger yards, and where there were excellent schools and community facilities. At the same time, the loss of what had been a huge manufacturing base resulted in a dramatic reduction in the number of jobs in Newark. And then there was increased corruption of all kinds, from street crime to organized crime to scandals within the city government. A growing African American population, with dwindling job opportunities, being policed and governed predominantly by whites, led to severe racial tensions, culminating in the region-changing Newark riots of July 1967. The riots put an exclamation mark on the so-called "white flight," which had already been in progress. The "perfect storm" of my parents' generation, where it seemed as if all the energy and momentum was moving in a very favorable direction, had reversed itself. By the late 1960s, the momentum seemed to be heading in the wrong direction, resulting in a demoralizing and negative energy.

Newark surely was not alone in this change of landscape. Many, if not most urban areas, went through similar changes. But virtually all of the problems associated with urban blight seemed to be exaggerated in Newark.

Max Herzberg and his teaching staff might have been superstars in the 1930s and 1940s, though they never had to deal with drugs, gangs, or high levels of violence. But that's exactly what Ron Stone encountered when he started work as the Weequahic High School principal in 1999. Just as Herzberg had been the right person for the job in his time, marshalling all of the positive academic energy of WHS, Ron Stone proved himself to be the right person to reverse the daunting, negative energy (academic and otherwise) that had plagued the school in more recent decades.

Small steps. Stone, a former college wrestler and football star, took some unorthodox approaches to help improve Weequahic's academics and athletics. For example, Stone wrangled forty thousand precious dollars to open a weight training room and he hired a new dynamo of a football coach, Altarik White, who had been a great running back in college, known for his "never give up" attitude.

Stone's plan was bold—and optimistic: the weight room would strengthen the footballers, they would improve and gain confidence, their fortunes on the field would improve, a semblance of school spirit and pride would return, and so on, all with positive momentum. Stone was well aware that Weequahic has never been a football powerhouse—with the one possible exception of the 1951 team, which won the city championship. When Stone arrived, the team was at or near the bottom of the standings.

As Ronald Smothers noted in his *New York Times* article regarding the weight room: "He [Stone] said he hoped it would demonstrate that you have to work hard and prepare yourself in order to get results. And then you realize that you can't be successful on the football field and then be afraid to tackle math." Small steps.

So, what have been the results? Well, the traditional football doormats became a miracle team—if you can call hard work and talent a miracle. The team lost its opening game and then won the next eleven straight to capture the state championship in 2006! Marvin Feinblatt, Andy Zubco, Al Lubetkin and others from 1951 have been matched, if not surpassed, by Amara Kamara, Jamaal Perry, Dominick Brown, Obadiah Dykes and others on the 2006 team.

More importantly, the school has been improving steadily in its academic performance. Its cumulative proficiency exam scores are rising. Jahquill Turner, a senior, attending a pep rally (over 300 students attended!) before the championship game, told Smothers, "If they win, we *all* win."

There must have been something to Stone's theory that the weight room could become a catalyst for achieving some positive momentum. The players did get stronger and better, their fortunes on the field clearly improved, many of the students started to find a reason for pride in the school, and so on. Did this help, directly or indirectly, to improve academic performance? Improved test scores are not accidental. Clearly, Principal Stone and his staff had to fight many battles on many fronts, but for 300 students to show up for a pep rally, one has to assume that many were energized by the team's success, and that energy certainly could have helped change the academic performance momentum.

When I spoke by phone with Ron Stone in early 2007, I mentioned the book I was working on, and was excited to learn that he knew of Swede and his legendary sports reputation. "Of course I knew of your father," he told me. What greatly impressed me in this one telephone conversation was the principal's remarkable energy level. He exuded it! He also came across as being very pragmatic; knowing he would not be able to turn things around overnight, and knowing it was not a one-person job. He also did not believe it was realistic to expect the high school to become what it once was. But if Ron Stone wasn't going to succeed (and his expectations, while realistic, were high), it wouldn't be for lack of effort. Not with him in charge.

But as strong a leader as Ron Stone seemed to me, he was only one person. Remember all the mentors I referred to when my parents were at Weequahic? There were great mentors everywhere, and they helped nurture all of the students in their respective eras.

Fortunately, Principal Stone received some help from a surprising source.

Hal Braff is a Weequahic graduate (Class of 1952), and like so many others of his era, as well as folks from before and after, he loved the unmatched enthusiasm and pride he felt for the school at class reunions. There was so much brotherhood and sisterhood. And at some point he had an inspiration: how can this wonderful phenomenon, all this love at our reunions, all this positive energy, be used to improve the lot of the current high school?

As an attorney, Hal has at various times represented the NAACP and CORE, and has always had a passion for trying to help the African American community. In particular, he has been fervent in emphasizing the importance of education to help release people from poverty. Hal is an inspiring speaker; you can't help but be impressed with his positive approach to an enormous challenge, one that is bound to cause its share of discouragement and disappointment along the way.

For instance, Hal told me: "Look, I was the beneficiary of a wonderful education. All of us were. Ours was a culture that appreciated and emphasized education. Our neighborhood and our school ground out professional after professional ... educators, business leaders, doctors, lawyers, etc. The kids at Weequahic today are kids, just like we were."

But after floating his idea of mobilizing alumni from the Weequahic of old to help the current students improve their options in life, the response was unenthusiastic. There was more than a little uncertainty about what kinds of efforts would or could make a difference. He also met with the Weequahic principal at the time, and the response, though very polite, was similar. Everyone seemed to think the idea had merit, but there was confusion about how to act on it.

The day after Weequahic won the state football championship on December 3, 2006, Braff's efforts to help his alma mater were highlighted by Bridget Wentworth in the *Star Ledger.* "I found out the faculty had no idea of our history," Braff declared. "And I thought we could take our energy from the past and bring it up to the needs of the kids who were living in some of the very same houses we lived in." Braff expanded upon this when we later spoke by phone: "It occurred to me something had happened to the students at Weequahic. They no longer knew the old school songs and the cheers; they knew nothing about the legends of Swede Masin and other Weequahic greats. On the other hand, at some of the nearby suburban schools—say in Verona or Livingston—very little has changed over the decades. There's continuity. But at Weequahic, the continuity had been lost years ago."

The tenacious Braff met with the Weequahic faculty. He told them about the illustrious history of the school, and he delved into detail. He even sang the fight song! I would have liked to have been there for that. Connecting the current students to those of the 1930s, 1940s, and 1950s is a beautiful and inspiring idea.

Braff's inspiration began to gain traction. Key objectives were identified: the need for more male role models, more experience and interaction with the white community, more mentoring. The passage of time saw the addition of more key players to the effort. Sheldon Bross, Class of 1955, became very involved, sparking the effort to launch a new organization, the Weequahic High School Alumni Association (WHSAA).

The launch was to take place at the Newark Public Library one evening; and when Braff and Bross went to survey the facility that morning, they coincidentally ran into Phil Yourish, Class of 1964, who occupied an office inside the library as head of the Newark Literacy Campaign. Yourish introduced himself, and the rest is history. That night, the WHSAA announced its primary goal of giving back to the current Weequahic students.

Today Yourish is the association's executive director, thanks in no small part to people like Steve Dinitz, Class of 1965, and Eli Hoffman, Class of 1956, whose support, financial and otherwise, has been instrumental in getting this effort off and running.

Over time, as other influential people such as Al Attles and Les Fein have become deeply engaged in the effort, the financial support has continued to grow. As a result, the WHSAA has been able to contribute funds toward uniforms and instruments for the school band, money toward a trip to France for the school's French-language students (twice), and hundreds of thousands of dollars for scholarships toward college educations for literally hundreds of students. The trip to France must have been a terrific experience for these kids. I suspect that many students never dreamed, upon entering WHS, that they would ever have the opportunity to spend ten days in France. Talk about expanding one's horizons!

I can't help but think the trip to France was a spectacular, eye-opening experience for the French class. So many kids growing up in Newark today do not have the opportunity to experience new, exciting, interesting things. Thanks to the efforts of many people, (and in particular the leadership of the teacher, Lavinia Rogers), not to mention all those whose financial support made this possible, the class probably learned more in one trip than we might ever imagine.

And so the effort continues. It will take leadership, creativity, many great mentors, constructive peer leadership and parenting, and the positive momentum that only success stories can create. It will take earth-movers like Lavinia Rogers, Altarik White, Hal Braff, Phil Yourish, Al Attles, Sheldon Bross, Eli Hoffman, and numerous others. It will most certainly require dealing with disappointment and will require the patience to deal with baby steps. It will take the mobilization of more reinforcements; there is strength in numbers. It will also be necessary for the students themselves to realize their potential and show the world what they have. In my opinion, the importance of the students themselves taking the ball and running with it cannot be overstated. This has the potential to have a very happy ending, but not without some sweat and tears. Nobody has said it will be easy. More power to all those who are fighting the good fight.

* * * *

In October 2007, I traveled to New Jersey to work on some final chapters of the book. I especially wanted to learn more about the efforts being made by the WHSAA and the WHS administration to provide the students with a greater school experience.

I contacted Arnold Keller, Hal Braff, and Phil Yourish, asking if they would like to join me for dinner one night when I was in town. Arnold suggested expanding the group—and the result was a cocktail hour followed by a wonderful dinner with thirty guests! Weequahic's Principal Ron Stone was there, as were Johanna and Lonnie Wright.

As we sat down for dinner, Arnold gave a short speech, telling of the time when he was seventeen, and played catch with a seven-year-old boy who already "had muscles you wouldn't believe." Arnold said he showed the youngster how to throw and catch—and that the boy grew up to become one of the all-time great athletes, Lonnie Wright!

Arnold related this story with relish—though the best part for me was watching Lonnie and Johanna as Arnold was talking. They looked very bemused, and it was quite evident Lonnie had no recollection of this life-changing event. Later, tongue in cheek, Arnold decided he also had a similar influence on making Al Attles a superstar. When I asked Arnold if he had also played catch with Jim Thorpe back in the day, Arnold replied, "Come to think of it, I did!" It goes without saying that Arnold "bleeds Weequahic orange" and is one of the school's most appreciative and proud alumni. He was the greatest of hosts this evening.

Another guest at dinner was Beth Kruvant, who has filmed a documentary about Weequahic past and present, and who arranged for Phil Yourish to give us a brief tour of the Weequahic section on camera later in the week. We started outside the high school, stopped outside the house where Philip Roth grew up, and walked through other parts of the neighborhood. Phil Yourish knows his Newark history as well as anyone, so it was both interesting and nostalgic for me. I threw in a few Swede anecdotes for the camera, a subject I always enjoy talking about.

But the highlight of Phil's tour was a visit to the very same high school my parents had attended. I had never been inside before, and can't begin to express how wonderful it felt to be walking through the same hallways, classrooms, bathrooms, auditorium, and cafeteria as my parents did during Weequahic's glory years. For instance, I learned that the auditorium has not changed since the time the school was built in 1932. Even the wooden seats, and whatever may have been carved into them over seven-plus decades, remain unchanged. The new football field and grandstands looked great, as did the impressive weight and exercise room, painted in Weequahic Orange. It was crowded with many students that day, both boys and girls, working out—with a little bit of socializing thrown in. I especially loved standing in the same gymnasium where Swede played his games and saw the window out of which Swede tossed his best buddy, Stan Gilbert.

Phil introduced me to Athletic Director Gary Westberry, who was soon to be inducted into the Newark Sports Hall of Fame. And he also introduced me to Lorraine White, a 1964 Weequahic graduate, who at one time was the school's football coach, said to be "the only female football coach in the city."

"The city?" I responded. "How about the world?!" After all, there are not many female football coaches anywhere! But what may be Lorraine's greater achievement is serving since 1970 as a highly respected Weequahic faculty member. I asked Lorraine if she was a strict disciplinarian as football coach. She replied, "Oh yes, and I still am." Suggestion to the students: do *not* mess with Ms. White.

All in all, it was a great day. The high school looked terrific and thanks to the efforts of the Alumni Association, the staff, and the students, the magic of Weequahic may be coming back. As the school song goes, "We're on our way, to meet the foe."

A VERY SOMBER UPDATE

In November 2007, Weequahic's charismatic, energetic principal, Ron Stone, died suddenly of a heart attack. When I heard this, it felt like a punch to the stomach. Virtually everyone I knew felt that Ron was the perfect person to make Weequahic High School the great place that it once was. I had been extremely fortunate not only in talking with him by phone, but also meeting him at the dinner arranged by Arnold Keller one month earlier. My first impression was that for being so physically powerful, he was very warm. In his own way he was another gentle giant. He will surely be missed, but will not be forgotten. The challenge now will be for others to step up and carry on his mission. Not an easy task, considering Ron Stone's greatness.

CHAPTER EIGHTEEN:
ALZHEIMER'S

My father passed away in September 2005 of complications from Alzheimer's disease. His final three or four years were difficult for everyone, as we watched his mental capabilities decline. Remember, this was a man whose company we adored. He loved his family, and was always keenly engaged in the lives of his loved ones.

Even though his father, Max, had died of complications of Alzheimer's at age 85, the four Masin kids were somewhat in denial—and none more than me—when Swede started showing small signs that he was changing. After all, it's natural that elderly people are going to be forgetful, absentminded, and so on. So, with the exception of Susie who suspected trouble and gently suggested that my father needed testing, we all rationalized the reasons Swede was slipping. Part of his morning ritual (besides his bowl of Fiber One) was to read the *Star-Ledger*, cover to cover. He started mentioning that it was getting difficult to read because the newspaper had changed to a "fancier print." We assumed it was his eyesight. He was never comfortable with gadgets, so when he started needing more assistance with the TV remote control, we rationalized it as a combination of his eyesight and his traditional discomfort with things mechanical. When he struggled to understand things, we assumed it must be his hearing. When he forgot the names of people he knew for years, we figured it was because he was always terrible with names.

In the summer of 2000, during one of his many visits to Portland, Swede went for a long walk one day. He got lost on his return even though he walked right past the street leading into our neighborhood. Fortunately, our close friend, Kathy Peterson, was driving by and saw he was headed in the wrong direction. She picked him up and drove him home. We laughed it off at the time; Swede never had a good sense of direction. But this was another of many little signs we chose to write off as trivial and unimportant.

Whenever I had business in New York, I would usually stay at my father's house and commute to the city. Often I'd stay all or part of the weekend.

Unlike my siblings, who saw Swede much more often than I did, his changes in behavior were starting to appear more glaring to me.

But at the time we were very pre-occupied with my mother. Before Estelle's five-month battle with cancer finally ended on January 27, 2002, most of our attention was devoted to keeping her comfortable and keeping her company. But, even as we focused on my mother's battle, in the back of our minds we individually concluded that Swede's future would need to be planned.

For instance, when Patty went to pick up my father to attend my mother's funeral, she wasn't mentally prepared to deal with Swede's insistence that he not change his outfit. He was wearing a nice navy blue suit, but his shirt was a pajama top and he was wearing sneakers. Patty prevailed, but it was difficult having to convince my father, who was being stubborn about changing, while she was mourning the death of my mother.

So, for a significant stretch of time there were many psychological ups and downs as we observed Swede's behavior. When he remained as witty as ever, making his customarily clever remarks, we thought there was *no way* he was starting along the road to Alzheimer's. Moreover, he still looked great, and he took his lengthy, daily walks. He drove (though not much and not far, and never at night), went food shopping, took himself to the doctor, barber, and more. Physically, for his age, he looked freakishly fit, as fantastic as ever. He was still lean, and strong as an ox.

But some of the dreaded signs were getting worse. When I was in New Jersey in 2001, I took my father to a funeral. The brother of one of Swede's good friends had passed away, and my father wanted to pay his respects. Some of Swede's old cronies were there, but he had a very difficult time remembering names and familiar faces.

He also started to have challenges dressing. He'd put on two shirts, or he'd put his shirt on over his pajama top. He'd wear the same clothes for days at a time. He started to have an aversion to water, and we had to persuade him to take showers. This was an eye-opener for all of us. My father had always been very well groomed.

Dale and Patty decided to have my father tested by a neurologist. There was a time when this would have been difficult to suggest, but Swede had mentioned to Patty that he was worried about the state of his memory. This gave my sisters the opening they needed. A neurologist performed a brain scan in which he noticed evidence of some mini-strokes. One in particular looked damaging, so the doctor asked my father a series of questions: math problems, spelling tests, current events, picture identification, etc. The results were mixed. Swede answered the math questions quickly and accurately; he had no problem spelling the word "police" backwards; he identified most of the pictured objects, but not some of the obvious ones (such as a picture of a glove); and when asked who was the previous president (Clinton), he replied: "What's his name, the one who ran around with all the women." Bottom line, the test results were mixed, but he *was* suffering from some dementia.

Personally, I was probably looking for any positive signs, so I was somewhat encouraged. But the reality was that Swede was having more and more trouble with basic chores. One night he complained to Patty that the scrambled eggs he'd prepared didn't taste right; she later discovered he had tried to scramble the eggs on a plate placed directly on top of the burner. He became very frustrated more and more often, and would lose his temper from trivial inconveniences. Once while I was in New Jersey, my father complained he just could not get a clean shave. The problem I discovered was that he was using his toothbrush. This may sound amusing, but for me it was just another huge, discouraging reality check. I was terribly disturbed; couldn't my father see that it was a tooth brush, not a razor? Swede, in spite of his great sense of humor, was always a dignified man. Seeing him struggle with fundamental chores like shaving was brutal to observe. I worked very hard to be overly patient with my father during these episodes. But often, as hard as I tried, it didn't matter. His brain was just not processing the information.

One day in 2001 Patty took my father to the doctor. While waiting, she noticed he had his portable phone in his shirt pocket, so she held it for him in her pocketbook. Afterwards they grabbed some dinner and then Patty dropped Swede off at home. She went to visit my mother, three minutes away. While there, Swede called. He couldn't find his car keys *anywhere*. He said he looked in every room, including the "room" (garage) where he kept the car. While talking, Patty remembered she had my father's portable phone with her. She interrupted my father and told him, and let him know she'd be back to deliver his phone. Swede: "Phone? Oh, maybe that's what I was looking for."

We could tell my father was at wit's end in his house. Watching TV was hard due to difficulty with the remote control device, he had trouble shaving, he was certainly losing the competence necessary to drive, and his overall confidence level was low.

In June 2002, I flew east to join Susie, Max, and Julie in a house we had rented for a week in Bethany Beach at the Delaware shore. First, I had arranged to take Swede to his doctor's appointment, after which I would head south to Delaware. I showed up at my father's house, and he was very upset. The previous evening he had tried to cut his toenails, but somehow he had cut himself badly. Based on all the bandages it also looked as if he had trouble trying to stop the cuts from bleeding. Then he showed me a light on the front porch, which was broken. Apparently he had become confused, and instead of turning off the light switch, he fumbled with the light itself and broke it. I calmed him down and took him to his doctor's appointment. I called Susie at the beach house and let her know I wanted to bring my father with me. She said, absolutely, we'd make room.

I told him, "Dad, I'm taking you to Delaware with me." Normally, my father didn't like sudden, unplanned changes/decisions; but not this time. He really didn't want to be alone in the house, so it took him only ten seconds to agree. We took the five-hour trip later that same day. After living in his house for fifty-one years, a house his father had built, a house all his kids grew up in, my father would never spend another night at 60 Mountain House Road, South Orange.

We had a beautiful few days in Delaware. My father was a little confused by the surroundings, but he was with family, which gave him comfort. Four days later we would be leaving for Oregon. The big question now was what to do about my father's condition. Susie suggested bringing my father home to Portland with us—at least temporarily. Between the four of us we could make sure he would have good company, and more importantly it would allow time to make decisions prior to Swede's return to New Jersey. Again, the Swede of old would not have been comfortable making the decision to fly across the country on short notice. This time he was eager to do so.

My father spent close to a month with us. Julie, Max, and Susie (and our dog, Daisy) were great company for him. He was treated like a king. He always had company, he never had to worry about his meals, he didn't have to drive, he didn't have to figure out how to turn on the TV, and so on. I took as much time off from work as I could, and we would take frequent drives to nearby, spectacular Columbia River Gorge. On many of the day trips we would stop at beautiful Skamania Lodge, on the Washington State side of the river, and have an outdoor lunch in one of the prettiest environments anywhere. The Lodge has a golf course, so my father and I would spend an hour or so after lunch on the practice putting green and have contests. I would always give him a few strokes, but he won each time and didn't need the strokes.

Saturday morning is when I play basketball with my buddies, and my father enjoyed watching us play. He remarked how good the games were and how high the level of play was. In reality we were an old, overweight, motley group, so this was more evidence that my father's judgment was impaired.

Susie took my father to our internist, our close friend Jim Kern. After a few tests with Swede, Jim clearly and calmly broke the news to my father that he must not drive any longer. This was critical. In retrospect we realized that we had (thus far) avoided a potential catastrophe by not taking the car keys from my father. Most of us have to deal with this at some point in our lives, and it is painful any way you do it. Swede was clearly dismayed that he could not drive any longer. He understood the ramifications; his life was changing, and he did not know what his future held. But deep down, I think he was also relieved; driving had become an unnerving adventure for him.

Every morning Julie took my father to the Lincoln High School track and walked laps with him. He still wanted his exercise. And every day, while the two were walking, Swede would tell his granddaughter the same three stories, relating to his parents. Max kept my father company, gave him a tour, with Susie, of Portland's excellent zoo, and made sure he had plenty of snacks (something from which Max took full advantage). And Susie? She did the hard stuff—taking my father to the dentist, to the doctor, cleaning up after Swede, and much more.

All in all, it was a wonderful several weeks. I sensed my father had a great time. He felt secure, he had the constant company of loved ones, and he had no responsibilities. He did not have to figure stuff out. We were there to do that for him. He was probably more relaxed than he had been in a long time. But every once in a while, in his more lucid, back to reality moments, he would fret about his future. No driving? What was he going to do?

I asked myself if there was a way he could stay with us in Portland, permanently. But Julie was about to leave for college, Max would be at school, and my job, with all its travel, would take me away from Portland frequently. Moreover, Susie was on the Board of Directors of the Portland YWCA, a very important and time-consuming commitment. And of course it would have taken my father away from my three siblings as well as his friends back in Jersey. I felt torn, helpless, and guilty. One slight consolation was that Swede's visit with us in Portland was so lengthy. I hadn't spent that much time with my father in decades. I'll always remember that visit. And I remember thinking at the time that we could/would do this frequently. It would provide long, pleasant, care-free respites from wherever he'd be living. So that was my rosy plan: long, fun visits with us in Oregon. If only it had worked out that way.

One evening I took my father to the local supermarket to pick up a few items. While on line, a nice lady from our neighborhood appeared. I introduced her to Swede.

Lady from the neighborhood: "Oh, you're Bob's father? Are you anything like your son?"

Swede: "Why, do I look like a sissy?"

Let me explain. Swede was not homophobic. But he had a very quick wit, even as his mind was failing him. Luckily, this particular wisecrack did not appear to offend anyone, considering the woman from the neighborhood, the woman cashier, and a couple of other folks on line all laughed heartily.

Everyone laughed except for me. I was busy trying to explain my father's sense of humor.

Upon his return to Jersey, Swede stayed at either Patty's or Dale's place while the siblings arranged for getting my father into an assisted living facility. We found a very nice place within fifteen minutes of Patty and twenty-five minutes of Dale.

My father adapted okay to his new environment. The facility has different levels of care. Swede did not start in the Alzheimer's wing. In spite of some of the previous anecdotes, my father had plenty of lucid stretches of time. He still went for his walks, although the staff had concerns about him getting lost, getting hit by a car, etc. They gave him an ankle bracelet to wear so they could locate him … just in case.

Patty brought my father out for another visit a couple of months later and we had a very good time together. It wasn't quite as magical as the previous visit, but it was great having him with us. However, unbeknownst to me at the time, that trip to Portland would be his last; he would never leave New Jersey again. Months later I had business in New York. I visited my father with the intention of grabbing his duffle bag, putting a few items in it, and flying him to Portland with me. I was really looking forward to giving my father a happy, invigorating vacation with loved ones. But it was not to be. He was appreciative of the offer, but he would not budge. He was simply overwhelmed with the prospect, and he was not going to be convinced. It wasn't even close.

I was terribly depressed over this turn of events. I had been determined to get him to go with me. I really wanted to give him a good time, with family. I wanted so much to hang out with him, make him feel happy and secure. But that day I realized that things were never going to be the same again. I was *very* dejected on the flight home. I couldn't read, watch the movie, or eat. I sat in my seat and brooded the entire flight. I had planned, naively, to bring my father back to Portland with me quite frequently, and for lengthy visits. He would love it! We would make things easy for him, as we had during his previous, care-free, month-long visit, and he would get nice long breaks from being in the assisted living facility. But this was a different Swede, one who was entering a new, shrunken world. He was still alive, but he was barely "with" us. And here I was, heading back home, 3,000 miles away from my father, and for all intents and purposes, invisible from him. It was a horrible day for me.

It also got me thinking about the guilt I had felt in 1989, when I moved my wife and daughter (Max wasn't born yet) across the country for a great job opportunity with the Columbia Sportswear Company. Both my parents were very dejected at the time, my mother very outwardly. She was not only sad, but also mad (at me). My father tried to keep a positive face, but I could easily sense that he was very disappointed as well. I will always carry some guilt about leaving. Certainly, we worked very hard at staying as close as possible. There were frequent phone calls, endless sending of pictures, and at least one family visit every year, sometimes two. But with the death of my mother and the decline of my father, the guilt came rushing back.

One of the worst things for me was not being able to pick up the telephone and call my father. It became impractical for my father to have a phone in his room. He could no longer dial out and he wouldn't recognize someone calling in. For me this was terribly significant. I used to call my father all the time. Now, that opportunity was gone forever.

When my father was in good mental condition, we always had the same drill when I called:

Swede: "Hello"

Bob: "Helllooooowe Deh Deh!"

Swede: "*Hey* Bob!"

Then, towards the end of my father's run at his house in South Orange, it changed slightly:

Swede: "Hello"

Bob: "Helllooooowe Deh Deh!"

Swede: "*Hey*, how ya doin!"

I realized he couldn't come up with my name right away. It sounds like a small, subtle change, but for me it was a big deal. My father had crossed another negative threshold, and it was distancing him from me. Another discouraging reminder I was losing my connection with Swede, my idol.

Another little family ritual was the Masin whistle. Whenever I'd enter his house, I'd greet my father with a whistle that sounded like the tune of a doorbell ringing. Twice. As in ding dong, ding dong, only via a whistle. Swede would always respond with the reverse sound: dong ding, dong ding. He always remembered that response, even when his memory was becoming very meager. I'm happy to say that I still use that same whistle with my own kids.

Pretty soon the staff at Whispering Knoll, the assisted living facility, realized my father needed more help to do things and would have to be transferred to the Alzheimer's wing. This was logistically difficult for the staff. In this wing, there were about thirty residents, all but four or five were elderly women, and a significant number of them had wheelchair or walker needs. Many were small and slight. Swede, on the other hand was quite mobile, big and strong, and if he did not want to take a shower, or change his clothes, or go to the dining area … well, you get the picture. He was a load for the staff to deal with.

205

I remember visiting my father, and when I would walk in he would give me a big smile. Unfortunately, by then he did not know my name or that I was his son. The final transition was when he had no clue who I was. I would walk towards him and for all he knew I was another member of the staff or another visitor for one of the other patients. Swede was still with us, but we were losing a part of him every day.

In 2004 the Metro West Jewish Community Center was honoring the first inductees into its new Jewish Sports Hall of Fame. Swede was among the first group. His four kids and my Aunt Shirley attended, and it was wonderful. Doug and I accepted on behalf of my father.

Earlier that day I was visiting with Swede at Whispering Knoll. I tried to explain the honor he would be receiving, and how special he was, as an athlete, as a man, and as a father. He turned in his chair to face me better; he seemed to be trying his best to comprehend what I was saying. But he simply could not. Very frustrated, and wincing, he tapped his forehead and shook his head. Try as he might, he did not understand because, as he was saying with his motions, "my brain won't let me understand." I was so frustrated for him. It was terribly sad.

When I would visit Swede at Whispering Knoll, I would tell him I was his son, and I would make sure to tell him what a wonderful father he was. He'd struggle to comprehend me, and I remember my regrets for not having told him these things during his lucid years.

Two of Swede's cronies and lunch buddies—men he adored and two very impressive, accomplished men—were inducted into the Hall of Fame that night as well: Sid Dorfman, the legendary sportswriter, and Les Fein, the legendary coach. My father would have absolutely loved being inducted with them.

Moreover, the great *Star-Ledger* columnist, Jerry Izenberg, was the master of ceremonies. He said some wonderful things about my father. He finished his introduction of Swede by saying, "I never knew his real name was Seymour. We all knew him as the Swede, and he was the best." He didn't say he was "great," or "one of the best." He was "the best"—a description that was both succinct and very meaningful, from a nationally known columnist.

My father's mind and health would continue to decline, slowly but surely. He always had perfect posture. But towards the end he walked slowly and (like most of the elderly) a little bent over. The man who, when I was a kid, was the biggest person in the world was now much closer to my size.

My frustration and guilt feelings of being 3,000 miles away kept building. I used to check the time and then add the three-hour time difference to figure out what my father was doing. Seven p.m. my time? He's probably sleeping. Two-thirty p.m. my time? He's probably eating dinner.

The mother of my buddy Bruce Fad had been stricken with Alzheimer's years earlier, and I thought back to Bruce telling me how he would often think about his mother, and wonder what was going through her mind as she sat in her chair at the nursing home. Now I was doing the same thing. I wondered what was going through Swede's mind when he was alone in his room, sitting in his reclining chair, with his memories blurred. Did he have *any* pleasant memories or thoughts? Obviously, it was a question that could not be answered, but I found myself guiltily wondering if Swede wouldn't be better off if he went to sleep and didn't wake up.

Thank goodness, my siblings were in striking distance of my father. They visited as often as possible. But Patty, as usual, went above and beyond. She had a very heavy teaching workload. It included making time for reading journals written by her many students, and writing comments. This necessitated plenty of evening and weekend work. But still she made time to visit Swede almost daily. Sometimes she would be there during dinner, and she would help my father eat in the facility's small dining room. She made videotapes for him, and sometimes they would sit and watch movies with Fred Astaire and Gene Kelly, and tapes of the Lawrence Welk Show. My father loved music and those videos were great for him. He would smile all the way through them. Often he would turn to Patty and say "I *know* ya gotta be smiling." She also made sure to bring my father his favorite snacks, which he never turned down.

Also, during her visits Patty would try to stimulate my father's mind. She would repeat names of his friends, old teammates and classmates, and other names from his life, to see if he could recognize them.

Patty: "Dad, do you remember Stanley Gilbert?"

Swede: "Yeah, sure I do."

Patty: "What about Berky [Saul Berkowitz]?"

Swede: "Oh yeah."

Patty: "What about Sherm Harmelin?"

Swede: "Sure"

On and on. "Sid Dorfman? Les Fein? Lonnie Wright? Timmy Lesnick? Marty Friedman? Morty Goodkin? Irv Rothman, Eddie Denholtz? Irv Keller, Mike Purzycki, Gene Halper, Doug Shatzberg, Irv Botwin, Harvey Manders, Red Greenburg, Arthur Tzeses, Donny Kurtz, Herbie Deer, Maury Raff, Sid Lester, Elmer Konwiser, Nat Stokes, Sid Zimmy, Mike Woller, Monte Irvin, Abbey West, Al Attles, Frank Chenitz, Burt Manhoff, Art Lustig, Norman Ward, Abe Golum, David Fast, Pep Pfefferstein, Bruce McCarthy, Al Blozis, Herman Knupple, Irwin Traurig, Moe Berger, Prof Gorton, Bibby Martens, Allie Stolz," etc., etc.

Once in a while Patty would throw in a fictional name, and my father would not recognize it. So he truly did remember, at least to some extent, the names of many of his old cronies.

These little exercises would stimulate my father, especially when he did not recognize one of Patty's made-up names. He would be quite happy with himself when she praised him for his correct answers.

Even as my father had trouble expressing himself well, he loved to sing along with Patty. Apparently, the portion of the brain that "stores" music is separate from the portion that stores other data. Swede could remember many words and the tunes of hundreds of songs. I would do the same during my visits. And we'd always get to some old Weequahic songs:

"We're on our way ... to meet the foe ..." And Swede would sing right along. Singing often improved my father's mood.

We took a calculated risk and decided to take my father to the Bat Mitzvah of Doug and Sue's oldest daughter, Rachel. During the ceremony, every time the congregation sang the Hebrew prayers, my father sang along beautifully—singing every word, even though he did not know what any of the words meant. At the reception, my father had a great time. It was hard to get him off the dance floor. When the band took a break, he started fretting about when he would be taken back to Whispering Knoll. He would become nervous when he was away from the security of his assisted living facility. But as soon as the band started up again he was back on the dance floor.

As tough as it was to watch my father's decline, Patty kept visiting constantly. She knew the staff very well, which could only help with the attention Swede would get. She also got to meet many of Swede's fellow residents, including this one petite little lady in the facility who could get quite feisty. Her name was Estelle. One day, as Patty was walking through the lounge to leave, Estelle motioned to her as she passed.

Estelle: "Excuse me! Where am I supposed to be?!" in a loud, piercing voice.

Patty (patiently): "Just wait here Estelle. You'll be taken to dinner in just a few minutes."

Estelle: "But where am I supposed to be?!"

Patty, repeating: "Just wait Estelle. They'll be here very soon to take you to dinner."

Then Patty moved on. While still just a few strides from Estelle, Patty heard her shout to anyone in the area who would listen: "This one don't know her ass from her elbow!"

Such could be life in the Alzheimer's care unit of Whispering Knoll, where the patients have entered a different world known only to them. But I will say this for Patty, every once in a blue moon she *does* know her ass from her elbow. As our entire family knows, there is only one Aunt Patty.

One day most of the family, including grandkids, came to visit Swede in the Alzheimer's care unit. The youngest grandchild is Doug and Sue's third daughter, Elissa. She was too young to be aware of my father's ailment, so she was running around, being a little mischievous, nagging her older sisters, Rachel and Taylor, and her cousin Valery, and coaxing my father into playing catch with a beachball. Swede was a bit overwhelmed with all the visitors, but he really seemed to enjoy kibitzing with Elissa. His whole life, he always loved playing with little kids. And little kids loved playing with him.

Later, Patty and I were sitting with my father in the lounge area. Patty kept asking Swede to smile for the camera. For each shot he had a different expression—always other than a smile. He would look sad, angry, wild, perplexed, crazy, and more. He was being a wise guy, doing the opposite of what Patty was asking. Even then, he still loved to play around.

So yes, there were some light moments during my father's mental health decline. And we remember those small, positive nuggets well. But my father, always so down to earth, was also a very dignified person, and I used to wonder how he would react if he really knew the extent of his plight and his no-win situation.

Some of the best experiences I've had in working on this book have been my telephone conversations with Stan Gilbert. He has a great sense of humor, and his recall of growing up with Swede in the Weequahic section is remarkable. I think he misses my father as much as me, something that is hard to do. He and a few of my father's other buddies visited Swede at his assisted living home right up until the bitter end. They often took him to lunch at a nearby deli. Stan said Swede often mentioned regretfully that he had no money to pay for his meal. Stan would tell him not to worry, he could wash the dishes afterwards.

Seeing my father at this stage of his life could be more than sad. Towards the end he recognized no one. The Swede of old, who was the absolute best of company and the greatest of fathers and dearest of friends, was gone. But it never stopped his loving friends from visiting, and I will always remember them for that.

At the end, my father's physical strength was his biggest weakness. Some Alzheimer's patients are not as difficult to care for as others. Caring for my father became very, very problematic. If he didn't want to get his injection, or if he didn't want to be showered or changed, forget it. He was too big and strong to handle. We had hired around-the-clock private individuals to help the Whispering Knoll staff with my father. Once in a while he would urinate in the hallway or on the floor in his room. The facility did not want to send Swede away, but it was very problematic and disruptive for them to care for him. The additional aide helped, but not enough. Eventually my father was transferred to the Carrier Clinic for testing and observation. Before going there he had to be recommended by a hospital. So he went to the Robert Wood Johnson Hospital in New Brunswick. The process of getting him there was traumatic. Dale and Patty arrived there shortly after my father had arrived in an ambulance. They saw Swede's aide, and she was crying. My father had struggled mightily as six men were needed to subdue him as he was being taken from the ambulance to his room, where he was medicated to get him under control. It was a wild scene, as one of the security guys—a big, young guy who looked like a football player—had to wrestle with my father, and then told my sisters he was the strongest patient he'd ever had to deal with. He could not believe how difficult it was to restrain him, especially considering his age. When I heard this story, I was beside myself. The frustration and helplessness tore at me. My eighty-five-year-old father, always the gentlest of men, deserved better than what this horrible disease was putting him through.

He was at the Carrier Clinic for several weeks. They tried their best, but any time a caregiver tried to give care, Swede resisted. He was confused and frightened and fought everything. The rest of the time he was in a reclining chair and slept.

Eventually he was transferred to a nursing home in Atlantic Highlands, New Jersey, which was one of the few places that could/would accept him. He spent most of the last month of his life in bed, but still it took four staff members to change him and clean him. He was fighting—and frightened—to the end. What a horrible disease.

Swede contracted pneumonia, and it was clear the end was approaching. I for one kept hoping my father would go to sleep and not wake up. In fact, I felt that way for much of the last year of his life. That is when there was virtually no more pleasure in my father's life. I know what he would have wanted, and that is what I was wishing for.

My siblings and I sat with my father his last day. I remember sitting next to his bed, my hand on his forearm, just staring at him, watching him breathe, his face expressionless. So much was racing through my mind; memories of my father when I was a little kid, as a teenager, and on into my adulthood. He was always there for me, in the most positive way, and now it was coming to a close.

He passed away September 10, 2005. I still get emotional when I think about it. And by coincidence, not three minutes after my father was pronounced dead, Julie called me on my cell phone. She said she was checking on her grandfather's condition, though I knew she was really checking on *my* condition. I kept trying to calmly tell Julie the news, that her Pop Pop Swede had died, but I could not talk. Every time I tried to speak, I would be on the verge of totally losing it, and I just did not want to upset Julie. I kept having to press my cell phone against my body so Julie would not hear me burst out crying. Finally, I was able to blurt out the news.

Swede's obituary, which was beautifully stated, reminded me of his high school and college yearbooks. As well known as he was for his athletic accomplishments, there was a lot of emphasis on Swede the person. His obituary stressed his humility, his gentle nature, his warmth, and his modesty. In fact, the headline stated, "Seymour 'Swede' Masin, 85, Humble Newark Sports Icon." I was very proud that his humility was stressed.

Les Fein observed, "I really treasured his friendship. He was an incredibly warm, soft, and wonderful individual for his legendary prowess as a big, strong man. He was like a gentle giant."

Jerry Izenberg, the longtime *Star-Ledger* sports columnist, summed up Swede's athleticism: "For him to dominate in everything was amazing. He was the guy that the entire city of Newark knew. He was so complete, he had the physical strength to match his talent."

My friend Dave Geoghegan sent me a note, honoring Swede Masin, the gentle giant. Not a gentle giant, but *the* gentle giant. I always felt that phrase defined my father better than any other.

Athletes with my father's versatility are very rare. But much more important was the way he carried himself. He was all man, and yet he never, ever tried to show it. As Panzer's yearbook said upon his graduation: "Panzer's loss is the world's gain."

All in all, based on the way so many different people remembered my father, it got me thinking that the early passage in *American Pastoral* was pretty darn accurate: Swede really was a magical name in Newark's Weequahic section.

ACKNOWLEDGMENTS

Memories enrich one's life, and I am thankful that mine are so positive about growing up in a great family. Fortunately, I still can recall much of my past, but I was aided considerably by the many home movies taken by my father, the thousands of photos in our possession, my parents' yearbooks, Swede's scrapbook, and the interviews with Swede and Estelle that Patty videotaped in 2000, which make for priceless reminders of their personalities.

As a novice writer, I am grateful to many people for helping me along this adventure.

I want to thank my buddy Wayne Von Stetton and his father, Wayne Sr., whose family history book was my initial inspiration for this project.

For providing great advice and constructive comments along the way, a big thanks to professionals Nat Bodian, Shawn Levy, Shawna Shu, and Kerry Tymchuk.

My many conversations with my parents' friends and contemporaries was the best part about working on this book. They were so willing to help, they were so informative, and they were just plain fun. In alphabetical order, my heartfelt thanks go to: Bunny Berkowitz, Dotty Blackstone, Mike Cohen, Mary Connor, Frank Chenitz, Sid Dorfman, Zoom Fleisher, Julie Kramer, Hal Lefcourt, Julius Lehrhoff, Stan Levy, Milton Lurie, Hilda Lutzke, Vita Ornstein, and Judith Wilner Stein. Their insights and stories were nothing less than priceless. I hope I'm not forgetting anyone; if so, my apologies.

Linda Forgosh and Beth Kruvant were extremely helpful, providing leads and offering encouragement—for which I thank them. I also want to congratulate them on their highly successful Weequahic-related projects.

Special thanks to my great buddy Bruce Fad for his very thoughtful and lengthy critiques and suggestions. He spent much time and put much thought into his recommendations, and for that I am very grateful. As my college roommate, he obviously learned a great deal from me—such as how to throw darts.

Of course, I want to acknowledge many of my oldest friends, including Joe Abruzzese, Marty Brafman, Jim Deutsch, Dave Fargnoli, Bob Katz, Neil Kramer, Judy and Eric Perlmutter, and Joe Purzycki. They are teased in this book, and I thank them in advance for being such good sports about it, and not being the whiny little babies they usually are.

There is a Web site, http://www.maplewoodonline.com, which keeps me in my hometown loop. It serves South Orange, Maplewood, and the surrounding area, offering numerous discussions on topics such as education, sports, arts, and entertainment. I love the way it keeps me connected to my old stomping grounds. And it constantly references people and places that I remember from growing up in the area.

My telephone conversations with Stan Gilbert were absolutely wonderful. Listening to my father's life-long buddy and his strong recollections of growing up in the Weequahic section with Swede was as good as it gets.

I was also fortunate to connect with Gail Lustig, daughter of my father's beloved football and basketball coach, Art Lustig. I want to thank her for her insights into her father, whose name was revered in the Masin household.

Few know the game of basketball better than Big 10 Commissioner (and my old South Orange friend and neighbor) Jim Delany. It was great catching up with Jim and hearing his gracious comments about my father.

I will always appreciate Jerry Izenberg's casual response when I asked him about Swede: "Your father was God-like." For someone who's been around endless superstars in his day, his "God-like" response sure made an impression.

I feel very fortunate to have met Ron Stone. Weequahic's dynamic principal passed away in November 2007, but his inspiration will live on at the high school.

Weequahic High School Alumni Association leaders Hal Braff, Arnold Keller, and Phil Yourish have been wonderful. Their efforts, along with many others, on behalf of Weequahic High School are making a huge difference. They provided me with a wide range of valuable information about my father and his incomparable school. I'll always remember Hal's response when I asked him if he knew of my father. He said "There was Superman, and then there was your father. He was huge. A legend." Arnold Keller, who has been one of my biggest supporters, deserves special recognition. Whenever I felt stalled, Arnold would call with the latest Weequahic news, and I'd once again be stirred to action. Thanks, Arnold.

To the doctor in Manhattan who sent us the letter about my mother—but whose name I am keeping private: your letter had a most powerful impact on me and my siblings. We thank you so much for providing us with this prized possession.

I also acknowledge a larger-than-life Weequahic icon, Philip Roth, whose Swede Levov character in *American Pastoral* provided my father (and us kids) with endless amounts of fun. Swede had a blast with the attention your great book generated for him. Thank you.

For a huge sports fan like me, meeting and/or conversing with Al Attles, Monte Irvin, and Lonnie Wright, three of this country's greatest athletes, was an incomparable experience. I'll always cherish my conversations with them, and their gracious words about my father. The same goes for Johanna and Jazmine Wright, two of Swede's all-time favorites.

A huge thank you, posthumously, to Saul Berkowitz, Les Fein, and Sherm Harmelin. They were great friends of Swede's, and they all contributed to the book. But as a sad reminder of the rapid shrinking of our nation's greatest generation, all three passed away as the book was being written. These great people will be missed.

Also missed will be Marie Purzycki (Mrs. P.) who I always considered a second mother and a very special person in my life. She passed away peacefully in January 2009, but I will never forget her enthusiasm and sense of humor when we spoke by phone these past few years. Mrs. P. loved her Weequahic years and her remarkable memory provided me with endless details about that time and place.

My buddy since grammar school, Jim Deutsch, was a savior. I may not be the most organized guy, but Jim's editing skills gave me my bearings and put me on the right path. He has been indispensable to me on this project, and for that I am most grateful.

Dale, Patty, and Doug have been my biggest cheering section, and it is only thanks to them that many of the anecdotes and facts in this book can be told. As hard as they tried to revise history to portray themselves in a better light, I was always one step ahead of them. I'll forever appreciate their ongoing support. And a special nod to Patty, the most organized Masin by light years. As Max and Julie always say, "There's only one Aunt Patty."

A special thanks to Susie, Julie, and Max. Their critiques have been most constructive, and their support and enthusiasm with this effort has been as strong as mine.

And then there's Aunt Shirley, my best source of Masin family lore, and a true lover of all things family. She deserves special thanks for having maintained Swede's scrapbook, starting about seventy-five years ago. Aunt Shirley has always been very special to my sisters, my brother, and me.

Most importantly, thank you Estelle and Swede. For everything.

INDEX

Photographs are indicted by *italic* page numbers. Ex: Masin, Estelle (Lepore), *30*

LaVergne, TN USA
09 March 2011
219279LV00001B/82/P